British Cultural Identities

In *British Cultural Identities* Mike Storry and Peter Childs assess the degree to which being British impinges on the identity of the many people who live in Britain. They analyse contemporary British identity through the various and changing ways in which people who live in the UK position themselves and are positioned by their culture today. Using examples from contemporary and popular culture, each chapter covers one of seven intersecting themes:

- place and environment
- education, work and leisure
- gender, sex and the family
- youth culture and style
- class and politics
- ethnicity and language
- religion and heritage.

This new edition is fully updated to include environmental concerns, devolution, the infantilisation of culture, binge-drinking, reality TV, 7/7 and terrorism, and the increasing shift from a literate to a visual culture.

Mike Storry was Senior Lecturer in English at Liverpool John Moores University and is now retired. He is co-editor of the *Encyclopedia of Contemporary British Culture* (Routledge, 1999).

Peter Childs is Professor of Modern English Literature at the University of Gloucestershire, author of *Modernism* (Routledge, 2000) and *Contemporary Novelists: British Fiction since 1970* (2004).

British Cultural Identities

THIRD EDITION

■ Edited by Mike Storry and Peter Childs

 Routledge
Taylor & Francis Group

LONDON AND NEW YORK

First published in 1997 by Routledge
Second edition published in 2002 by Routledge

Third edition published in 2007
by Routledge
2 Park Square, Milton Park, Abingdon, Oxon OX14 4RN

Simultaneously published in the USA and Canada
by Routledge
270 Madison Ave, New York, NY 10016

Reprinted 2005, 2006

Routledge is an imprint of the Taylor and Francis Group, an informa business

© 1997, 2002 selection and editorial matter,
Mike Storry and Peter Childs

© 1997, 2002 individual chapters, their authors

Typeset in Sabon and Futura by
Florence Production Ltd, Stoodleigh, Devon
Printed and bound in Great Britain by
MPG Books Ltd, Bodmin, Cornwall

Every effort has been made to ensure that the advice and
information in this book is true and accurate at the time of going to
press. However, neither the publisher nor the authors can accept any
legal responsibility or liability for any errors or omissions that may
be made.

British Library Cataloguing in Publication Data
A catalogue record for this book is available from the
British Library

Library of Congress Cataloging in Publication Data
British cultural identities / edited by Mike Storry and Peter Childs.
– 3rd ed.
      p. cm.
    Includes bibliographical references.
  1. Great Britain – Social life and customs – 20th century.
  2. Popular culture – Great Britain – History – 20th century.
  3. Great Britain – Civilization – 20th century.   4. National
  characteristics, British – History – 20th century.   I. Storry, Mike,
  1943–   II. Childs, Peter, 1962–
  DA589.4.B75 2007
  941.082—dc22   2007011780

ISBN 10: 0–415–42459–3 (hbk)
ISBN 10: 0–415–42460–7 (pbk)
ISBN 10: 0–203–08957–X (ebk)

ISBN 13: 978–0–415–42459–2 (hbk)
ISBN 13: 978–0–415–42460–8 (pbk)
ISBN 13: 978–0–203–08957–6 (ebk)

We would like to dedicate this book
to the memory of our dear friend
and colleague Edmund Cusick

Contents

1   Places and peoples: nation and region   37
Peter Childs

2   Education, work and leisure   77
Mike Storry

3   Gender, sex and the family   119
Roberta Garrett

4   Youth culture and style   147
Jo Croft

5   Class and politics   177
Frank McDonough

Conclusion: Britain towards the future   **269**
Mike Storry and Peter Childs

Figures

Tables

Contributors

Peter Childs is Professor of Modern English Literature at the University of Gloucestershire. He has edited, with Mike Storry, *The Routledge Encyclopedia of Contemporary British Culture*.

Jo Croft is Lecturer in Literary Studies at Liverpool John Moores University.

Edmund Cusick was Head of Department for Writing at Liverpool John Moores University until his untimely death aged 44.

Roberta Garrett is Lecturer in Literature and Cultural Studies at the University of East London.

Frank McDonough is Reader in Modern Political History at Liverpool John Moores University.

Gerry Smyth is Reader in Cultural History at Liverpool John Moores University.

Mike Storry was Senior Lecturer in English at Liverpool John Moores University. He has taught widely in Britain and abroad. He has published fiction and poetry and edited, with Peter Childs, *The Routledge Encyclopedia of Contemporary British Culture*.

Preface

The government decided in mid 2006 that schoolchildren should be taught core British values, which were deemed to be freedom of speech and democracy, for example. A response in *The Times* newspaper suggested that these were not British, and should be supplemented by more distinctive national characteristics: irony, modesty, snobbery, insularity, anti-intellectualism, pragmatism, self-deprecation, pessimism, politeness, nostalgia, slobbery and emotional repression. These are not defining traits but they are recognisable – nobody says 'sorry' more or means it less, no one has less sartorial style or eccentric flair for self-fashioning, no one is more famed for both kinkiness and prudery: 'no sex please, we're British'.

There are thus many things about the British, many of them trivial and even more of them debatable, that are unlikely to find their way onto a school syllabus designed by the government.

This is a book that aims therefore to explain something about the British from the bottom up rather than the top down. The year 2007 is the 300th anniversary of Britain's creation and so, while Britain is still in crisis about itself, it has been around for a very long time and much can be said about its evolving sense of identity, just as much more needs to be said about the fact that contemporary Britain is fast changing as new ethnicities mingle with old. Which is partly why the official pressure to define Britishness is so great, and is minded to do it in terms of citizens' responsibility towards a political contract within the life and liberty enjoyed under the welfare state as well as the social contract predicated on shared British experiences of the National Health Service, pubs and clubs, schools, the BBC, public transport, television and sport, to choose the clearest examples.

British Cultural Identities is aimed at people interested in certain questions: Whose Britain? Whose culture? Whose identity? Do a majority of people in the UK think of themselves in terms of being British anyway – a question that will be initially answered by the government's Census in 2011, which for the first time will ask, 'What do you consider to be your national identity?: English/Scottish/Welsh/Northern Irish/British/Other.' Our book approaches the idea of British identities through contemporary practices and activities: not through institutions or economics, but through culture. The book is written in a clear, accessible style, making it especially useful to the student, in the UK or abroad, who wishes to be introduced to the variety of British experiences at the time of this third centenary. In the first, second and now third editions, it has aimed to be a different kind of book about the contemporary UK: one which looks at Britain in not sociological or historical but cultural terms. Each chapter is clearly structured around key themes, has a timeline of important dates, a list of recent cultural examples, and a section of questions and exercises. The book is illustrated with photographs and tables throughout.

All the contributors to this collection outline the plurality of identities found across the UK. The essays begin from the belief that identities are the names we give to the different ways we all are placed by, and place ourselves within, our culture. The contributors have been asked to think of culture as the practices and beliefs that people encounter and share – events, ideas, and images that form their lives everywhere and everyday. The introductory chapter deals with some current views on Britishness and with the issues being discussed in Britain at the present. The remaining seven chapters cover intersecting areas: gender and the family; religion and heritage; places and peoples; youth culture and age; class and politics; language and ethnicity; education, work and leisure.

The chapters are organised in the following way. At the beginning of each one you will find a timeline, usually of the most significant dates for the area covered. There follows a structured discussion of ways in which that area can be understood in different ways and at different levels. The conclusions drawn by each chapter are open because all the contributors believe there are many Britains and many British cultural identities. You will find many opinions expressed, but all the writers aim to outline current debates, key moments and speculative questions rather than to supply definitive answers. Consequently, our collective aim is to explore the face of British culture today, while at the same time suggesting that it will have changed tomorrow.

At the end of each chapter, you will find some questions and exercises, preliminary answers to most of which will be contained in the text. However, some of the questions are designed to stimulate your thoughts and to encourage you to go online or to libraries where necessary to conduct research or to test our suggestions by looking at the numerous cultural products that supply a way into an understanding of cultural identity in contemporary Britain. The further reading shows you where to go next for more detailed study. Some of the books suggested will also have been chosen because they cover aspects which the chapter itself has not been able to treat at length. In an introductory text such as this we cannot cover the minutiae of all social, ethnic, or even regional groupings; however, we intend to sensitise readers, particularly those outside the UK, to Britain's cultural diversity. Lastly, we have also listed at the end of each chapter some recent cultural examples which we feel will give you an insight into concerns, anxieties and tensions within contemporary British culture. These novels, films and TV programmes are of great importance because they provide specific British cultural representations relevant to the issues under discussion. We have chosen to select books, movies and programmes that are either current and particularly helpful or widely available and time-tested.

Introduction: Britain in the modern world

Mike Storry and Peter Childs

Timeline

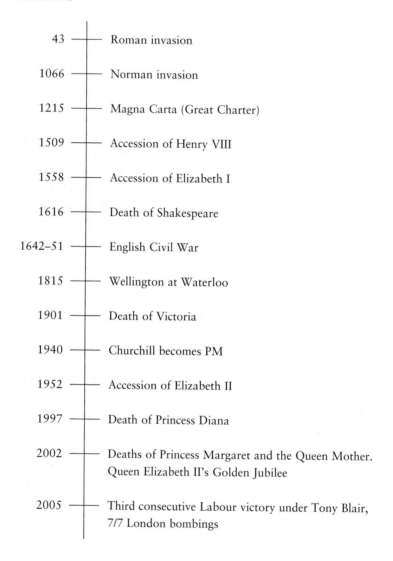

43	Roman invasion
1066	Norman invasion
1215	Magna Carta (Great Charter)
1509	Accession of Henry VIII
1558	Accession of Elizabeth I
1616	Death of Shakespeare
1642–51	English Civil War
1815	Wellington at Waterloo
1901	Death of Victoria
1940	Churchill becomes PM
1952	Accession of Elizabeth II
1997	Death of Princess Diana
2002	Deaths of Princess Margaret and the Queen Mother. Queen Elizabeth II's Golden Jubilee
2005	Third consecutive Labour victory under Tony Blair, 7/7 London bombings

THIS IS A BOOK ABOUT contemporary Britain and British people. On the one hand, Britain is a country with defined boundaries, a recognisable landscape, a long history, and a position in the various international economic, social and political league tables. On the other hand, British people are much harder to describe. To begin with, some British people do not live in Britain. Also, many people living in Britain do not think of themselves as British. Nationality is a matter of allegiance and cultural affiliation. Some people say that your nationality is indicated by where you choose to live or by the team you support at sports events; others say that it is a question of who you would fight for. It has also been argued that nationality is no longer a powerful force in Britain, that it is simply a matter of circumstance, and that today it is far less significant than local or global identities: relatives, friends and communities are more important to us and so is transnational culture.

Above all, nationality is a question of identity and so is crossed by other kinds of identity, such as ethnicity, gender, sexuality, religion, age and occupation. This book aims to outline some of the kinds of identity found at those intersections in Britain at the beginning of the twenty-first century. As such, it will be implicitly questioning the difference between British cultural identities and cultural identities in Britain. Fifty years ago, T.S. Eliot famously said 'culture' was something that included 'all the characteristic activities and interests of a people'. He thought that this meant for England: 'Derby Day, Henley Regatta, Cowes, the twelfth of August, a cup final, the dog races, the pin table, the dart board, Wensleydale cheese, boiled cabbage cut into sections, beetroot in vinegar, nineteenth-century Gothic churches, and the music of Elgar.' Fifty years on, conceptions of English and British identity have changed enormously and, for example, few people would attribute any significance to the twelfth of August, the opening day of the grouse-shooting season. Moreover, TV, which didn't feature for Eliot, would appear from Table 0.1 to be the main cultural bonding agent between British people.

The term 'British' is itself contentious. In recent years, partly as a response to the devolution of political power to Scotland, Wales and Ireland, there has been much questioning of what it means to be British. If we are

TABLE 0.1   Subjects of conversation between friends and family (2006)

Subject	Percentage of people who ever talk about subject
Advertising	2
Big business	2
Bringing up children	26
Clothes and fashion	19
Cost of living	43
Education	20
Gardening	16
Law and order	16
Neighbours or workmates	21
Politicians	8
Religion	6
Sport	25
Television programmes	48
The government	19
Trade unions	1
Newspaper articles	19
Health and welfare services	18
Unemployment	16
Personal health	21
None of the above/don't know	3

Source: *TOM Attitudes to Advertising Survey* (2006)

all British, then why should people feel a need to revert to their previous 'nationalities'? And if others in the UK have power devolved to them, what becomes of the formerly dominant English?

In examining nationality we should add the caveat that Britishness is often used instead of Englishness. People from Wales, Scotland, and Northern Ireland believe that making Englishness synonymous with Britishness erases their identity. R.S. Thomas, the Welsh poet and clergyman said 'Britain does not exist for me. It is an abstraction forced on the Welsh people.' For him it was just an aspect of imperialist domination and he wanted no part of it. Further, many people regard the concept of nationality itself as imprisoning and threatening to personal identity. The Englishman Tim Robinson, author of *Stones of Aran,* says for him Englishness represents 'a set of limitations to be wriggled out of if I can'.

FIGURE 0.1   Elvis: American culture permeates transport café and rural Britain in this and the next figure

FIGURE 0.2   Jimi Hendrix

The debate has broadened out into questioning whether we are anyway determined by nation any longer. Some commentators suggest that it is easier to define British cultural identity by looking outside than inside. The argument goes that Britain is just another constituent of Marshall McLuhan's 'Global Village' – the product of various world influences, rather than the outcome of home-grown social developments. Doubtless there is some truth in this. One has only to see the popularity of McDonalds, American branded clothing, or the prevalence of overseas restaurant cuisines. (Britain has eight thousand Indian restaurants.) Don't we live in a global culture, don't we enjoy influences from many geographical areas, and isn't identity different for everyone? Some people are influenced by the fact of their age, or that they live in a big city, are well or badly off financially. In short hasn't nationality been overridden by 'cultural' identity? This book seeks to address those questions.

Cultural identity is something which is partly imposed by background and partly chosen. All people have a number of influences bearing on them, from both Nature and Nurture: 'I am my genes and my generation.' That is, they inherit their ethnicity, physical abilities, intelligence and so on, in large measure from parents. But many other 'environmental' factors affect their development. For example: family, region, schooling, religion, music, etc. determine their experience. To a degree they form their own cultural identities by selection from a range of options. So for example they are Beatles fans or Manchester United supporters, or opera-lovers or film fanatics. They conform with or react against the values of their parents and accept or reject society's expectations of them. These influences, absorbed wittingly or unwittingly, determine identity.

DIY identities

So, where once identity was seen as innate, internal, it is now seen more as the product of external influences. The body itself has become the site of identity. There is a proliferation of fitness centres where you can lose weight and produce a new you. Through Pilates or yoga you can reshape your body in an image and likeness which appeals to you, instead of having to accept what nature gave you. Thus you can control your own identity.

People also assemble their identities from their make of car or their shoes or their ski-wear or their hobbies. Lidl and Aldi have identified a market niche missed by their supermarket rivals. They direct their special offers towards people who see themselves as anglers, equestrians, divers, cyclists, skiers, etc. This reflects the proliferation of niche markets and most retailers, especially online, try to gather as much information as they can on consumer choices in order to target their products.

Likewise, young people assert their identities as members of groups of their own choosing. There is a long tradition in Britain of groups appropriating brands used by other classes, often in other historical periods, and subverting them to their own uses. Examples would be: 1950s Teddy boys who wore Edwardian gentlemen's jackets; 1960s mods who rode Vespa scooters; 1980s football fans who 'adopted' Burberry scarves and Pringle pullovers; 1990s Goths attired in black; and contemporary gangs in Yorkshire who follow Leeds Football Club, see themselves as 'hard', and wear J. Arnold T-shirts (the name of a former Leeds pencil-maker and school-supplier). Such subcultural groups have established their own codes of communication which can be seen in their graffiti, tattoos and clothing and allow young people to form their own identities, very separate from those of their parents.

Many people's identity is bound up with the fact that they own a BMW or drive a Honda motorbike or minimise their carbon emissions for example. In an individualistic culture, the motor car is associated with freedom and individual expression. There is a huge number of personal number plates

FIGURE 0.3   4x4 with blackened windows illegally parked on a suburban street

and customised cars. Four-wheel-drive cars (US: Sports Utility Vehicles; UK: 4x4s) have become very popular, and controversial. They are known as 'Chelsea Tractors' and their drivers are attributed with arrogance and a reckless disregard for pedestrians. Jeremy Clarkson, presenter of BBC2's motoring programme *Top Gear*, is the larger-than-life leader of the 'petrolhead' culture, who has also become popular for his outspoken views voiced on the programme *Grumpy Old Men*. His love of fast cars and his larger-than-life personality have made him into a cult figure. This admiration for 'excessive' individualism may explain why Britain's train and bus services compare unfavourably with those elsewhere in Europe. In a climate of emphasis on freedom of the individual, it is hard to promote the concept of public transport.

A negative side to this individual selection of identity is that migrants can continue to live in a sort of 'ghetto of the mind'. For example, there are forty Asian TV channels in Britain and viewers select what they agree with from UK mainstream channels (where the 'trust' factor is 20 per cent), and 30 per cent of Muslim migrants watch only Asian TV. This is a deliberate turning away from the mainstream culture. A multiculturalism where everyone can opt out of the mainstream has been challenged with Jack Straw's attack on the Muslim veil in October 2006; Trevor Phillips, former head of the Commission for Racial Equality attacking the ideology of 'separate development'; and the establishment of the government's Integration and Cohesion Commission.

We have used the plural 'identities' in our title to make the point that no single mould fits British people. The population is diverse in all sorts of ways and this is one of the strengths of the culture which has evolved over the past 2,000 years. Many races and continents have contributed to its development. For example, most people don't know that in Roman Britain a garrison of African soldiers, under Septimus Servius, guarded Hadrian's Wall. Modern Britain contains numerous elements, often in tension with one another, but more usually complementary. For example, many people, who elsewhere have come to blows: Hindus and Muslims; Protestants and Catholics; Greeks and Turks; in Britain have for the most part found ways of working together in peaceful coexistence. Their liking for stability, quality education, healthcare and robust economic conditions has overridden their ideological differences. One of the aims of our study is to identify elements of British culture which have brought about this benign effect. In addition, in recent years communities from many overseas countries have settled successfully in Britain, including the following: Poles and Somalis in Wales, Portuguese and Filipinos in East Anglia, Indians in Northern Ireland, Bangladeshis and Pakistanis in Scotland.

British Cultural Identities describes how people in Britain see themselves. It is concerned with the culture they generate and are in turn formed by. 'Culture' is meant in its broad sense as shared experience – that which comes out of a dynamic mix of ages, races, regions, sexes, income levels and interests. The identities which are produced by this culture are personally and collectively fluid. Because what we are examining is complex and changing, our conclusions will be tentative and general. Our constant is the fact that the people who live on the islands are the way they are, partly because they live there.

In conducting our study, we will look at specific current political, social and cultural events. This will enable us to give basic background information on Britain: who is in power, what is the racial mix, the size of the population, the key institutions, the main sports, religions and so on. We will include some succinct contrasts with the past to fill out that background. Recent events chosen for examination reveal some basic truths about Britain in the political, social and cultural arenas and lead us to emphasise the complexity of British society and the need for careful analysis.

Institutional Britain

A list of traditional pillars of mainstream Britain would identify the key 'official' institutions as Parliament; a legal system which enforces the rule of law; an educational system of good quality; the Anglican Church; the

Bank of England; the Stock Exchange; the BBC. These are all elements of a stable society, but examination of them doesn't really begin to tell the story of the culture, for which they are prerequisites. There are several other 'institutions' which are equally or even more dominant in people's lives, and whose significance, though 'unofficial', is widespread. There is Henley Royal Regatta (rowing); cricket at Lords in London; Badminton Horse Trials; yachting at Cowes; rugby at Twickenham; the Glastonbury Pop Festival; the Edinburgh Festival; the Notting Hill Carnival. None of these events is 'institutional' but each figures largely on individuals' psychological calendars and forms part of the cultural menu from which some British identities are chosen. They are supplemented with numerous other sporting and social entertainments: soccer matches, greyhound and horse-racing, darts tournaments, snooker matches, pub quizzes, Townswomen's Guilds. These are all seen by their fans as indispensable to their individual cultural landscapes.

This broad British cultural scene has a further supporting infrastructure of self-regulating organisations that serve to channel the talent which in another culture would not find an outlet. These include the Football and Amateur Athletic Associations, private art galleries showcasing the work of Damien Hirst, Tracy Emin and Martin Creed with their sheep in formaldehyde, bed with used condoms, or The Lights Going On And Off; publishing houses making the Harry Potter phenomenon possible; film and video production companies, which create soaps like *EastEnders* and *Hollyoaks*; the advertising and design industries; the music industry, from small recording studios to major artist recruiting houses like EMI and Virgin. These are part of Britain's cultural fabric yet they have no official status and no state funding.

Popular culture

One consequence of examining the nation through its official institutions is that large cultural areas will always be unexplored. Immigrant communities will have no place. Teenage fashions, clubs, comics, pubs, around which many people's lives revolve, won't get a look in. The Britain covered in the myriad special-interest magazines will not feature. Examining the experience of the man or woman in the street will give a more comprehensive picture of contemporary British culture. By and large, he or she is exposed to the culture which has welled up from below, not been imposed from above. This experience may be read through elements of popular culture such as music, magazines, TV and film, examples of which are offered throughout this book.

Popular culture, which comes from below, (soaps, tabloids, 'reality TV' such as *Big Brother*) can be more useful for our analysis than high culture (opera, theatre), because it reflects widespread, particularly youthful, public taste and thus enables us to explore Britons' psychology, motivation and aspirations. High culture, on the other hand, 'enforced' initially, via school curricula, deliberately ignores life as lived experience, and contemporary social trends. The most vibrant cultural developments in Britain come from the margins not from the centre. The following, for example, have become incorporated into the mainstream: in music, hip hop and bhangra; in fashion, saris and kimonos; in style, dreadlocks, body-piercing, and tattooing; in literature, novels by Hanif Kureishi or Zadie Smith, poems by Benjamin Zephaniah.

Schooling

Concentration on popular culture enables us to keep pace more easily with the rapid changes in society. For example there have been significant shifts in patterns of education. The fee-paying private schools have always had a disproportionately significant influence throughout British society, largely through their reinforcement of class structures. Ambitious members of ethnic minorities see Britain as a place where 'the old school tie' matters and, faced with latent racial prejudice, see their way forward as through private education. This is leading to profound cultural changes in one of Britain's dominant mediums for social advancement. There has always been an ethnic-minority presence in such schools, but pupils were usually sons of powerful overseas dynasties. For example, in Billy Bunter's school Greyfriars, in the 1930s *Magnet* comic, there was an Indian boy Hurree Jamset Ram Singh who was the Nabob of Bhanipur. The presence in popular culture of such figures has undoubtedly contributed to the mystique of the great public schools, such as Eton and Harrow, whose prevailing ethos was nevertheless predominantly white, Anglo-Saxon, Protestant, Establishment. Today however, private-sector schools have proportionally more ethnic minority students than do state schools. These pupils are 'domestic' rather than from overseas, and this leads to greater integration into the corridors of power of British society for some ethnic Britons.

Other factors in the current cultural transformation are: the re-negotiation of the whole concept of the family; the new technology: computers, mobile phones, the internet, DVDs. People's daily lives are adapting to shifts in career patterns, new skills requirements from employers and new entertainments. The majority of those who attend university today for example are taking courses which didn't exist ten years ago. There are degree courses in web design, tourism, nursing, film, media, football and pop music studies, to name a few. For a conservative country like Britain that is a fundamental change.

Methodology

In this period of flux, where the only constant is change, what it means to be British today is markedly different from what it meant ten years ago. Enduring stereotypes are not a great deal of help. For example a 1999 poll of young Europeans associated five elements with Britain: Shakespeare, London, the BBC, the Beatles and the Royal Family. This is very out of date. Any single snapshot of British identity will also be blurred. So what we have chosen to do is to look at a number of recent studies of the way people live, and to see how helpful they are in explaining the way our society works. Our first example: every year the *Sunday Times* publishes a list of the 1,000 richest people in Britain. This is one way of making a judgement about the people who live here. It assumes that their wealth reflects not only their commitment and work, but also their aspirations, their values, and their outlook. Secondly, in March 2001 the *Observer* Sunday newspaper published a study 'Britain Uncovered' dealing with 'the way we live now: money, work, love, sex, crime, youth, race, religion, education and ignorance'. It contains an eclectic mix of things happening on the cultural scene which represent significant trends. Thirdly, Channel 5 produced *An A-Z of Britishness* which was another attempt to pin down the essence of contemporary British culture. We will fourthly, look at a list of 'Quintessences of Englishness' offered in Julian Barnes' novel *England, England*. We will examine each of the above attempts to describe the moving target of British culture and will see how useful their various approaches can be, but first a look at a number of political, social, cultural and sporting events and incidents will let us see how people reflect and inform the culture around them.

Politics

The General Election of June 2001 gave Labour, which came into power in 1997 on a wave of euphoria, a second term of office with 413 MPs to the Conservatives' 166. This was an astonishing majority. It was 31 per cent greater than Margaret Thatcher's landslide second victory in 1983. In 2005 this majority was reduced, probably because of Britain's involvement in the war in Iraq. (An anti-war march in London in February 2003 had between 750,000 and 2 million people, depending on police' or organisers' estimates, and was claimed to be the largest protest march in British history.) But the Labour majority remained comfortable, and in 2007, 'New' Labour appear to have the broad support of the people. However, a better indication of how people feel about their country and their politicians might be the fact that in both the 2001 and the 1997 Elections, two single-issue candidates, standing as Independents, were elected without the benefit of any elaborate party machine. These were: in 1997 Martin Bell; in 2001 Richard Taylor. Bell, a former war correspondent, stood as an Independent candidate on a 'decency' manifesto, and defeated the sitting Tory MP Neil Hamilton, who had become embroiled in accusations of corruption. Taylor, a retired hospital consultant standing on the single issue of the downsizing of his local Kidderminster hospital, unseated a Labour junior minister by 17,630 votes! Both Bell and Taylor countered elaborate, sophisticated and expensive political machines, during electoral landslides.

There is a maverick element to the British electorate, who periodically, almost whimsically, decide who they do or do not want to govern them. For example, in 1945 they rejected Winston Churchill, a continuing favourite of the Americans to this day, who had been a successful wartime Prime Minister, but whom they did not want in peacetime. Meanwhile today, young voters are so disaffected from the whole political process that, to try and secure their votes during the last election, the parties resorted to texting them on their mobile phones.

Conclusions we can draw from this are that, although Labour is in power, and although Parliament is sovereign and elected by the people, British voters are still wary of having their lives determined by professional politicians and are prepared to drop them instantly when opportunity knocks. This signals a long-standing distrust, by British people, of pro-fessionals (Disraeli was Britain's first full-time Prime Minister, only in as late as 1868) and professionalism (Rugby Union held on to its amateurs-only status until the mid 1990s). People have in the past preferred to be governed by the 'gifted amateur' or the aristocrat whose inherited wealth made him (rarely her) less likely to be corruptible. Nowadays, when professionalism is more accepted, they are still prepared to elect people who operate without the benefits and constraints of a party machine.

However, both the 2001 Twin Towers bombings (9/11) and the London Tube attacks of 2005 (7/7) have led to subtle shifts in Britain's political and cultural atmosphere. In the past, society has been worried about 'the enemy within' (1940s: fifth column; 1960s: communists, 'reds under the beds'), that is people whose political ideology differed from that of the Establishment. After these terrorist attacks and the general 'War on Terror', the focus switched to fear of the outsider: xenophobia, despite the fact that the 7/7 bombers were largely 'home-grown' in that they lived and were educated in Yorkshire.

Society

In the social arena, when the Queen Mother celebrated her 101st birth-day in 2001, the Royal Family gathered around for the happy occasion.

The Queen Mother was personally popular with all social classes. Hitherto, Buckingham Palace had not handled public relations well, but now, trying to be 'user-friendly', the Royals organised a photo opportunity for the benefit of the media. However, an unplanned outcome of the event was that newspapers took the Royal Family to task for literally wheeling out Princess Margaret, the Queen's sister, in an invalid chair. She was clearly seriously ill and it was seen as inhumane – a violation of her rights as an individual, to display her to the masses. So what was meant to be an orchestrated moment of celebration became an opportunity for anti-monarchists to express their hostility to royalty and the Royal Family.

Here we can conclude that once again characteristic British individualism kicked in. People do not like to feel their emotions and responses are stage-managed. One of the effects of Britain's Protestant Reformation was that the individual retains his or her right to a personal view. This Protestant tradition of independence is linked to ideas of egalitarianism and fair play. It favours the views and behaviour of the individual over those of the herd. Consequently people resent attempts to manipulate and orchestrate their private views. They want to accord themselves and others freedoms and that includes the freedom of privacy when necessary.

The Queen's handlers seem to have since learned some lessons in PR. For her 80th birthday in 2006 they invited 2,000 children to a party at Buckingham Palace with figures from children's books, such as Postman Pat, Winnie-the-Pooh and Paddington Bear.

Culture

The building of the Millennium Dome at Greenwich was an attempt by the government to display aspects of Britain which it felt were important. It was also undoubtedly meant to lend authority to the government that produced it – a precedent set by the Great Exhibition of 1851 at the Crystal Palace in London's Hyde Park. Tony Blair called the Dome 'a triumph of confidence over cynicism'. The Government spent a billion pounds of taxpayers' money erecting a tent at Greenwich and filling it with amusements. There were several 'zones' including a 'Faith Zone' and a 'Body Zone' which were meant to inform and to entertain.

However, from the beginning the project was a disaster. It was intended to represent Britain, but the people weren't consulted and didn't feel they had any stake in it. People contrast the Dome with the successful Eden Project in Cornwall, which thrives and which started as a community project. People saw the Dome as a further example of money being syphoned from the regions to be spent in London. They didn't like being managed into visiting it, and the more they were hectored by government ministers to attend, the more reluctant they were to go.

The low attendance figures illustrate two things: the mixture of elements chosen to be celebrated was awry (the Faith Zone was partly financed by the subsequently disgraced Hinduja brothers), secondly, people do not like to be told, least of all by government, what they should like or what they should do. This rejection of the authority of government is a major aspect of British cultural identity. People will not be bullied. (The song 'Rule Britannia' contains the line: 'Britons never never never shall be slaves'.) The failure of the Dome project illustrated the cultural powerlessness of government in a democracy.

Sport

Taking pride in the sporting achievements of one's nation is clearly a significant indicator of one's attachment to one's homeland. That this persists, and even increases, despite political devolution to the regions and Britain's integration within Europe, is a paradox and shows the persistent interest taken in sport. It is even suggested that now that England lacks its own institutions (because they are all 'British'), discrete language or even national dress, its cultural identity is invested in sport. As English football fans re-establish their identities, they have replaced the Union Jack with the flag of St George and are reclaiming their Englishness. Sociology professor Tim Crabbe says that it is now sport 'which creates the spaces for people to form intense relationships with one another'.

Traditionally, Britain's sports stars have been lionised: W.G. Grace the nineteenth-century cricketer; Roger Bannister, the first four-minute miler; Jonny Wilkinson, captain of the English rugby team; Sir Steve Redgrave, the Olympic rower, and so on. Britons particularly welcome the success of sporting heroes in football, or soccer, as it is known elsewhere. The game of football is central to Britain's view of itself and is supported fanatically by people of both sexes, from all social classes, ages and regions, so for example any football match between England and Germany assumes more than sporting importance. There is national glee in remembering Britain's 4–2 defeat of Germany in 1966. The commentator's 'They think it's all over ... it is now' became a famous *Sun* newspaper headline after that match (and is the name of a popular BBC sports quiz programme). After England's 5–1 victory over Germany in 2001 (following a 1–0 defeat at Wembley nine months earlier) all sorts of genies good and bad came out of the bottle. Even people who don't normally follow football were exultant. This was reflected on TV and radio where newsreaders, male and female, did not even try to appear dispassionate. The so-called 'black-edged voice' reserved for describing the normal disasters of the news, disappeared in the reporting. Sport here proved cohesive and positive. The fact that one section of British society, rampaging English hooligans, went round Munich after the match chanting 'there's only one Bomber Harris', went largely unnoticed in the British media. Overnight there was a shift from middle-class apprehension about the prospective behaviour of hooligan-fans overseas, to a display of triumphalism where 'a few hotheads' must not be allowed to detract from the very real victory which took place.

Xenophobia

The way in which news is reported reveals much about British readers and viewers. The coverage of immigrants and asylum seekers, for example, has revealed sharp differences in British attitudes to foreigners and in generally accepted notions of what it means to be British. Ex-Tory party leader, William Hague applied the phrase 'bogus asylum seekers' to refugees, presumably in the belief that it would endear him to his followers. In practice it raised the anger of opponents and supporters alike. For the former it was evidence of Tory racism, for the latter it failed to distance him from the lack of compassion of his predecessor-but-one, Margaret Thatcher.

Events like this can enable a latent nationalism to arise. This happens instantly, and newspapers can rally support against an 'enemy' overnight. In 1981 the *Sun* orchestrated hatred for 'the Argies' over the Falklands conflict. Most *Sun* readers were unaware where the Falkland Islands were, but they rose to the invitation to be xenophobic anyway. That Iraqi leader Saddam Hussein, the Serb Slobodan Milosevic or Zimbabwean Prime Minister Robert Mugabe could equally be vilified at a moment's notice indicates a xenophobia always ready to be ignited, in certain sections of the British public. Opposition to the takeover of Manchester United by the American Malcolm Glazer (ostensibly because he wasn't a fan) was undoubtedly partly based on his nationality: the MU supporters who opposed him called themselves the 'Manchester Education Committee'. Even the 2001 Royal Variety Performance featured a comedian who centred his act around the British prejudice against the French! Dislike of other nationalities is not far beneath the psyche particularly of some of the older generation and of the unthinking.

However, there are also some promising straws in the wind to come from Britain's ethnic mix. The popular Rabbi Lionel Blue suggested on Radio 4 that one of the benefits of recent immigration to his neighbourhood in London was an increased respect for elderly people – something inherent in immigrant communities but disappearing from native British culture.

Recent immigrants from the enlarged EU have dissipated prejudice, as British people have become impressed with their work ethic.

The above examples from current affairs show how complex a country Britain is. It is an amalgam of paradoxes. It is generally conformist and conservative but is also in a constant state of change. It is governed by Parliament, but the people's voice is strong. It has a monarch but many people are republicans. It generates a lot of popular and much 'high' culture, but also philistinism and hooliganism. Constituency of its population also is in flux. The majority of the population is Caucasian, but 6.8 per cent of people are now from ethnic minorities – predominantly from the Caribbean, Africa and the Indian subcontinent. It is hard to embrace such contradictions and tensions. It is much easier to talk about 'Britains', or for that matter the 'identities' of our title.

Postmodernism

It might be argued that modern Britain is no different from any other developed state. In a postmodern world of surfaces, public relations, stylistic fusions and so on, new urban developments are the same everywhere. Manchester's Trafford Centre shopping mall, for example is a collage of global culture. It has trompe l'oeil artwork, Greek statuary, Art Deco mouldings, Whistleresque murals, Venetian frescoes, a mock-up of the deck, deck-furniture and lifeboats of the Titanic (presumably designed to dredge up from shoppers' unconsciouses, images of upper-class travel, as well as the teenage, heart-throb film *Titanic*). There is also a fibreglass statue of Sammy Davis Jr! This shopping mall and others like it, steeped in global 'culture' (or kitsch?), are now firmly entrenched on the cultural map for British young and old alike. Are these people 'consumers' defined by the products they are made to buy, or Britons who assert their multicultural identities and individuate themselves by shopping?

Media

More important perhaps than global influences is the role played in British life by home-grown media. Everything is now played out on television. Moral and ethical dilemmas, from gay rights and cosmetic surgery to euthanasia and abortion are illustrated and aired in soap operas. Everyone in the public eye, all organisations, and corporate Britain have P(ublic) R(elations) people to help to present themselves to the world. Investors buy shares on the promise of 'newsflow'. Politicians are forced to resign in time for *The Six O'clock News*. Ministers must respond to news quickly in order to seem decisive, rather than, wisely, having considered in depth. Government has been accused of making announcements to the media first and circumventing Parliament, so important is it to 'get the message out'.

Nobody in Britain can claim to be unaffected by the barrage of noise coming from these external influences, however people distinguish between what they tolerate, what they accept and what elements of the culture (or counter-culture) they welcome and choose for themselves as a buffer against the outside world.

Language

We should also be careful with language. In any discussion of nationalism, identity, or current affairs, language is never 'innocent'. The choice of words reveals the underlying outlook of the speaker. So, for example, the word 'foreign' in English is much more severe than the *étranger/estrangeiro* found in most romance languages or than the German *auslander*. Latent British xenophobia is revealed in the offensive tabloid expression 'Johnny Foreigner'. Our chapter 'Ethnicity and Language' says a lot more about this, but for now think about the impact on national relations and culture of the following uses of language: to welsh is to cheat or renege; to scotch is to thwart, to squash, to prevent; an Irish lanyard is an untidy rope. In other words, the names of the three 'subsidiary' nations in the British Isles have negative connotations in the language of the dominant one. Thus national prejudice is encoded in the English language. One only has to consider the number of discrete disparaging names for other nationalities in English ('Krauts', 'Frogs', 'spics' and so on, versus the single word 'gringo' in Spanish) to suggest that the language is racist. This is a negative legacy of the British empire.

Bearing these points in mind, we will now turn to examine the approaches of the three recent studies refered to earlier, each of which uses a list or key words to identify salient characteristics of British people.

The *Sunday Times* 'Rich List'

Financial status is clearly one determinant of cultural outlook. The *Sunday Times* evidently believes that, as F. Scott Fitzgerald said: 'the rich are different'. They may be distinguished by the flamboyant garishness of their taste, rather than by their discernment. Ruby Wax conducted viewers around the Duchess of York's 'distinctive' home in a famous TV programme. But even if they are philistines individually, the rich collectively tend to be patrons of the arts. For decades Maurice Saatchi has been buying the work of contemporary British artists. Their sense of identity is determined by the fact that they are rich and therefore insulated from the constraints and inconveniences of the less well-heeled – who often wish to emulate them – hence the fascination of the Lottery and money-based TV programmes like *Deal or No Deal*.

Many ordinary people, such as public servants, teachers, social workers, postal employees, workers in the civil service are defined by their usefulness. However, the rich, as a group, would rarely claim that their chief aim is public service. So, in the *Sunday Times* richest 1,000 list we see that the fashion sector has forty-one entries, including familiar high street names such as Joseph, French Connection (now FCUK) and Russell & Bromley. The aim of these companies is the continued creation of wealth for the benefit of the families which own them and of wages for the people who work for them, rather than public service.

In 2001, after the dotcom bubble burst, old money continued to do rather well. The land-owning Duke of Westminster (300 acres of Mayfair and Belgravia) was the richest man in Britain. But that does not mean the rise of Britain's meritocracy is faltering. In 2001 there was another drop in the proportion on the list of those who inherited their wealth. Only 241 of the 1,000 in the list inherited their fortunes. This is the smallest proportion since the list was first drawn up in 1988. Then about 70 per cent of the 200 entries had inherited their money. This represents a significant shift in a culture in which inherited wealth plays such a major part. Financial change fuels the process of social and cultural change. The *Sunday Times'* focus on money reveals very little about the rich people profiled or the lives of the mass of the population, however, the fact that most of those on the list are 'household names' indicates that they are part of a social community, as well as a purely financial British hierarchy, and in a celebrity culture the rich are admired and emulated.

(See the full *Sunday Times* 'Rich List' in Chapter 5).

The *Observer*: 'Britain Uncovered'

Whereas the *Sunday Times'* list offers a snapshot of a segment of British society whose primary motivation and identity is financial, the *Observer's* 'Britain Uncovered' supplement takes a 'sociological' approach to contemporary culture and covers a broader spectrum. It contains a survey of public attitudes (69 per cent are against same-sex marriage; most popular European country: Spain; only 19 per cent of people would not take out private healthcare or educate their children privately, if they had plenty of money) and behaviour (37 per cent would keep a wallet they found with £200 in it). It also looks at people's activities across the age range from deprived teenagers to pensioners; attitudes to work; drug culture; education; and finally eccentricity. Two sections deal with the spiritual state of the nation – broadly speaking the decline of institutional religion in favour of 'house churches' and the appeal to young Muslims of traditional Islam.

As a barometer of 'the health of the nation', the supplement is quite hopeful. Society is changing, but the fixed standards from which people are straying hover in the background. For example, the journalist Burhan Wazir complains about the severity of his own upbringing in Pakistan, but reports that young British Muslims are managing to combine the practice of their religion with the freedom to go clubbing if they want to. The film *East is East* (1999) highlights similar dilemmas. The section on eccentricity suggests the impossibility of pigeonholing people. Miranda Sawyer, author of a book on suburbia, *Park and Ride* (2001) meets a pensioner who is feeling wobbly 'because he'd taken two Es' (Ecstasy tablets). In her view, eccentricity is what keeps the culture vibrant and makes Britain interesting, because unpredictable.

The *Observer*'s approach is trying to present a snapshot of the real Britain as opposed to that of the tourist brochures. It is partly limited by factors surrounding any inquiry based on questionnaires. Questions and the scope for replying to them can be limited. Respondents do not always tell the truth. The funky and the bizarre sell newspapers, etc. and hence figure larger than life. But by and large we are given a dispassionate overview, within the constraints of the *Observer*'s liberal, left-wing leanings.

Channel 5: An A-Z of Britishness

In 2001 Ian Russell produced a programme called *An A-Z of Britishness* for Channel Five. Using twenty-six headings, the programme makers looked at various aspects of contemporary Britain. Their list of topics was random and eclectic, and the tone flippant with, for example, taxi drivers from the north and south voicing prejudices about either side of the divide. However most viewers of a programme intended for home consumption, could relate to the items raised. The list is reproduced in Table 0.2 and might be used for a classroom brainstorming exercise.

Many of these items are obvious, but a few require explanation. Deep-fried Mars Bars and fluorescent green peas are comical northern food delicacies; Britons are evidently the highest per capita consumers of jigsaw puzzles; there is an attempt to introduce the kilt as a fashion garment for men; Thomas Crapper, an inventor, popularised the lavatory in the nineteenth century; Routemasters are red London buses; 16 million saucy postcards were sold in 1963 – the company is now defunct; the rating 'X' for films, which gave them a forbidden-fruit status, was abandoned in 1981; yobs are thugs – the cartoonist Tony Husband got his own back on his

TABLE 0.2   *An A–Z of Britishness*

Alcohol	North–South divide
Bingo	Older people
Cockney	Pantomime
Dome	Queue
Eccentricity	Routemaster
Food – peas, Mars bars	Saucy postcards
Gnomes	Thatcher
Housing crisis	Union flag
Inventors	Victory
Jigsaw	Weather
Kilt	X-rated
Lavatory	Yobs
Manners	Zebra crossings

Source: *An A–Z of Britishness*, Channel 5 (March 2001)

muggers by drawing 'Yobs' cartoon for *Private Eye* for fifteen years; the idea of black-and-white zebra street crossings was exported around the world.

The programme was a lighthearted venture, but made some telling points. For example it interviewed three people, Scottish, Irish and English respectively. The two former knew the dates of their respective national saint's days (St Andrew: 30 November, St Patrick: 17 March), but the English person did not know that St George's Day is on 23 April. This tends to support the idea that it is English people who are least aware of their nationality and whose sense of identity is now most in crisis.

The programme included a comment from the writer Ross Benson that Britons have good manners in order to mask their underlying violence. He said that during the Falklands conflict, the Argentines found it very difficult to deal with the good manners of British diplomats: 'They subject you to their charm, and if you don't agree with them, they kill you.' The programme concentrated on some of the more outrageous elements of Britain. Many of the people featured were 'oddballs' – a cockney Pearly King, a gnome collector, a man who walked the length of the country barefoot and lived in a cave.

The limitations of the approach in this case are: programme time constraints; the appeal of the bizarre rather than the ordinary – presenting a wackier Britain than the norm; the absence of all the 'ordinary' features of British life – work, sport, family, landscape and perhaps the most dominant element of British culture: TV itself. However, largely because of its idiosyncratic approach, this was a successful programme bearing a message, broadly speaking celebrating eccentricity, which British people wanted to hear about themselves.

England, England

In Julian Barnes' novel *England, England*, a powerful businessman plans to turn the Isle of Wight into a theme park, so that tourists will not have to traipse from Buckingham Palace to Stratford on Avon to Chester and so on. His business blueprint lists 'Fifty Quintessences of Englishness' (see Table 0.3).

Some of these items are tongue-in-cheek, and one could argue about the order in which they are prioritised, but they represent some common perceptions and will be familiar to many within and outside the United Kingdom.

Examining the list we can see that it contains some physical monuments, some historical figures, some works of the imagination, some ceremonials. Most people can easily relate to these elements of Englishness even if they don't apply them to themselves.

The monarchy, for example, is a common topic of conversation, though most Britons have never seen the Queen in person. Members of all social classes, and older people especially, support the monarchy but draw the line at the minor royals who they see as contributing nothing to the welfare of Britain. They point, for example, to the moral lead meant to come from royalty. The marital breakdown rate of the present incumbents, at three out of four, is worse than the national average of one in three. Despite this disillusionment, 70 per cent of Britons say they prefer to live as subjects under a monarch rather than as citizens in a republic. However, 68 per cent of them believe that we will not have a monarchy fifty years from now.

As regards the classic serials category listed below, most people could name *The Forsyte Saga*, or Jane Austen adaptations, but they would be just as likely to include preferred TV sitcoms such as *Blackadder*, *Fawlty Towers*, or even *Little Britain*, as well as detective series like *Inspector Morse* and *Midsomer Murders*. These programmes are based on a nostalgic view of England – John Major's 'warm beer, cricket and ladies cycling'. Set in beautiful locations, they are essentially about restoring order and calm to an idyllic place whose waters have been ruffled by the odd murder or two.

Partly because of its context in a nostalgic novel, Barnes' checklist has an historical bias. Past glories overshadow such present-day banalities as 'whingeing', 'emotional frigidity' and 'shopping' and this list, more than the others, records the traditional British vices of snobbery, hypocrisy and perfidy. There is a dated feel to such an approach. The tenor of the items is before the past half century. It is Britain in aspic, disabled by its past, and

TABLE 0.3   Quintessences of Englishness

Royal family	Bowler hat
Big Ben/Houses of Parliament	TV classic serials
Manchester United FC	Oxford/Cambridge
Class system	Harrods
Pubs	Double-decker buses/red buses
A robin in the snow	Hypocrisy
Robin Hood & Merrie Men	Gardening
Cricket	Perfidy/untrustworthiness
White cliffs of Dover	Half-timbering
Imperialism	Homosexuality
Union Jack	*Alice in Wonderland*
Snobbery	Winston Churchill
God save the King/Queen	Battle of Britain
BBC	Francis Drake
West End	Trooping the Colour
The Times newspaper	Whingeing
Shakespeare	Queen Victoria
Thatched cottages	Breakfast
Cup of tea/Devonshire cream tea	Beer/warm beer
Stonehenge	Emotional frigidity
Phlegm/stiff upper lip	Wembley Stadium
Shopping	Flagellation/public schools
Marmalade	Not washing/bad underwear
London taxis	Magna Carta
Beefeaters/Tower of London	

Source: Julian Barnes, *England, England* (1998)

really has little relevance for the contemporary British student population for example, who are more tuned in to travelling through Europe, music and the drink and drugs culture.

Individualism

One thing all these studies have in common is their admiration for British individualism. They praise British people's dissent, scepticism, lack of conformity, the ability to set rather than follow fashion trends, and individuality over the herd instinct. Eccentricity is one stage further on from this and is admired even more. Undoubtedly for a country of eccentrics to thrive, fundamental tolerance of dissent or difference is necessary, and clearly this exists in Britain. Environmental protesters become national heroes, through media exposure. Ken Livingstone was elected mayor of London despite the Government's best efforts to thwart him. It would be nice to think that Britain could supply a model of diversity which could be exported to other post-industrial democracies. However, that may be less possible in future in a global climate of mistrust, where the prevailing belief is that individual freedoms must be curbed in the interests of the freedom and safety of all.

Heroes

A pragmatic way of looking at British identity and of examining the aspirations of ordinary people is to look at the kind of contemporary heroes they have created. These heroes reveal a lot about the people who have created them. They reflect how people would like to be themselves, or what they see as admirable in others. As a group, heroes represent the values of their culture. Significantly this cynical age has thrown up many anti-heroes or stage villains, such as Jade Goody from *Big Brother* (fourth in Channel 4's *100 Worst Britons We Love to Hate*), and Anne Robinson from *The Weakest Link*. Previous generations tended to admire Establishment figures or politicians, such as Churchill or Macmillan, but today sports people tend to predominate. For example Jonathan Edwards, the long jumper is also well known outside his sport. Others well known enough outside their sports to appear in TV ads are: Frank Bruno the boxer, Gary Lineker and Vinny Jones the footballers, Steve Redgrave the Olympic rower and Steve Davis the snooker player. Steve Redgrave won five Olympic medals for rowing at successive Olympic games. In 2001 it took him around six hours to run the London Marathon because so many well-wishers impeded his progress. As a national hero he embodied virtues of doggedness and determination, good humour and stability which even the MTV generation of slackers can evidently relate to.

Today's heroes are decided much more by the young than they were hitherto, and consequently TV and media personalities such as Carol Voordeman and Chris Evans tend to feature, as well as those from sports, business and commerce. So nowadays the range of heroes is much wider. In order to examine this phenomenon, we will consider in more detail a small number of select prominent examples.

Princess Diana

An unlikely hero was Princess Diana. She was born into privilege, the daughter of Earl Spencer and, after her fairy-tale marriage to Prince Charles, had several palaces to choose from. She became a fashion icon and her appearance was widely imitated. The other side to her was her compassion for victims of Aids and her opposition to landmines – a product of the military-industrial complex of which she herself was arguably a part. Perhaps for this reason, people saw the latter as a particularly principled stand.

She was a paradoxical heroine in that her wealth could have separated her from people in the street, but it didn't. She was genuinely liked by her future subjects: so much so, that Tony Blair could make political capital by calling her 'the People's Princess' – at her funeral. The arrival of Princess Diana was a watershed in attitudes to the monarchy. Buckingham Palace completely misread the public mood with their muted reaction when she was killed with her lover in a car crash in Paris in 1997. The Queen remained at Balmoral in Scotland and Diana was not given a state funeral.

People already knew from a TV interview with Martin Bashir that Diana was at odds with the palace, and when the latter appeared to be prepared to give her a low-key funeral, they were outraged. There was a national outpouring of grief. It was a moment when the nation came together in sorrow because Diana represented values which were theirs as well as hers: compassion for the sick in an uncaring world; frustration at restrictions in a society hidebound by hierarchy; open-mindedness in a Britain needing to become multicultural; an evident belief in the need for women to break out from the stultifying conventions of marriage and assert their sexual freedom – although arguably the latter was just the continuation of an upper-class practice made much harder to hide nowadays from paparazzi. Her funeral was one of the periodic, unscripted moments in current affairs which unleash genuine feelings of solidarity among British people. It is as if they wake up from their traditional passive conservatism and realise how much they really care about certain issues. There is a subtle shift in the public mood and in people's relations with one another. The topic is so alive, ten years later, that a Stephen Frears film dealing with the case, *The Queen*, has attracted large audiences. Helen Mirren is uncannily like the Queen, and the depiction of relations between members of the Royal Family, the Blairs and Palace flunkies has the ring of truth.

It should also be said that many other Britons were totally nonplussed by this public display of grief. They speculated bemusedly on the spiritual bankruptcy of those whose emotional lives were driven by the need to hero-worship public figures. They were astonished by the uncharacteristically British public expression of emotion. We can conclude that Britain contains many opposites, and also note that some British heroes are more unequivocally revered abroad than at home. So, Diana's saint-like media image was drawn on by the 2001 French film *Amelie* (directed by Jean-Pierre Jeunet), in which the heroine's life as a do-gooder is inaugurated at the moment she is watching the news report on Diana's death in Paris.

The Beckhams

Two contemporary heroes for young people are David Beckham, the ex-Manchester United footballer and England captain, and his wife Victoria. Posh and Becks, as they are known, are style icons and are observed minutely by the media, their fans, and detractors. In *On Beckham* (Jonathan Cape, 2001), for example, Julie Burchill said that David displays 'Diana-faced gravitas . . . [and] seems so aristocratic', while [Victoria] is 'so delightfully common'. The couple feature as key characters in Alistair McGowan's impressions on BBC1. Posh was formerly a member of the manufactured group the Spice Girls. Today they are very real trend setters – parents worry that teenage pop fans will copy Posh's wearing of a lip ring. Boys copy Beck's haircut.

They both have jobs to do and theoretically the intense media interest which surrounds them 'just happens'. Although what is reported is made to seem spontaneous and natural, it is in fact the product of an elaborate public-relations campaign. In August 2001 the British national press contained 450 stories about Victoria Beckham. This cannot have been accidental. Becks has his child Brooklyn's name tattooed in gothic script on his lower back, where press photographers can see it, and now also that of young Romeo. As an ambitious young couple they have realised that for them life in the media is money in the bank. So they set about cultivating their public personas.

In a sense the 'Posh and Becks' phenomenon is too closely orchestrated to be genuine popular culture, despite its dependence on mass support. Whereas most youth culture is about iconoclasm, rebellion and anarchy, their fame is orchestrated by PR firms. Posh and Becks are part of a process of the transfer of wealth and power from a previous generation to a new one. In 2001 they went by helicopter from their Cheshire mansion to the home of Lord Leverhulme, the soap magnate, for the dispersal auction sale of its contents. They spent £2.1 million on purchases of antique furniture. The effect of this was to strengthen the position of Establishment antique-collectors; to spread the message to their own fans that the past contains items of value; and to transfer the proceeds of other people's consumerism into wealth for their own future generations. Hence they consolidate the wealth of Britain past, while engaging in processes (pop music and football) which are seen as transitory and ephemeral.

Media celebrities

Another young contemporary hero whose career has risen on the strength of media publicity is the TV chef Jamie Oliver. He does everything in the eye of the media. He televised his cooking academy. He fronts TV ads for Sainsbury's. He writes for *The Times* magazine. He travels to New York. He is a talented, hard-working individual but he also benefits from the publicity machine which sells him. He is a 'media hero' who is valued for his appearance, passion, style and presentation. He lives his life in public and never seems to have private moments. All his T-shirts are ones the audience would like to own. They are never crumpled. Their owner looks confident. He never appears depressed or having moments of introspection. He is forever cheerful and cuddly. In reality such people don't exist. He has capitalised on being in the right place at the right time and is evidently the twenty-first-century version of the renaissance man whom people want to admire.

Business

Young people today particularly esteem achievers in business, commerce and finance. The businessman Richard Branson is the most admired figure. He is self-made, rich, zany and takes part in dangerous sports such as ballooning and powerboat-racing. He deals in elements of youth culture such as CDs, videos and DVDs though his Virgin Megastores. Young people admire the megalomania of his ambition – he also owns an airline and a train company – as much as the City distrusts him for his lack of focus.

Anita Roddick who founded the Body Shop is also admired for the stances which she takes on matters such as the testing of cosmetics on animals. As a female entrepreneur she is mould-breaking and serves as a role model for a younger generation of women who want to make power and principles a part of their identities.

Finally, a most unlikely 2000 overnight heroine, at the age of 24, was Derbyshire-born Ellen MacArthur. The young yachtswoman came second in the Vendée Globe single-handed round-the-world race. It was a phenomenal achievement for her and what struck a chord with people from all walks of life was the fact that she was not well connected, nor well-heeled and was not a particularly media-savvy person. In demeanour she was modest and didn't seem particularly confident. However, she was obviously extremely self-sufficient and competent, and had worked single-mindedly for her fame. She had started as a sailing instructor in Hull, had lived in a container in France, and gained her achievement on her merits. For these reasons, including also the nautical connection for an island people, she

…d to young and old. She currently holds the record for the fastest
…ound-the-world trip.

…lity TV

Such is the power of TV in Britain, that some heroes can be blatantly manufactured and presented to the audience, rather than chosen by the population
at large. This is done in a semi-documentary format. The public are voyeurs
who see behind the scenes of auditions, etc. People collude with the pretence
that they are a part of the programme-making and delude themselves into
believing it is all real. The sense of empowerment they are thus given makes
them more likely consumers of the eventual product. In 2001 an ITV series
Pop Stars set about auditioning young hopefuls from all over the British
Isles to form a band. The programme masqueraded as a talent competition,
and the band which was produced, called *Hear'Say* was presented as
something that rose commercially on its own merits. The audience was
bamboozled into not seeing the paraphernalia of the production process
(editing, promotion, stage-management). The group was put together in
front of the viewers' eyes week by week on TV, and yet spectators were quite
happy to be hoodwinked by a process which they were bankrolling.

The series was very like 'reality TV' where people's lives are turned
into soap opera. Successful candidates' families were interviewed. We vicari-
ously experienced emotions with them. And yet the whole system of heats
and talent spotting was a sham in the sense that it pretended to replace a
haphazard system where talented singers sink or swim, depending on their
luck, with one where merit is all. So, for example, Claire Freeland a Glasgow
call-centre supervisor was widely considered the most talented singer.
However, the verdict of the programme producer Nigel Lythgoe was Voice:
10. Looks: 3. So she was dropped from the group.

The show was really about generating interest to fuel a market for
a product which it was creating. This will ultimately sell CDs, make the pop
group stars and the programme producers rich and subvert the previous
norm, under which it was consumers, not manufacturers, who decided what
they wanted to consume. The formula is commercially successful and
promoter Simon Cowell has a new series *Pop Idol* for ITV which seeks a
solo performer.

Dumbing down

Many, particularly older people see standards of all sorts being lowered
in society and in the media generally. They call it 'dumbing down'. They

complain about the quality of TV programmes and attribute this perceived decline to deficiencies in the educational system. For years it has been suggested that the median level at which TV is beamed is the third form at school (age: 14). If that link is retained, media standards will fall even further, so the argument goes.

Similarly, every year GCSE and A-level results are greeted with complaints from the newspapers that the exams are getting easier. There is a ritual denial of this from teachers and teaching unions who say that people should give credit to the young for their hard work and achievement instead of undermining their morale. The government supports the examiners' line that standards have not in fact declined and that 'grade-inflation' is a mirage, but the government would, wouldn't it?

Reflecting this debate about standards, *Private Eye* runs a column called Dumb Britain. Sample recent extracts include:

> Steve Wright's *Big Quiz* (Radio 2)
> WRIGHT: Who wrote the novel *Lady Chatterley's Lover?*
> CONTESTANT: Chaucer.

> *National Lottery Jet Set* (BBC1)
> EAMONN HOLMES: Who wrote *Treasure Island?*
> CONTESTANT: Robinson Crusoe.

> *The Weakest Link* (BBC1)
> ANNE ROBINSON: Which is the only letter in the alphabet
>   with three syllables?
> CONTESTANT: Z.

It is tempting to suggest that this anxiety about dumbing down is a result of Britain's diminished economic and military significance in the world. Or again, it is one of the effects of devolving power to regions hitherto controlled by England. A former Chief Scientific Adviser to the government said in 2001 that universities are under-funded and must not be seen 'simply as a substitute for National Service to keep youngsters off the dole queue'.

Whatever the reason, fear about dumbing down of radio and TV programmes, turning ideas into soundbites that can be assimilated by a not-very-well-educated audience, is rife, and we will see later whether there is just cause for this view, or whether it is a symptom of a moral panic.

The debate about standards is like an annual game that is never satisfactorily resolved and which mirrors other social and cultural divides and anxieties. People who have themselves been to grammar schools and attended the old universities feel that they worked harder than the present generation and became more competent. Progressives, on the other hand, welcome the new ways, applaud the sloughing off of Britain's imperialist past and attribute the complaints to traditional British snobbery and conservatism.

Pessimists suggest that the under-educated young, having lost interest in the pursuit of knowledge are politically unconcerned and merely dissipate their energies in drugs, sex and pointless consumerism.

This is harsh. One has only to point to the Canadian writer, Naomi Klein's anti-globalisation book *No Logo*, which sold very well to the 18 to 30 age group in less than a year in Britain in 2000. Education may be changing and evolving, but it is by no means certain that standards are declining. Young candidates on Jeremy Paxman's *University Challenge* are frighteningly bright at answering both general knowledge and specialist questions.

British Cultural Identities structure

Having reviewed a number of potential approaches to the question of British cultural identity, we have chosen to structure our book into eight chapters. We have headed each chapter with a timeline because one needs to be aware of 'public' events which shape people's private experiences. After each of the chapters we have included review exercises which allow the development of discussion on issues which British people themselves debate. In order to inform discussion we have included some 'cultural examples'. These are items, mainly from popular culture, which people value. They include films, TV, drama, novels, social commentaries and other artefacts which illustrate the cultural state of the nation. They are not academic references, but signposts towards cultural understanding.

Our first chapter 'Places and peoples', deals with the cultural geography of Britain. People are products of their biology and environment (Nature and Nurture) and we try to determine what they have in common – what the British 'system' produces. The chapter considers how far people pride themselves on being from a particular area. There is a well known North–South divide but there is also a continuing historic rivalry between Lancashire and Yorkshire. People from Cornwall and Devon (the West Country) feel they are different from those in London, which is 300 miles away and yet rules them. Londoners see themselves as at the authentic heart of Britain, and so on.

'Education, work and leisure' deals with the formal and recreational aspects of living in Britain. It assesses the extent to which people accept the shared cultural values which schools and universities transmit to them. It looks at attitudes to employment, and the trauma for members of a social group who defined themselves as 'working' class but who are often no longer working. It asks whether leisure-time in Britain is spent productively, to promote the physical and psychic well-being of the population – or is it wasted in hedonism?

'Gender, sex and the family' traces the change in attitudes and patterns of behaviour of the sexes. Sex is biologically, but gender socially determined. So, where has a questioning of traditional gender roles led to in modern Britain? Attitudes to sex and sexuality, among young people particularly, are very different from their parents'. So how do families resolve these potential divisions? The concept of the nuclear family has undergone profound change. Male authority has been eroded. Marriage is less common and divorce is prevalent. Where is this leading not just in terms of social stability, but of how people see their family roles and futures?

In 'Youth culture and style' we examine the way in which 'teenagers', a concept first identified in the 1950s, have their own codes of communication, fashion, behaviour and cultural practices. We also look at the status of older people in a society becoming more youth-oriented.

'Class and politics' deals with the question of whether people's lives and psyches are conditioned by the socio-economic stratum in which they happen to have been born. The death of class has been repeatedly pronounced. We offer another view. We also look at the way in which class influences voting patterns and the extent to which people still see themselves as 'political' or of the right or left.

'Ethnicity and language' looks at important questions around race, not just for ethnic minorities, who make up 6.8 per cent of the British population, but for speakers of Irish, Scots, Welsh and English whose identities are partly thereby determined. It discusses the colonising nature of language and its effects on immigrants and Britain.

The chapter 'Religion and heritage' assesses how far people living in Britain maintain a spiritual dimension in their lives. Religious observance appears to be in decline. But that is not the whole story. Linked to the idea of religious belief is the collective endorsement of a set of values from the past, worth handing on, and preserved in the form of heritage. Heritage is more complicated than the preservation of historic monuments. It involves the idea of theme-park Britain, the Notting Hill carnival, distinctive foods. It is very often about the incorporation of influences from the margins into the eventual mainstream.

Some of the questions we are posing are: Will British culture be annihilated by, or will it incorporate global culture? Why does one cultural influence, one's gender for example, override another, one's Scottishness say? Is the present generation in Britain radically different from its parents? If so, in what ways? If not, why not? Do the British media reflect or direct people's views and perceptions? Is Britain a melting pot of cultures, does it allow and encourage diversity, or do newcomers become conformist and conservative? What does it mean to be British in the twenty-first century? If 'British' is a brand, what does it signify? Quality? Style? Snobbery? Popular Culture? Heritage? Social change? Stability? Perfidiousness? Good manners . . . ?

 ## Exercises

1   How important do you think mythology and folklore are to a 'sense of identity'? From the descriptions in this chapter, and from your own knowledge, what common images of England and of Britain have you noticed, and what characteristics do you think they represent?

2   In the next chapter, you will find it suggested that the British, and the English in particular, are being presented in a certain way in Hollywood in the 1990s. Before you read this however, we'd like you to consider the following exercises:

  ■ Thinking of the American films you have seen, how many English actors can you remember? Have they usually played English characters? How have the English been stereotyped by Hollywood in the past?

  ■ In terms of recent Hollywood films, James Bond is perhaps the most famous English character (first played by Sean Connery, a Scot). What other similar larger-than-life images of British people has Hollywood produced? How many of these originated in British novels?

  ■ Does Hollywood portray British women differently from British men (you might think of Deborah Kerr, Joan Collins, Glenda Jackson, Julie Andrews, Emma Thompson, or even the Americans Katherine Hepburn in *The African Queen* and Bette Davis in *The Virgin Queen*)?

3   How important do you think wider geographical perspectives, such as those offered by Europe or the Commonwealth, are to understanding British identity? How is national culture altered by these larger communities? Can you name fifteen countries that are in the Commonwealth, and can you list them by (a) size of population? (b) year of Independence?

4   British daily national newspapers are extremely varied, from the tabloid press to the broadsheets, and so are their readerships. A long-standing characterisation of newspapers categorises them in terms of the people who buy them. Listed below are the newspapers (a) and the descriptions of their readers (b) – can you match the one with the other:

(a)   *The Times; Daily Mail; Sun; Financial Times; Guardian; Daily Telegraph; Daily Mirror; Morning Star.*

(b)   ■   Read by the people who own the country.
      ■   Read by the people who think they run the country.

- Read by the people who think they ought to run the country.
- Read by the people who do run the country.
- Read by the wives of the men who run the country.
- Read by people who don't care who runs the country.
- Read by those who think the country should be run by another country.
- Read by those who think the country is being run by another country.

5   In this chapter we have looked at traditional British identities. What do you know of the following people and characters who have become important or comic cultural figures to the British: Lady Godiva, Henry VIII, Queen Guinevere, Dickens's Mr Podsnap, Shakespeare's Falstaff, Biggles, Bulldog Drummond, Robert the Bruce, Lord Nelson, Lawrence of Arabia, Clive of India, and Bunyan's Christian? What are the problems with continuing to advance these characters as icons of Britishness?

6   How important do you think it is to consider language when describing other people? For example, the word 'immigrant' has not been used in this chapter but you will come across it elsewhere in this book because it is the common term used by most of the British to describe other people who have come to settle in the UK. By contrast, the British abroad are almost never regarded (by the British) as 'immigrants' in other communities or even as 'emigrants' from Britain. Most often they are called 'expats' (short for expatriates). Why do you think this is?

Reading

Clifford, Sue and Angela King. *England in Particular* Hodder & Stoughton, 2006. Best-selling catalogue and celebration of local English phenomena from Quaker Meeting Houses to Horse fairs.

Fox, Kate. *Watching the English* Hodder & Stoughton, 2005.

Gascoigne, Bamber. *Encyclopedia of Britain* revised edition, Macmillan, 1994. Impressive reference work, meticulously researched, which contains an A to Z guide to almost every aspect of British culture, from pre-Roman times to the present.

Moran, Joe. *Queuing for Beginners* Profile Books, 2007. A quirky study of the detail of everyday life, partly based on Mass Observation studies. Using the format of a single day, it reveals the 'infra-ordinary' routines through which British people conduct their lives.

Room, Adrian. *An A to Z of British Life* OUP, 1992. Handbook containing a lot of information on background detail to British culture, history, idiosyncrasies and 'institutions' such as Ascot, Henley and Glyndebourne.

Samuel, Raphael (ed.). *Patriotism* 3 vols, Routledge, 1989. Detailed examination of kinds of British identity in terms of history, gender, race, politics, cultural icons, and much more.

Cultural examples

Films

Bridget Jones's Diary (2001) dir. Sharon Maguire. Deals with the efforts of a thirty-something woman to find a man. A 'chick flick'.

Billy Eliot (2000) dir. Stephen Daldry. Funny and shrewd treatment of class and work.

Lock, Stock and Two Smoking Barrels (1998) dir. Guy Ritchie. Four London working-class men pool their money in a high-stakes card game. Things go wrong and they end up owing half a million pounds with one week to come up with the cash. Ex-footballer Vinny Jones stars in this gangster movie with 'real' background.

Harry Potter and the Philosopher's Stone (2001) dir. Chris Columbus. Orphan Harry goes to Hogwart's Academy, learns the practice of magic and has adventures. Good overcomes evil. Blockbuster film of J.K. Rowling's novel, filmed in 'heritage' Yorkshire. She insisted on British actors.

The Queen (2006) dir. Stephen Frears. Lavish portrayal of conflict within the Royal Family over Diana, Princess of Wales.

Books

Ian McEwan, *The Cement Garden* (1984). Details adolescents' response to the death of their mother in a bleak Midlands environment. A key text for unlocking UK teenagers' minds.

Joanna Trollope, *The Choir* (1992). Presents a typically British conflict between appearance and reality, change and tradition, when a venal Dean wants to close a cathedral choir school.

Nick Hornby, *About a Boy* (1998). Deals with the problems facing a laddish central character who thinks he has his life sorted out. The son of one of his girlfriends introduces him to his own emotions. Filmed with Hugh Grant.

Tony Parsons, *Man and Boy* (2000). Written with autobiographical hindsight, this novel laments the myopia of a central character who loses everything through an irresponsible fling with a colleague. Discussed in a prison as Book of the Month, on Radio 4.

Graham Swift, *Last Orders* (1997). A group of four working-class Londoners travel to the seaside when their friend dies, to scatter his ashes in the sea. A high-profile British film followed in 2002.

Penelope Lively, *A House Unlocked* (2001). Though Lively is one of Britain's best contemporary novelists, this is a non-fictional collection of memories of English country life in the twentieth century inspired by Golsoncott, the Somerset country home occupied by her family.

TV programmes

Cold Feet. Very popular British equivalent of Friends (as is the sitcom *Coupling*) but with more orientation towards drama than comedy.

EastEnders. Enduringly popular soap with fans of all ages. Set in 'Albert Square', London.

Who Wants to be a Millionaire? Quiz programme, hosted by Chris Tarrant. It caught the imagination for its options of 'ask the audience' or 'phone a friend'.

The Weakest Link. Scathing Anne Robinson acts as a dominatrix in this quiz programme and rudely dismisses contestants who don't make the grade.

Deal or No Deal. A quiz show with Noel Edmunds, where contestants get a lot or a little money.

This Life. Ground-breaking documentary-format drama series where a group of lawyers in their 20s live together in a large house.

Power of Nightmares. dir. Adam Curtis. Powerful documentary suggesting that politicians are fearful of being seen as mere managers. So they invent enemies to protect against.

Websites

www.ons.gov.uk
> Office for National Statistics. UK Government Agency, produces social, health, economic, demographic, labour market and business statistics.

www.statistics.gov.uk
> The official UK statistics site. Up to date and accurate.

www.time.com/time/daily/special/diana/
> An archive of pictures from the life and death of Princess Diana.

www.private-eye.co.uk/
> Online version of very influential satirical magazine. Presents alternative view of contemporary Britain.

www.bbc.co.uk/history/programmes/greatbritons/
> The BBC's 'Greatest Briton' site.

www.wikipedia.org/
> Authoritative contemporary encyclopedia of useful facts and articles.

www.the-times.co.uk
www.telegraph.co.uk
www.guardian.co.uk
www.independent.co.uk
> These broadsheet newspapers offer daily comment and analysis which reflect and inform the culture.

Places and peoples: nation and region

Peter Childs

chapter 1

Timeline

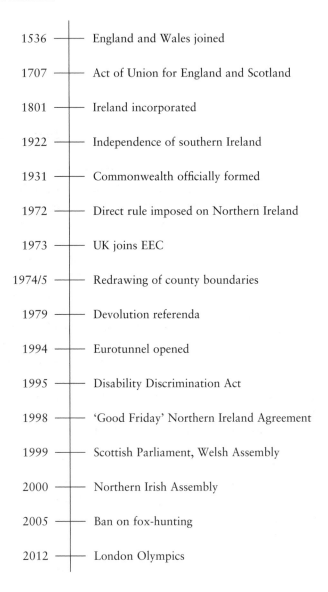

1536	England and Wales joined
1707	Act of Union for England and Scotland
1801	Ireland incorporated
1922	Independence of southern Ireland
1931	Commonwealth officially formed
1972	Direct rule imposed on Northern Ireland
1973	UK joins EEC
1974/5	Redrawing of county boundaries
1979	Devolution referenda
1994	Eurotunnel opened
1995	Disability Discrimination Act
1998	'Good Friday' Northern Ireland Agreement
1999	Scottish Parliament, Welsh Assembly
2000	Northern Irish Assembly
2005	Ban on fox-hunting
2012	London Olympics

Introduction

'B RITAIN' IS A COMMONLY used short form of the full name of the United Kingdom of Great Britain and Northern Ireland. Great Britain (GB) strictly comprises the countries England, Wales and Scotland, whereas the United Kingdom (UK) also includes Northern Ireland. On the one hand, these four countries have become part of one nation over the last 500 years: Wales was linked with England in 1536; an Act of Union joined the crowns of England and Scotland in 1707; Ireland was incorporated in a Union lasting from 1801 to 1921, when all but Northern Ireland gained independence (taking effect in 1922). On the other hand, as European history repeatedly demonstrates, political union is not cultural union, and it has often been maintained that Scotland and to a lesser extent Wales should have greater devolution of power from the government in Westminster, if not full-blown independence. The pressure of this view, following referenda of the populations, resulted in the creation of the Scottish Parliament and the Welsh Assembly in 1999, which give not autonomy but increased self-government (unlike the Scottish Parliament, the Welsh Assembly has no legis-lative or revenue-raising powers). These elected bodies can be perceived as part of a transition to full national government in Wales and especially Scotland, though at present they are seen by some as an extra layer of bureaucracy between the people and the UK government at Westminster, which retains overarching financial control and has generally centralised power rather then devolved it, especially in relation to local government below the regional level. By contrast, Northern Ireland had self-rule in most governmental areas except foreign affairs and defence prior to 1972, at which date direct rule from London was reintroduced following increased sectarian violence between Protestant and Catholic factions. However, fol-lowing the Peace Agreement in 1998 and in line with Scottish and Welsh devolution the previous year, a Northern Irish Assembly and Executive was created in 2000 to end direct rule from Westminster, though continued violence and a lack of political commitment to the Agreement has led to suspensions of the Assembly, of which the longest began in 2002 and continues into at least 2007. However, in 2006, the Northern Ireland Act

FIGURE 1.1 Map of the British Isles, showing locations of counties, cities, towns and villages discussed in this chapter

made it possible for the members to meet oncemore with a view to advising the Secretary of State concerning 'matters referred to it by him to support preparations for devolution'. A *Guardian* poll in August 2001 reported that 41 per cent of Britons believed Northern Ireland should join a united Ireland, while only 26 per cent believed it should be a part of the UK. By the end of 2006, Belfast and Northern Ireland in general were fast becoming top tourist destinations and relations between the north and south of the island were on a better footing than they had been in living memory. A culturally based, political problem remains for the British government however, as Northern Irish Catholics identify with the rest of Ireland in the south, while Northern Irish Protestants (of generally Scottish and English ancestry) see themselves as part of Britain and so oppose both Ireland's unification and devolutionary steps that would force them to come to a settlement with the Catholic population. Yet, it would be wrong to conclude that Northern Irish Protestants identify themselves with the English. Instead, they have developed their own identities while maintaining their religion and their allegiance to the crown as evidence of their Britishness – traits repeatedly revealed in polls which show them to be more religious and more conservative than people on the British mainland.

In terms of natural, as opposed to political geography, it can be argued that Britain is marked by great contrasts but few extremes. Its highest mountain is Ben Nevis (4,406 ft or 1,343 m) in Scotland, and its longest river is the Severn (220 miles or 354 km), which rises in central Wales but also wanders as far east as Gloucester in England, while the UK's largest lake is Lough Neagh (153 sq. miles or 396 sq. km) in Northern Ireland. Officially, the mainland stretches from Dunnet Head in the north of Scotland to Lizard Point in Cornwall, but most people will describe Britain as running from the famous names of Land's End, in the south, to John O'Groat's.

However, when situating British identity in terms of place in relation to culture, we should both turn to smaller geographical units, such as the ancient counties whose boundaries were contentiously redrawn in 1974, and look to the larger outside world, not least because many British people do not live in the UK. Britishness in modern times has often been defined in relation to the Continent as European political and physical links have become stronger: since 1973 the UK has been a member of the European Community (now European Union) and in 1994 the Channel Tunnel was opened, providing a rail connection from England to France. From another perspective, their eventful history means that British people have ties throughout the world, particularly with those more than fifty countries who are still members of the Commonwealth of Nations, a loose association of independent countries formerly of the British empire. In between all these geographical and political groupings there has arisen not just a few but a multitude of British cultures and identities.

To give an initial outline of the UK in terms of place, we can begin by looking at three aspects: size, population and people. The United Kingdom has a land area of just over 93,000 sq. miles (242,000 sq. km), a little over half of which is in England. This is one reason why England is sometimes mistaken for Britain abroad, but a stronger factor is the relatively large size of England's population – an imbalance that allows it to dominate the union, beaming its television programmes to the rest of the nation for example. The UK population size is stable but slightly on the increase because immigration and greater longevity are compensating for a declining birth rate. It topped 60 million in 2005, and the average age was 38.8, almost five years higher than in 1971.

However, we should not assume that strength of cultural identity increases with size of population – indeed, many people would argue that the opposite is more likely to be the case. It is therefore not surprising that to confuse Britain with England (which has 84 per cent of the population) can cause grave offence. History provides ancient reasons for vehemence of feeling: England is named after the Angles, a tribe who invaded Britain's south-east coast from northern Europe in the fifth century and, with other conquering tribes such as the Saxons, drove the older inhabitants, the Celts, to the west. Celtic influence is still notably present in Ireland, Scotland, Wales and Cornwall, and this ethnic difference remains one basis on which England, of the UK's four countries, is sometimes considered to have the least in common with the others. On the other hand, the breakdown into English, Welsh, Scottish and Irish histories can also be misleading when it comes to contemporary cultural identity. The domestic histories of these four countries do not adequately represent the people of the UK today because Britain now has a far richer mix of ethnicities than those associated with the ancient Anglo-Saxon or Celt. Over the last century and before, the connections created by the empire have led to the arrival in Britain of many people from the Caribbean, the Indian subcontinent and Africa, such that, for example, the number of British people of Asian descent is now greater than the population of Northern Ireland. Similarly, recent migrants from Eastern European members of the EC, older refugees from countries like Bangladesh and Uganda, plus communities uprooted from Cyprus, Vietnam and China, have added to the different cultural identities found in Britain. In 2000, the number of people who classified themselves as members of an ethnic minority stood at 3.8 million, a rise of nearly a million in ten years. Again, while this book deals with people within the UK, there are strong British identities to be found in, for example, Hong Kong, a British crown colony up to 1997, the Falkland Islands, over which Britain fought with Argentina in 1982, and the vast Commonwealth of Nations. So, while this chapter will focus on places within the UK, the cultural life of people in Britain is both always in flux and much wider than geographical boundaries might suggest.

Lastly, in amongst this discussion of British identities, it is also salutary to note that there are many rumours circulating about the end of Britishness. Tom Nairn's 1981 book *The Break-Up of Britain* (Verso Books) is a key point of orientation in the debate, followed up by his *After Britain: New Labour and the Return of Scotland* (Granta, 2000). But, in the context of Europe and devolution, there is, of course, a range of other books on the same subject with different angles, such as John Redwood's anti-Europe *The Death of Britain* (Macmillan, 1999).

There are additionally voices from abroad, one of which I shall quote. An article by expatriate Andrew Sullivan in the *New York Times* in 1999 (21 February, 'There will always be an England') uses the headline 'Farewell Britannia' on every page. Sullivan anticipates a post-imperial attempt at dismantling:

> By quietly abolishing Britain, the islanders abolish the problem of Britain. For there is no problematic 'Great' hovering in front of Scotland, England or Wales. These older deeper entities come from a time before the loss of empire, before even the idea of empire. Britain ... is a relatively recent construct, cobbled together in the seventeenth century in the Act of Union with Scotland. ...

And there are of course voices from Scotland and Wales that also look forward to the end of Britishness as the route to a fuller and better national future free from England. Both Tom Nairn and Andrew Marr have written books that foresee an English-free Scotland that would effectively end the 'idea' or 'experiment' of Britain. The Welsh poet R.S. Thomas writes: 'Britishness is a mask. Beneath it there is only one nation, England' while Gwynfor Evans, the former leader of Plaid Cymru published a book entitled *The End of Britishness* in 1981, arguing that 'Britishness is Englishness'. Another poet, Robert Crawford, from north of the border, maintains that: 'It is hard to think today of what could be confidently called "British" culture rather than English or Scottish culture ... Scottish culture seems to have moved into a post-British phase.'

While we can therefore still talk about 'British Cultural Identities', the emphases need to remain on the multiplicity and plurality implied by the third word, particularly given the resurgence of regionalism in recent years, suggesting that the weakness and strength of Britain is the fact that many people see themselves as primarily some other nationality or ethnicity, and 'British' only secondarily. This trend is likely to continue. The Office for National Statistics predicts that by 2031, the population will have grown by another seven million. Proportionally, this increase will represent still greater migration into the country and rising numbers of children born to migrant parents or grandparents, enriching the mix of international identities still further.

Nation

The British mainland, separated from the European continent by the English Channel, is the eighth largest island in the world but the third most populous after Java and Honshu in Japan; with a total population over five million, Ireland is the twentieth most populous. The UK's inhabitants are therefore islanders, and their attitude towards the rest of the world has sometimes been said to reflect this, though some would say this is merely an English trait.

While the Commonwealth offers many indications of the cultural and ethnic influences on modern Britain, and is at the same time a sign of the UK's international links and Imperial past, it is Europe's economic policies, legal dictates and bureaucracy that is increasingly forcing the British to reconsider their identity. For some people, 'Brussels' has become a major opponent, in the face of whose recommendations and legislation they are trying to assert a national culture that they feel is coming under attack. Alongside genuine fears, such as that of a loss of local languages, there has also arisen a mythology of European Union policies: rumours maintaining that traditional British foods, such as dairy milk chocolate, crisps, fish and chips, and Cornish ice cream are under serious threat because of EU standardisation. Through appeals to such recognisable staples of national heritage, a powerful resistance to the EU has been built up, but other voices maintain that Britain's political, economic and legislative future has to lie within a united Europe. Consequently, the split over the EU within the Conservative Party has constituted its major policy stumbling block for the many years. While the majority of British people are happy in principle to participate in an economic union they are also defensive of their distinctive traditions and their cultural separation from other European countries: in other words, of their traditional identity.

Country

To illustrate some familiar ways in which the countries of the British Isles have developed separate cultural identities, we can begin with examples of their various images and emblems. England's patron saint (and also Portugal's) is the probably fictional St George, a knight who slew a fire-breathing dragon in medieval English mythology. St George's cross is the name of the English flag, which depicts a red cross on a white background – and English national teams still play rugby and football predominantly in white. The English emblem has been the rose since the War of the Roses in the fifteenth century, when the House of Lancaster, whose symbol is a red rose, fought for the English crown against the House of York, whose symbol is a white rose. More recently, as a symbol of both tradition and socialism, the red rose has been adopted as its emblem by the Labour Party. Red is also the colour of Wales, whose mascot since 1801 has, interestingly, been the red Welsh dragon, which is the central figure on the country's flag. The patron saint of Wales is a sixth-century monk called St David (*Dewi Sant* in Welsh), and his day, 1 March, is regarded as the country's unofficial public holiday (in a 2006 poll, 87 per cent of people in Wales wanted it to be a Public Holiday, and 65 per cent were willing to give up another holiday in lieu). Wales's twin emblems are the leek and the daffodil. English and Welsh hostility is rooted in history, the relative size of populations arguably giving rise to English condescension and Welsh resentment. Welsh identities are distinctive in terms of language, literature and culture, but Wales is also divided by language (most people speak English and not Welsh), politics (between those who want a republic and those who would wish for a self-governing nation within a federal UK), and geography (as in England, there is a split between north and south). The Welsh emphasise a sense of community more than the English (except those in the north of England who can be as hostile to southern Englanders as the Scots or Welsh are), and according to surveys see themselves as more caring, genuine and responsible than their English neighbours. Economic regeneration, the new Welsh Assembly, the resurgence of the Welsh language and the characteristic landscape of the valleys have all added to a growth in Welsh national feeling.

Intranational rivalry is suggested by two other adopted animals: the warring lion (England) and unicorn (Scotland). Since James VI of Scotland became James I of England in 1603, these animals have featured on the Royal Arms holding the monarch's shield. The lion has become a symbol of the strength of the crown and Britain in general, while the Scottish unicorn represents purity. In politics, the Scottish Nationalist Party is the strongest voice for the country's distinctive identity, and its most famous campaigning supporter, Sean Connery, has vowed to move back to Scotland if the country wins independence. The Scots have a stronger sense of national identity and allegiance than most English or Welsh, perceiving themselves as tough, friendly, outdoor people who are proud of their traditions and history. Consequently, and partly because of the distinctive Scottish accent(s), they have a higher profile abroad than the Welsh, and in some ways a more positive profile than the English. Scotland's patron saint is one of the twelve apostles, St Andrew, and its emblem is the thistle, a symbol of defence. St Andrew's cross forms a part of the British flag, known to most British people as the Union Jack, together with the crosses of St George and St Patrick, the patron saint of Ireland.

A fifth-century ex-slave, St Patrick made the base for his gospel preaching in Armagh, and from there led the successful resurgence of Christianity against chieftains on the British mainland. His feast day, 17 March, is an official holiday in Northern Ireland and his cross is the country's flag (it is not that of the Republic of Ireland). Northern Irish identities contain strong English, Scottish and Irish connections, although there are people in the six counties who identify neither with traditional Irishness nor with Britons from

FIGURE 1.2   Mini with Union Jack design

the mainland, seeing themselves instead overwhelmingly in terms of their own local culture, with its emphasis on both hard work and an easy-going character. Ireland's emblem is the shamrock, whose three-in-one leaf was supposedly used by St Patrick to demonstrate the Holy Trinity, but on the British coat of arms Ireland is represented by a harp, now most widely recognised as the logo for Guinness, the famous Irish stout. The majority of these symbols have become signs of a collective heritage and the degree to which people align themselves with such images today is negligible, but on the saints' days a few individuals do wear badges with their country's emblem in their lapels. In terms of popular culture, the Union Jack had already become simply a minor fashion design in the 1960s and 1970s, appearing on watch faces and T-shirts. It was also taken up in the 1980s by football fans, who since then have visited Europe with the flag daubed on their faces (reminiscent of the Ancient Britons who would paint their faces blue with a substance called woad to frighten their enemies). Today, individuals are more likely to turn to television personalities, film and pop stars, or sports players for their country's heroes and icons.

Ireland is the second largest of the British Isles. However, unlike smaller islands which are wholly British, such as the Isle of Wight and the Shetlands, Ireland is officially partitioned. In 1921, when an agreement was signed giving the rest of the country independence, six of the nine Irish counties that constituted the ancient province of Ulster remained part of the United Kingdom – these were the north-eastern counties that were predominantly Protestant. Though people and communities place their allegiances according to their different beliefs and associations, Northern Ireland therefore has national and official links with the rest of Britain while its people share deep roots with histories and traditions south of the border, and since the Anglo-Irish agreement of 1985 the Republic of Ireland has participated in its political and legal matters. Ireland is politically divided but in several respects it is culturally united for many people, not least because the Irish have retained a national distinctiveness despite the globalising influences that are so evident in England. In the 1960s, traditional Irish music saw a resurgence that has continued; government policy has been to revive the Irish language; indigenous sports such as hurling and Gaelic football have remained popular; and Irish literature is flourishing. For example, in Seamus Heaney, the Irish have arguably produced the finest poet writing in the English language since W.B. Yeats – who was also Irish. Also, in 2005 the Booker Prize for fiction, Britain's best-known literary award, was won by *The Sea*, a complex work by Wexford-born John Banville, who many critics consider both the heir to James Joyce and Samuel Beckett and one of the supreme living prose stylists in English.

In 1994, the Booker was won by James Kelman, a Scot, with his novel *How Late it Was, How Late*. This is a story written in Glaswegian slang and its part-abusive, part-aggressive patter is peculiar to that city, such that its idioms are not always readily intelligible in much of Scotland outside Glasgow, let alone in the rest of Britain. In addition to a unique vocabulary, the Scots have their own legal and educational systems, a stronger Calvinist tradition than the English, and a history which has forged closer links with the French and Irish than the English. When the Scots move abroad, it is said that their national identity emigrates with them, which is significant when approximately four times as many Scots live outside of Scotland as within. It is important to remember that such feelings of belonging do not cease at the border and, in England for example, there is a strong sense of Scottish identity – as any 25 January spent at thousands of English pubs will demonstrate. This is Burns' night, when the birth of Scotland's national poet, Robert Burns, is celebrated with drink, song and dance in a way that Shakespeare's very seldom is. Scotland retains a strong and sometimes antagonistic cultural identity separate from England and sceptical of the idea of Britain in which the centre of power is so remote and Scottish oil, the economic foundation for any possible independence over recent decades, has always been British North Sea oil. After the 1707 Union, Scotland continued with distinct legal, educational and religious institutions and Scottish affairs are still largely managed at the Houses of Parliament in London by Scottish MPs.

Officially, the most closely tied countries in the UK are England and Wales, which includes the large island of Anglesey across the narrow Menai Strait. Often mentioned as one unit for purposes of surveys, censuses and polls, England and Wales are joined administratively as well as politically and economically. However, many of the arguments for devolution have rested upon the view that Wales, as well as Scotland, is readily distinguishable from England in terms of language, culture and history. For example, a traditional cultural event which identifies Wales separately from the rest of Britain but which is held in many forms is the Eisteddfod, a bardic competition from pre-Christian times. The name, meaning 'chairing' or 'session', derives from the ceremonial seating of the bard or poet whose work has been awarded the first prize. The Royal National Eisteddfod, conducted entirely in Welsh, is held annually in different locations throughout the country. It involves music, drama and other arts, as well as poetry. The Eisteddfod is announced over a year in advance at a harp ceremony conducted by the Gorsedd, or Court, encircled by specially laid stones. The festival is associated with a nationalistic Welsh identity and *Plaid Cymru*, 'the party for Wales', was founded in a hotel room in Pwllheli during the Eisteddfod in 1925. As a cultural event the Eisteddfod remains identifiably Welsh even though there are English language spin-offs, just as Highland reels and sword dancing are Scottish. In terms of place, it is country rather than nation that remains the major cultural, though not necessarily political, grouping with which people identify.

The Welsh are more socially and politically integrated into Britain than any other non-English country. The stated aim of its nationalists is to gain as much freedom as possible within the union, rather than seek full independence, though this may be for practical, economic reasons rather than any other, with Welsh industry and agriculture dependent on the British market and economy. It is cultural self-determination and the preservation of Welsh heritage that are of most importance, and this stance has been largely successful. According to the 2001 General Household Survey, people in England are most likely to describe themselves as British (48 per cent), followed by the Welsh (35 per cent), and then the Scots (27 per cent), with those aged over 65 less likely to accept the 'British' label.

Region

It is important to remember that culture varies for Irish, Welsh, Scottish or English people depending on which region of their country they come from. In Wales, three-quarters of the population live in the valleys and coal regions of the south, which instil a different sense of Welsh identity from the mountains and seaside towns of the more militantly anti-English north; while in England it is the heavily populated metropolitan areas that have created several of the strongest regional identities. People from these different areas are associated with specific names and local characteristics, though it is their dialect that most obviously distinguishes them. For example, those from Newcastle and Tyneside, in the north-east of England, are called 'Geordies' after a mining lamp designed by George Stephenson, while people from Liverpool are known as Scousers, after a sailor's stew of meat and potatoes called lobscouse, and anyone brought up in the vicinity of London's Cheapside is known as a cockney, originally the name for a spoilt city child. The importance of regional identity can also be understood from any phone-in radio programme where presenters will almost invariably cite the area that callers are from, thereby eliciting subject matter for discussion and adding interest for listeners who have connections with the area.

Since 1994, England has been divided into nine regions (North West, North East, Yorkshire & Humberside, East Midlands, West Midlands, South West, South East, London, and East), and as from 1999 these have been used as European Parliament constituencies. The country is often talked about in terms of a North–South divide, which is cultural, economic and political (the Labour Party has far more support in the north and the Conservative Party in the south). The perceived divide does not occur in the middle of the country, however, and southerners sometimes refer to a cold, industrial region that is everywhere 'north of Watford', a town not particularly far north of London. In turn, some northerners caricature many southerners as 'soft' or as emotionally 'cold'. This is because people from the South East, and particularly London, are sometimes seen as fast living, career minded and unfriendly, while they are also more comfortably off and enjoy better weather than those further north. Differences between north and south have evolved over the last two centuries and are more cultural than simply industrial or economic (during parts of the nineteenth century the north was more prosperous than the south). In August 2001, *The Times* published a special issue of its Saturday Magazine, proclaiming 'It's Cool Up North' (punning on the phrase 'It's Cold Up North'). The reasons for this assertion are several: the economy is diversifying and shifting from traditional manufacturing areas, currently in recession, into more prosperous service industries (e.g. a quarter of workers in Leeds are now in financial and business services); culturally, the north has provided the most prominent groups, from the Beatles (Liverpool) through Oasis (Manchester) to the Arctic Monkeys (Sheffield); in football, Manchester United and Liverpool have greater pedigrees than Arsenal and Chelsea; plus London no longer has a monopoly on fashion, and Manchester's Joe Bloggs label, for example, has broken several sales records since its foundation in 1995.

However, the largest number of 'enterprise zones' and development areas, assisted by government funding and incentives for industry, are in regions such as the Midlands, the North East, east central Scotland and South Wales – but this economic difference from the south of England is frequently exaggerated. That a southern English region such as south-west Cornwall is also a development area is often ignored because it is distant from London and the financially dominant South East. The greatest financial distinction between London and the rest of the country is the cost of housing, with average national house prices usually insufficient to buy a home anywhere in London.

Other regional differences are evident in sport, food and housing: the north has rugby league, the south rugby union; the north has butties, barmcakes, and baps (all breadcakes) while the south has sandwiches and rolls; terraced housing is more common in the north, detached houses and bungalows in the south. Between these two regions lies the Midlands, a band of counties such as Staffordshire and Nottinghamshire across central England which, caught between two cultures, often seems to be regarded as the north by people in the south and vice versa. However, a strong regional identity associated with the dales, hills and moors is felt by people in the Midlands, and the countryside of a county such as Derbyshire is often considered the most beautiful in England (by Jane Austen in *Pride and Prejudice*, for example). Also, a distinct personality attaches to Birmingham, the UK's second-largest city, and the distinctive 'Brummie' accent is as recognisable as a Scottish or Welsh.

Language, accent, vocabulary and idioms of speech f[...]
regional differences. For example, Welsh, a version of which [...]
Britain when the Romans invaded in 55 BC, is one of the ol[...]
in the British Isles. Tens of thousands of people still speal[...]
educational institutions run language courses, and, since 197[...]
Wales, or *Cymru*, has been bilingual. About a quarter of the [...]
tion speak both languages, and because Welsh and English ar[...]
supported it is usual to see signs written in the two languages. Also, Gaelic,
another variant of the ancient Celtic languages, is still spoken by some
people in Ireland, Scotland and, to a lesser extent, the Isle of Man. Accent
and idiom vary enormously throughout Britain, although since the 1990s
there has been concern expressed over the spread of 'estuary English': an
outer London accent and dialect characterised by features of pronunciation
such as lisped 'r's and by words such as 'basically' (it is thought by some
to be reducing speech variations). In England there are still great differences in regional accent but the clearest boundary is that between north and
south. No English person is likely to mistake the long, soft vowels of a West
Londoner who could rhyme 'garage' with 'large', for the short, hard ones
of a Lancastrian, who could rhyme 'garage' with 'ridge'. As for local
vocabulary and idioms, if we take Scotland as an example, some words have
become national expressions and most British people will understand 'ken'
(know) or 'wee bairn' (small baby). However, an English person would be
unlikely to know the meaning of such words as 'wabbit' (tired and weak),
'toom' (empty) or 'reidh' (smooth).

Scottish words come from different languages that lie either side of an
ancient regional divide. The majority of Scots are Lowlanders and have an
ancestry that is part-Teutonic and part-Celtic. In the past, they were
considered different from the traditionally more aggressive, independent,
Gaelic-speaking Highlanders, who were a minority but supplied the national
symbols of the tartan, bagpipes, kilt and sporran (like the Highland games,
these are largely produced for tourists nowadays). However, except in the
crofting (loosely, farming) communities of the west, this division is historical more than contemporary, and religious denomination, football team
allegiance and city of birth are more likely to form points of cultural identity,
especially for Lowlanders. Today, Gaelic is the principal language only in
the Outer Hebrides and a few other, mainly island communities.

While it is small in comparison with many countries, Britain still has
regional television companies which, as well as making and carrying the
nationally transmitted programmes, provide localised information to areas
such as Granada in the north-west of England and Central in the Midlands.
Since the 1980s, regional accents have been increasingly welcomed onto the
BBC airwaves, which were previously saturated by announcers with the
clipped tones of received pronunciation, an upper-class accent used to

standardise speech by public schools in the nineteenth century. Today, there are also local radio broadcasts in Welsh and since 1982 there has been a Welsh-language television channel called *Sianel Pedwar Cymru*, which means Channel 4 Wales and is abbreviated to S4C. However, national stations are more culturally influential for most people, and satellite stations for some. While there are regional weekly and even daily papers, a similar picture is true of newspapers: even locally, national media are frequently more popular than regional.

County

After region, the largest area with which the British identify themselves is their county, a geographical fusion of landscape, culture and administration most likely to affect people in terms of its natural scenery and its historic landmarks. County boundaries partitioned ancient Britain and three counties in the south – Sussex, Kent and Essex – were Anglo-Saxon kingdoms. Modified in 1975, counties still form the basis of local government in England and Wales, though reorganisation in 1997 again changed the map (for example, Gwent used to be a county in south-east Wales but, since the 1997 local government reorganisation, it officially no longer exists). In terms of county types, the most famous grouping in England is the 'Home Counties', a nineteenth-century phrase referring to the counties around London, such as Kent, Surrey, Berkshire, Middlesex and Essex. Some counties are known for their countryside: Cumbria's Lake District (made famous in Wordsworth's poetry) and Hampshire's New Forest (a royal hunting ground for William the Conqueror); others for their industry: Lancashire's factories and mills (described in novels by Charles Dickens and Elizabeth Gaskell) and Nottinghamshire's mines (as in D.H. Lawrence's *Sons and Lovers*).

Northern Ireland is sometimes known simply as 'the six counties'. Local government there operates now on the basis of small district and borough councils, but ancient county identities are stronger. To take one example, Antrim, which derives its name from the fifth-century monastery of Aentrebh, occupies the north-east corner of Ireland. A county of moorlands and wooded glens, it is bordered by the sea on three sides. On the north coast is the famous Giant's Causeway. This is a promontory of vertical basalt columns formed by a volcanic rift which stretches under the sea to the Hebrides, islands off the west coast of Scotland. However, Irish legend holds that a giant built this as a walkway from Ireland to a cave on the Hebridean island of Staffa, so that he could attack the legendary Scottish hero Fingal. The roof of Fingal's Cave is also formed of straight six-sided rock columns which the two giants supposedly threw at each other. Celtic mythology adds a magical dimension to local identities and has been used in Ireland in attempts to forge a national consciousness, but even English Romantic poets such as Keats, Wordsworth and Tennyson have written about Fingal's Cave.

Most of England's modern counties are based on the thirty-nine ancient counties established between the twelfth and sixteenth centuries. They have a recognisable identity and will be said to have their own particular characteristics and distinctive inhabitants. Counties have given their names to famous stretches of countryside (e.g. Surrey Hills or Devon Moors), to types of people (unsophisticated socialites are 'Essex girls' and those with determination have 'Yorkshire grit'), to food (Cumberland sausages and Cornish pasties) and even to breeds of animal (Staffordshire bull terrier and Berkshire pig). However, one of the strongest ways in which county loyalties are continued is through sport. For example, one of the twenty county cricket clubs, Yorkshire, refused up until 1992 to allow anyone not born in the county to play for the team. Despite this, Yorkshire has won the County Championship more often than any other team.

Of course, geographical features are also significant. Yorkshire is separated from its historic rival Lancashire by the Pennines, a range of limestone hills popular with walkers and sometimes described as the backbone of England. Yorkshire is famous abroad for the moors on which the Brontë sisters used to live, but the county is also well-known in Britain for a section of the Pennines, the Yorkshire Dales, which was designated a National Park in 1954. These Parks are areas of significant natural beauty in England and Wales protected under an Act of 1949. The Act prohibits building or development in such areas as Dartmoor and the New Forest in England, Snowdonia and the Pembrokeshire coast in Wales. Similar protection applies to 'listed buildings', usually those dating back before 1840. Such measures preserve the past for the heritage and tourism industries and, partly in consequence, listed buildings and National Parks are sometimes put forward as representative of an authentic Britishness that is at threat from the architecture, pollution and city-oriented life of the present.

Yorkshire is particularly famous for having a strong identity, but this is actually true of most counties. For example, in 1995 inhabitants of Britain's smallest ex-county, Rutland, which was merged with Leicestershire in 1974, were trying to have the county officially recognised again, by raising funds through a 'Rutland' credit card: they succeeded and Rutland was one of the forty-seven ceremonial or geographical counties recognised in the Lieutenancies Act 1997, named for the appointment of Lord-Lieutenants, who are historically the Crown's representative in a county. In the 1970s, this sense of local county identity was satirised in a TV series called *Rutland Weekend Television*, a spin-off from *Monty Python's Flying Circus* that had nothing to do with the county – it just pretended to be run on a low budget by a small community of amateur enthusiasts.

In 1975, the Welsh counties were rearranged with others to reduce their number from thirteen to eight. Powys, in mid-Wales, covers the old counties of Montgomeryshire, Radnorshire and most of Breconshire, but the name itself is that of an ancient province dating from about the fifth century. Like all British counties, it is steeped in history. The county contains Powis and Montgomery Castles, the Dan-y-Ogof Caves, Brecon Cathedral, and Gregynog Hall, but its most famous landmark is the Brecon Beacons, or *Bannau Brycheiniog* in Welsh. These are a collection of mainly red sandstone mountains, designated a National Park in 1957, that run for forty miles away from the English border. Along and between the mountains are standing stones from 5,000 to 6,000 years ago, ancient castles, and cairns (hill markers made from piles of stones). The forests, mountains and reservoirs of the Beacons provide excellent grounds for outdoor activities such as angling, gliding, riding, boating, trekking and cycling. Since 1996, Wales has been divided into unitary authorities, but county identities remain for many people.

Though Scottish local government is now conducted by 'council areas', Scotland has thirty-three traditional counties, of which Fife was the only county not to be renamed as a region in the local government reorganisations of 1974/5 when Scotland was divided into nine large administrative regions and three island areas. The administrators of the Local Government Act had intended that the county be split in two but the people of Fife protested so vehemently that the plans were dropped. It is also nationally and politically significant that off the coast of Fife are the drilling ships and rigs that have been exploring for oil and gas in the North Sea since the 1970s. Some of the arguments put forward for devolution by the Scottish National Party, which has seats at Westminster and campaigns for an independent Scottish Parliament, turned on the standpoint that North Sea gas and oil are Scottish and would enable the country, free from England, to run a prosperous economy. England, for its part, makes occasional gestures at Scottish inclusion, as when the economist Adam Smith became the first Scot to feature on an English banknote when he replaced the composer Edward Elgar on the Bank of England's £20 note in 2007 – a fact that left the leader of the Scottish National Party, Alex Salmond, distinctly unimpressed given that Smith already featured north of the border on the Scottish £50 note.

City

In all, the United Kingdom currently has sixty-six cities, a title many British people wrongly think is given to a town with a cathedral. City is actually a title of dignity conferred on towns of religious, commercial or industrial importance by statute, royal charter or tradition (for example, Coventry,

Exeter and Norwich are mentioned as cities in William the Conqueror's eleventh-century *Domesday Book* of landholdings). Occasionally, new cities are created, sometimes bidding for the status, as Brighton did successfully in 2000. Britain's cities vary enormously, from the nineteenth-century industrial giants Manchester and Newcastle in the north to the southern ports such as Southampton and Bristol. There are also the cities noted chiefly for their cathedrals, such as Hereford and Ely, and the heritage cities such as the Roman town of Chester, whose entire medieval surrounding wall has survived, or Winchester, a small city of only 30,000 people which in Anglo-Saxon times was the capital of England.

According to the EU's 'Exploring Europe' publication, the first five things that spring to mind when someone thinks of the UK are Shakespeare, the BBC, the Beatles, Royalty and London, the capital of England. Within London there is a 'square mile' of offices and banks that encompasses the original walled area that is also sometimes referred to simply as 'the City' and is the financial hub of Britain's business activities. At over eight million, London has the largest population of any city in Europe and has a claim to be the most ethnically diverse of the planet, although many people have been steadily moving away to the outer suburbs and commuter zones since the Second World War. Britain's capital is one of the best-known cities in the world but in many ways it is different from the rest of the UK, its growing population largely fuelled by migrants. The cultural meetings of established and new citizens illustrate the blended histories that London now represents because its 'conglomerate nature', as Salman Rushdie records in his controversial 1988 novel *The Satanic Verses*, now echoes the cultural diversity of the old empire. To reflect London's particular interests and identity, the position of Mayor was revived in May 2000, and its first elected incumbent was Ken Livingstone, the ex-leader of the former Greater London Council, which was itself reborn in the form of a Greater London Assembly created to run affairs in the capital. A 2006 survey commissioned by the government concluded that Britain's cities were in economic recovery after years of decline, with the biggest secrets to regeneration being a university and an airport. The research, based on 56 cities, found that most English cities still lagged behind European counterparts with London only 23rd out of 61 in the European league table of economic performance (Bristol is 34th, Leeds 43rd, Newcastle 58th and Liverpool in last place at 61st).

Britain's high culture is famously represented everywhere in London from the National Gallery in Trafalgar Square and the Royal Academy of Arts in Piccadilly to the Royal Opera House in Covent Garden and the National Theatre on the South Bank. Museums in central London are around every corner; from the Museum of the Moving Image (MOMI), which celebrates film and television, to the vast British Museum which was the world's first public museum and is one of Britain's most visited tourist attractions. As much as anything in London, the British Museum serves as a reminder of Britain's Imperial history, and yet it is only one of around a hundred major museums in the capital. These, from the Museum of the Jewish East End and the Museum of Eton Life to the Sherlock Holmes Museum and the Florence Nightingale Museum, represent the variety of Britain's lucrative cultural heritage industry.

Tradition is still celebrated all year round, from the Lord Mayor of Westminster's New Year's Parade through to the Lord Mayor's Show in November. However, in a modern consumer culture such as Britain's, the past is often used for commercial profit or for charity: 'punks' are quite likely to be art students looking to supplement their grants by simulating a Britishness for photographers; Pearly Kings and Queens, who were originally arbitrators in arguments between traders, are now usually on show, with their coats covered in mother-of-pearl buttons, to raise money for local causes.

To many people outside the capital, 'London' conjures up a collection of buildings, landmarks and monuments such as Buckingham Palace, St Paul's Cathedral, the Tower of London, Westminster Abbey, Big Ben and Piccadilly Circus. However, London is best seen as not one city but a patchwork of cities stitched together: the cockney East End, the Docklands development, the Parliament at Westminster, the administration at Whitehall, the parks and the Thameside areas, the museums, theatres, shops and galleries of the West End, the residential areas such as Hampstead and Belgravia, the City, the exhibition area around Earls Court, and the famous suburbs from Richmond in the west to Greenwich on the east. Despite this diversity, it is the tourist attractions that survive in the popular imagination as representative of London: a fascination with Britain's past that was illustrated in the 1960s when London Bridge was bought by wealthy Americans who had it taken apart and rebuilt in Arizona.

A further less well-publicised characteristic of London and other British cities is the rise in the number of homeless people sleeping on the streets, which exceeds 2,000, and a parallel increase in begging, which is now common in the central metropolitan areas. In London and elsewhere, 'inner-city' areas are generally less well off than the suburbs, to which the more affluent sections of society have moved (a small counter-trend has brought the middle classes into the renovated dockland areas of London and other cities). Lifestyles are different too: in the inner cities the neighbourhood and street in which people live impinge more on their sense of identity than they do in the suburbs where people's home and garden are major preoccupations and sources of pleasure. Inner-city regeneration has become a central policy for successive governments since the war, and more especially since the 'riots' that broke out in the early 1980s in the inner cities of London, Liverpool, Bristol and Birmingham, and led to violent clashes between police

FIGURE 1.3 London Bridge (the most photographed site in Britain)

and protesters against the government's race, housing and employment policies.

Until recently, the capital city of Northern Ireland was most famous throughout the world for its violence, but this is changing as social and commercial regeneration takes hold and the country welcomes increasing numbers of tourists who might not have visited before. Since 1968, Belfast has chiefly made the front pages of British newspapers for its sectarian killings, although statistically it has been a safer place to live than many American cities. Separated as they are by the fortified wall of the 'Peace Line', the Falls Road (Catholic) and the Shankhill Road (Protestant) have become notorious throughout Britain and 'the Troubles', as they are locally known, have contributed to Belfast's population of around 300,000 having one of the highest unemployment levels in Britain. Following the peace negotiations begun in 1995, the Northern Ireland Tourist Board has been actively trying to bring visitors back to the country through a publicity campaign including newspaper and television advertisements, to see sights ranging from the newly restored Albert memorial clock and the magnificent City Hall to the houses of the late footballer George Best and the musician Van Morrison. A largely rural country without the crowded motorways or the fast-paced life of England, Ireland's difference from the rest of Britain is illustrated by the fact that Belfast is the country's only industrial city.

The capital of Scotland is Edinburgh, cut across by the famous Royal Mile – central streets that run through the old town marking the area walked or ridden by numerous kings and queens. Though it is Scotland's first city, Edinburgh is smaller than Glasgow whose population is in excess of half a million and about 100,000 greater. Culturally, while Glasgow is currently deemed by some to be one of the 'coolest' cities in Britain, Edinburgh is probably most famous for its annual summer Festival and Fringe, which has grown since the war to be a series of different festivals devoted to drama, film, literature, music and dance. The Festival, where the Fringe alone in 2006 hosted a record-breaking 28,000 performances in 260 venues, sells tickets to hundreds of thousands of visitors and claims to be the largest arts festival in the world. But to the residents of the city, a greater celebration takes place on New Year's Eve, which is known as Hogmanay in Scotland, when people gather round Tron Church in Edinburgh, just as they do in Trafalgar Square in London, to celebrate the coming year and sing 'Auld Lang Syne'.

Cardiff, or Caerdydd in Welsh, in the county of South Glamorgan, is the capital of Wales and its largest city with a population of around 320,000 in 2006, which includes large numbers of Bangladeshis and Pakistanis but also many thousands of Somalis who settled in the 1950s. Built on a site originally developed by the Romans in the first century, the city of Cardiff stands alongside the river Taff (though the common nickname for the Welsh, 'Taffy', does not come from this but derives from the pronunciation of the Welsh equivalent of David, 'Dafydd'). In the nineteenth century, Cardiff became a major port when it provided an outlet for the coal mined in local valleys such as the Rhondda. In more recent decades, as the coal industry has declined so have the Cardiff docks, which used to export more coal than any other port in the world. However, since the 1990s Cardiff's docklands, like London's, have been greatly renovated and the extensive redevelopment has meant the entire waterfront has been restructured. Cardiff is also home to two strong Welsh passions: rugby union and singing. Cardiff Arms Park is the centre of Welsh rugby football and stages international matches as well as the Welsh. Since 1946, Cardiff has also been the base for the Welsh National Opera, which started from amateur roots and is the oldest of Britain's regional opera companies (the others are Scottish Opera and Opera North). A new Opera House was being commissioned for the inner harbour of Cardiff Bay as the centrepiece for the docklands area development, but after difficulties it was shelved and a more impressive and welcomed Wales Millennium Centre, to house an international arts and cultural complex, opened in 2004 instead, along the bay from the new Richard Rogers' designed Welsh Assembly building. These add to the Millennium Stadium in west Cardiff, built on the site of the old Cardiff Arms Park rugby ground in 2000. The impressive new stadium even staged the English FA Cup Final in 2001, and again in subsequent years because the completion of the new Wembley national football stadium in London was repeatedly delayed.

Town

On the one hand, many people regret a creeping sameness in British cities and towns – for example, in most high streets you will see more or less the same shops, such as Boots, Marks and Spencer, Next, Mothercare, Debenhams, Burton, Woolworths and WH Smith. On the other hand, British towns are still enormously varied, from the seaside towns, market towns, country towns, tourist towns and industrial towns, to the post-war 'new' towns. Some coastal towns such as Blackpool and Bournemouth are chiefly known as seaside resorts and these are extremely popular with British holidaymakers, although overseas tourists are more likely to visit historic towns such as Roman Colchester or Shakespeare's Stratford. Other popular spots, famous since the seventeenth century for their 'healing waters', are spa towns such as Harrogate, Cheltenham and Buxton. Many northern towns like Wigan and Huddersfield retain for southerners the unfair image of industrial decline they gained between the wars, while market towns in the Midlands such as Melton Mowbray in Leicestershire still suggest the traditions of the English countryside. Towns do not have the large cultural life of cities or the close-knit community feel of small villages, but they combine aspects of each, providing a balance that many people feel is preferable to the bustle of the urban areas or the relative isolation of the countryside, though fears have been growing over the phenomenon of binge drinking at weekends, driving all but pubbing and clubbing partygoers away from town centres on Saturday nights. Each county also has a 'county town' which traditionally, but in many cases no longer, was the seat of county government. County towns can often be inferred from their names, such as Lancaster in Lancashire and Shrewsbury in Shropshire.

Traditional English towns retain many of the architectural signs of the nineteenth century. Victorian, iron-framed, glass-roofed, covered markets remain in the centres of Bolton and Halifax, for example. Many towns still have magnificent municipal buildings from their heyday over a hundred years ago and grand public houses from the turn of the century. Impressive corn exchanges, where samples were auctioned or sold, still stand in many country towns like Bury St Edmunds and Bishop's Stortford, while imposing workplaces like the Bliss Valley Tweed Mill at Chipping Norton in the Cotswolds and the Clocktower Mill in Burnley stand out as reminders of the industrial revolution in mill towns. Every sizable British town has a central park such as Jephson Park in Leamington Spa or Avenham Park in Preston, and while each town is different its development of terraced housing, shops, factories and schools around church, railway station, market, town hall and square will be familiar.

Many modern towns have arisen because of the New Towns Act of 1946. These include Harlow and Stevenage near London, East Kilbride near Glasgow, and Cwmbran in South Wales. However, of the total of thirty new towns the most well-known and recent example was created in 1967 in north Buckinghamshire: Milton Keynes. The new towns were designed to enable

FIGURE 1.4 A typical small-town street scene

a redistribution of the metropolitan populations and they had to cope with the preferences indicated by commuter life: a traditional English liking for the countryside wedded to a practical need to be able to reach the city. The intention was always to plan towns for modern living in every aspect by blending industrial and residential areas with full leisure facilities, and by separating traffic from pedestrians through a network of underpasses and walkways. However, Milton Keynes was not built up from nothing: it was designed to unite thirteen existing villages which are now enclosed by sweeping 'bypass' roads. Britain's largest new town in terms of area and population, Milton Keynes covers fifty square miles and had about 207,000 inhabitants according to the 2001 census. Despite its image of cleanliness and hi-tech living, much of the large town is still underdeveloped and underused, and yet its diverse range of amenities and accommodation, from solar-powered to timber-framed houses, make it a more ambitious town project than any other since the war. More recently, the south has witnessed the increased popularity of once disparaged dormitory towns, which have seen huge rises in house prices as part of the recent property boom. These are towns outside the M25, London's ring roads, that are still commutable distances from the capital. Towns like Tunbridge Wells, St Albans and Farnham have seen house price growth in excess of 100 per cent in the space of ten years but there is an increasing trend for many city workers with young families to choose these new hotspots to raise their children.

Most British towns have their own distinctive characteristics or annual events that promote a local cultural identity. For example, two Welsh towns in the county of Powys are Hay and Brecon. Hay-on-Wye is a small town that has become the book trade capital of Britain. Almost every shop in the town is an antiquarian or second-hand booksellers, and people drive great distances to spend a whole day searching the shelves; club, university and school trips are sometimes especially arranged to come and browse at what has become the largest collection of second-hand books in the world. While Hay has developed a prestigious annual literature festival, the nearby town of Brecon is the site of a distinctly Welsh community-based jazz festival each August which attracts over 30,000 people and takes place throughout the town in the Cathedral, halls and pubs, as well as the streets themselves. Partly because jazz is enjoyed by its fans for its musical anarchism, flair and improvisation, its celebration at such festivals has been seen as one of the less obvious assertions of Welsh independence from English culture.

However, against this individuality, we must also note that the look of larger modern British towns has been greatly influenced by the United States. British planners, in the light of a general cultural imitation of American trends, have adopted stateside practices such as the 'doughnut effect' where town centres become abandoned by shoppers for malls on the outer ring. A largely consumer culture has been imported across the Atlantic and modern buildings reflect this: shopping complexes, multiplex cinemas, theme parks, out-of-town supermarkets, Disney stores and fast-food restaurants, some of them drive-ins. The result is a sameness that is convenient and reassuring but also, on a national scale, numbing. Most cities and towns in Britain can be expected to have a number of fast-food outlets such as Burger King, a range of clothes shops like Gap, a Tesco or similar shopping centre away from the town, a Super Bowl, Laserquest or ten-screen cinema complex, leisure centres and heavily subscribed workout gyms. Milton Keynes is a prime example of this cultural saturation. It has imitation sheep and cows, acres of Astroturf, a grid road network, huge parking lots, a Milton Keynes Bowl for rock concerts, and 'California Collection' houses. The planners' aim has been to emulate the values and facilities of the ideal American town: efficiency, convenience, easy access, cleanliness and even air-conditioning, plus such unBritish aspects as indoor gardens, straight roads and parking for thousands of cars. In this, the city's designers have probably succeeded, but Milton Keynes more than any other town remains the butt of numerous contemporary jokes for the many British who unfairly caricature it as a place lacking culture, history or interest.

The British town is a halfway house between the milieu of the city and the country. It is usually a safe place, and a sedate, traditional and pleasant environment by day, but binge drinking is making it a no-go area on Saturday nights for non-drinkers. On such occasions the town may seem an unsophisticated place. The expensive jewellery of the city will not be on show but there may well be plenty of fake blonde hair, 'bling', and layers of flesh (especially around the midriff) on display. Some towns now also sport many of the wider, loud-and-proud, in-yer-face excesses of the modern rebellion against gentility, restraint, class and repression. This makes British towns unlike almost anything that would be found in Continental Europe, but they might well contain echoes of eighteenth-century Britain if a historical view were taken. This common caricature of the town these days, is very different from the British towns of the past, prior to the advent of youth culture and American influences.

Village

By stark contrast, very little international influence will be found in Britain's villages, some of which can still be described as rows of thatched cottages nestling in country fields between hedgerows and small streams. Since the war, people have moved back to rural areas, reversing the trend started by the industrial revolution. In recent decades, the number of people living in villages has increased by several million to be around 25 per cent of the total population, though only 2 per cent of the overall workforce is employed in

FIGURE 1.5   Summertime British musical village concerts (perfect for picnics)

agriculture, fishing and forestry. Agriculture accounts for about 1.5 per cent of the Gross Domestic Product and there are a little under 250,000 farms in Britain. Over half of these are devoted to dairy farming or to beef cattle and sheep, while the farms primarily involved in arable crops are chiefly found in eastern and central-southern England or eastern Scotland – the main crops by area are wheat and barley though the production of potatoes and sugar beet in tonnes exceeds that of barley.

Villages in Britain are traditionally associated with a close-knit society centred on a hall, which serves as a kind of community centre, a market, parish church, pub and a 'green', which is a grass area for fairs, fetes, cricket matches and other sporting events or public gatherings. Most villages therefore promote a strong blend of social identity, because people usually have a number of roles within the community, and personal identity, associated with land ownership and family history. A village's focus is likely to be on continuity and familiarity, and it is often said that everyone will know everyone else's business. Village life, it is said, is synonymous with community, which is symbolised by church-going, jumble sales, charity collecting, fetes and flower shows: those who join in are welcomed and those who do not are treated with suspicion.

However, village life is slowly changing. A modern phenomenon is the commuter village. These are hamlets or villages which have sufficiently good transport links for office workers to travel by road or rail to the major cities, such as London and Birmingham, sometimes on journeys that take several hours. Many city business people live in villages for the peace and quiet, the clean air, scenery and wildlife – but they probably have little involvement in the life of the village unless they also have children they want to bring up locally in the comparatively friendly, unpolluted and safe environment of the country. Similarly, second homes in villages throughout, for example, the Yorkshire Dales, are not unusual. City workers come out to them at weekends or just in the summer for holidays. Such city people are sometimes resented by the local villagers because they force up property prices and they also pose a threat to the continuity of village life. In the 1980s, 'holiday homes' in Wales were occasionally targets for arsonists resentful of this intrusion by outsiders, particularly from southern England. The increase in village populations since the war has also occurred because more and more people, who are also living longer, are retiring to the countryside from the city. Historically, village work has been based around a farming community, but the size of the agricultural workforce decreases year by year. Britain now has nine counties that are classed as rural and, to give an indication of how they are still in some ways isolated from city life, about a quarter of the villages in these areas still have no food shop, post-office, or doctor's surgery. An article in *The Times* in 2001 claimed that there was still a 'village pecking-order', with landowners and farmers at the top, long-established residents, of thirty or more years, in the middle, and newcomers, of less than fifteen years, at the bottom. The article claimed that slightly below this last echelon came 'new incomers', and way down at the bottom, Londoners.

Oddly, Britain's most talked about village is fictional. Ambridge is the setting for *The Archers*, the world's longest running radio serial. Begun by the BBC in 1950, the programme is broadcast during the week for fifteen minutes, twice a day, and by radio's standards it has a large, devoted following. In the serial, Ambridge is close to the market town of Borset in the fictional county of Borsetshire (shire is a term for the central English counties whose names have that suffix – *The Archers* was initially broadcast just in the Midlands). The ongoing saga revolves around the Archer family at Brookfield farm and portrays a close-knit village community in which everyone interacts with everyone else. Episodes are full of domestic incident and minor moral dilemmas but there are fewer exaggerated, intense emotional scenes and revelations than in the television soaps. The programme has always aimed to reflect realistically and unsensationally the concerns and interests of a village community and it has a farming correspondent who ensures the serial's treatment of agricultural issues is factual and accurate. Ambridge's counterpart in reality is Hanbury in Worcestershire, where some outside location scenes have been recorded and the programme also has a tradition of including real people, the most noted of whom was the Queen's late sister, Princess Margaret, in 1984. In 1989, the Post Office issued a set of commemorative stamps to mark the 10,000th episode, and by 2006 the series had run for more than 15,000. A similar stalwart of BBC Radio 4 has been *Gardeners' Question Time*, which has taken a panel of experts around the country from village hall to village hall since 1947, with occasional programmes recorded in France. Like much of Radio 4's broadcasting, the programme thrives on consistency and from 1951 to 1980, the trio of gardening authorities remained the same, but in 1994 an entirely new panel was introduced. Such changes, seemingly trivial, are extremely contentious for the station's loyal and conservative following. Gardening is the number one outdoor pursuit in Britain, and just as one patriarchal saying runs that 'a man's house is his castle', it would be fair to say that an English country garden would be the preferred castle grounds.

Unsurprisingly for a people who are statistically more likely to give to animal charities than to the homeless, the British have long fashioned themselves as a nation of animal lovers, and Britain has a great variety of wildlife, with an estimated 30,000 animal species. Television reflects this with many shows such as *Animal Roadshow*, supplementing the broad appetite for nature and wildlife programmes, where the venerated national icon is Sir David Attenborough, whose TV series from *Life on Earth* to *Planet Earth* are among the most watched and praised. Yet attitudes to animals vary between town and country, as witnessed by the struggle, discussed on pp. 66–7, over the fox-hunting ban in 2005, which was largely supported by city dwellers who saw it as a barbaric activity of the landed gentry, and the country dwellers who saw it as a traditional activity to help keep down the numbers of a predatory pest around farms. Another issue in 2001 centred on animals, tested this affection and also pointed up many differences between town and country: the foot-and-mouth crisis, which by September 2001 had resulted in the killing of three million sheep and over half a million cattle. The crisis arose in February 2001 and soon pointed up several areas of disagreement: some resented farmers the compensation they received for culled animals because they refused to use vaccines and also because they have long been subsidised, to the tune of a third of annual turnover (this is because when Britain joined the EC in 1973, land prices more than doubled because the Common Agricultural Policy raised the prices paid for arables, milk, beef and sheep); farmers felt that walkers and others, as much as the movement of livestock, spread the disease; tourist agencies resented the closing of country paths in spring while farmers disagreed with their reopening months later; farmers were dismayed that compensation (£926 million by August 2001) was paid in euros which, because of the strength of the pound, was less than it otherwise appeared; towards the end of the initial crisis, in the summer of 2001, an outrage was sparked by accusations that some farmers had deliberately contaminated their livestock to get compensation. The priorities in the toing and froing were foregrounded by the spring general election that year, which farmers wanted postponing until after the crisis so that the disease was not spread by the large movement of people, while others argued that postponing the election would give out the wrong signals internationally, suggesting that Britain had been 'closed down' by the disease. The crisis added to growing concerns over food scares and the general safety of meat products, which have been added to since 2001 as people's concern over genetically modified crops and their appetite for organic produce both increase alongside the broader environmental as well as health concern over 'food miles': the distance travelled by food ingredients before they reach the store.

Conclusion

In this concluding section, as well as summing up we will look at four thematic aspects to British culture that are linked to place but are shared by everyone throughout the UK: the country–city divide, travel, the weather, and the environment.

Apart from political borders, one of the strongest kinds of geographical division in Britain is that between those who look for the natural life of the countryside and those who prefer the amenities at hand in the city. This is a long-standing difference of taste and in the eighteenth-century, the poet William Cowper, in his poem *The Task*, wrote the famous line 'God made the country and man made the town'. Today, culture in cities tends to be diverse, reflecting the highly concentrated rich mix of different peoples with varied lifestyles: life is mostly anonymous, formal and based around groups with specialised interests. Country life by contrast is generally associated with tradition, custom, community, cultural unity and 'the outdoor life'. The antipathy between the two is pointed up by the common expressions of pity each makes towards the other: those in the towns are stereotyped as believing country people are deprived of life's 'basics', ranging from adequate heating to convenience stores, while those in the country are caricatured as feeling that their lives are morally superior and that urban people only live in cities because they have to (according to the *Observer*'s 2001 survey 66 per cent of people would rather live in the country).

An article in *The Times* observed that 'although there is a part of every Anglo-Saxon soul that is pastoral . . . there is a tradition of antipathy between yokel and townie which runs through English history.' It is often maintained that rural and urban people have different attitudes to the traditions of British life and, for example, one cultural pursuit that many feel marks a division between people in cities and villages is fox-hunting: a bill to ban it was passed by the House of Commons but overwhelmingly rejected by the

House of Lords in March 2001 only to be forced through by the government in 2005 (the ban applied to fox-hunting, deer-hunting and hare-coursing with dogs in England and Wales). It is a frequent generalisation that city people want what they call 'blood sports' banned; and it is just as common to hear from those in favour of what they call 'field sports' that anti-hunting campaigners do not understand, as villagers do, the need for control of the population of predatory animals in the wild. For reasons such as this, the kind of cultural division in England between north and south is also sometimes found throughout the country between 'townies' and 'yokels'. As farmers are considered by those in the towns to provide the country's food, they are blamed whenever prices are thought to be too high, as they usually are, but farmers are also resentful because they claim it is the supermarket chains who are hiking-up prices while forcing producers to accept low payments or be dropped. Similarly, feeling that again they have been penalised, farmers led the fuel-duty protests that brought Britain almost to a halt in the summer of 2000. The feeling that the priorities of the countryside are being sacrificed by the government was concentrated in the formation of the Countryside Alliance, whose slogan 'Listen to Us' expresses its belief that in the face of London's policies it is powerless. The Alliance has arguably had little success even though its rallies in the capital have brought out more protesters on London's streets than any other recent cause apart from the Iraq War in 2003. The Alliance fashions itself as the countryside fighting for its liberty, and it defends hunting, fishing, shooting and the interests of farming communities as well as campaigning on conservation and the environment.

Lastly, before moving on to consider travel and the weather, we must note that in addition to the country and the city, there is a third place of escape for people from either of these communities: the coast. Because all Britons live on an island there is a strong coastal culture incorporating trawler fishing, watersports, ports and docks, shipping, yachting and, for visitors, the British tradition of seaside holidays, with its staple ingredients of piers, buckets and spades, postcards, amusement arcades, deckchairs, donkey rides and promenading. Again, there are also dozens of smaller islands off the British mainland, and the largest of these, the Isle of Wight below the south coast of England, is a county in its own right.

These areas are of course linked by travel on road, rail, air, river or sea. More than three in four British households today own at least one car. In the 1930s, more miles of road in Britain were covered by bicycle than by car, but now it is mainly those conscious of their health and the environment who choose two wheels over four. Current high traffic levels are also projected to increase by 30 per cent between 2006 and 2015, prompting renewed calls for 'green taxes' to ensure people pay by the mile for their road usage. Commuting by train, on the main network or the London

Underground, is a daily activity for millions of Britons – many of whom will complain that the rail services are far worse than on the Continent. In response to this constant criticism, a charter was introduced in the early 1990s to compensate people for delays, cancellations and poor reliability. London's main airport, Heathrow, is the busiest in the world, although only 20 per cent of its seventy million customers take domestic flights. Additionally, though they were superseded as a mode of transport in the nineteenth century by the railways, Britain is carved across by hundreds of streams and rivers, some with houseboats, and over 4,000 miles of canals and waterways. Also, trams have been reintroduced in cities such as Manchester and Nottingham, while an automated light railway links the city area in London with the docklands.

An influence that on another level links city, country and coast is a shared climate. In the eighteenth century, Samuel Johnson said: 'When two Englishmen meet, their first talk is of the weather.' Throughout Britain today the weather is still the most frequent topic of conversation, and not usually for agricultural reasons but simply because it is so changeable. Many British people will be only too willing to offer a forecast of likely shifts in the weather. On top of experience and barometers, several other, often proverbial methods of prediction are sworn by. For example, a herd of cows lying in a field is thought to indicate rain, as do twitching bunions and rheumatic attacks. Similarly, the old saying, 'Red sky at night, shepherds' delight; red sky in the morning, shepherds' warning' is passed down from generation to generation as a sure method of anticipating fair or foul weather throughout the country. The national hobby of predicting rain, sunshine, hail, thunder, snow or sleet is nicely summed up by the annual bets on whether there will be a white Christmas. Perhaps because of their obsessive interest in the weather, the British are generally sceptical of official forecasts. While this scepticism is distinctly unfair, it was famously bolstered in October 1987 by a freak hurricane which a BBC television weather forecaster asserted would pass Britain by. The storm blew over fences and light buildings, brought down telegraph wires and poles, put television stations out of action, resulted in eighteen deaths and left many cars crushed by fallen trees. Memories of 1987 were frequently invoked in the winter of 2000, when 'freak' floods left many villages under water and thousands of people homeless, and Britain does occasionally suffer minor earthquakes such as the one that hit the West Midlands in 2002, measuring 4.8 on the Richter scale.

Britain in fact has a moderate climate in terms of its temperature, which has never been recorded as high as 100° Fahrenheit or as low as - 18°F. Generally, it is between 35 and 65°F, and the climate is milder in England and Wales than in Scotland. The weather remains a constant talking point in Britain because of its local variations and its seasonal oddities: for example, though winter runs from December to February, a cricket match has been 'snowed-off' in Buxton, Derbyshire, in June. August, in high summer, is one of the wettest months of the year and many Britons will swear that May and September are usually sunnier months. Rainfall differs greatly between regions and average annual levels vary from 500 mm in East Anglia in eastern-southern England to 5,000 mm in the Scottish Highlands. Britain's climate has in general been even less harsh in recent years, contributing for example to an increase in the popularity of camping, but the downside to this phenomenon is the environmental impact of global warming.

Lastly, therefore, we might consider how a country is discussed in terms of its environment. For different reasons, the human maintenance and manipulation of the environment is of particular interest to two groups of people: environmentalists and the disabled. While they have generally lagged behind other Europeans in terms of green issues, people in the UK have become increasingly sensitive to ecological concerns, and most people now understand that 'saving the planet' is not just for environmentalists and in fact 'everyone must do their bit', which is a typical British attitude. The Green Party of England and Wales, founded in 1973 as the Ecology Party, has ninety-two local councillors from the 2006 elections, and has a considerable presence and influence in certain towns, such as Oxford, Norwich and Brighton. Most large cities are now circled by a 'green belt' on which little development is allowed, but it is still the case that twenty-seven miles of greenfield land (equivalent to the size of a city such as Southampton) are built on each year. The Forestry Commission, which has its headquarters in Edinburgh, was set up in 1919 because of the timber shortage that became apparent in the First World War. By the 1980s, through grants and government administration, it had already reached its 2000 target of nearly five million acres of forest land. Recycling centres have also been stationed at shopping centres and other public places, for people to bring along their old newspapers, glass, clothes and aluminium, while the gathering of recyclable material is now a staple feature of rubbish collection from homes – yet Britain's recycling rate is a lamentable 22.5 per cent compared with, for example, the percentage in Austria, Denmark and the Netherlands of 60 per cent. Britain's green movement began in the radical 1960s, and the campaigning environmental group Friends of the Earth has been prominent in Britain since 1970, lobbying on world issues such as rainforests and global warming as well as on local British concerns including beach pollution and the privatisation of the water authorities in 1989. Greenpeace, the Campaign for Nuclear Disarmament, Earth First!, and various 'New Protest' groups, sometimes associated with New Agers, discussed in Chapter 7, have all also been active in Britain over the last thirty years. A major issue here is that of pollution and congestion. Car travel accounts for 80 per cent of miles travelled in Britain and there are now nearly thirty-five million cars on the road, twice the number thirty years ago. Congestion is such that the average journey speed is 25 mph even though the lowest speed limit is 30. Congestion is expected to increase by half again on motorways by 2015, adding hugely to concerns about gas emissions, compounded by the British love of short breaks abroad and cheap flights – the number of passengers flying out of the UK is set to rise to 470 million by 2030 unless fuel taxes or other measures intercede. It is also a factor that Britons in 2006 have a quarter of a million 'second homes' abroad, a rise of 100,000 in six years. A 'congestion charge' now applies to everyone who takes a car into central London, yet most British people also think the privatised train services are poor, with overcrowding on London commuter trains doubling between 1996 and 2006, while fewer and fewer people are using bus services outside the capital. Meanwhile, the number of air passengers is set to increase from 229 million in 2005 to 401 million by 2020. Overall, British carbon emissions, per person half those of the US, have fallen by about 10 per cent since 1990 but the rise in car and air travel in recent years has stopped the downward movement according to figures for 2004 and 2005. On the good side, such issues and facts are now in the mainstream of public debate, such that for example, most people will have read that the average family's Christmas lunch in 2006 has travelled 84,000 miles to get there, totalling the distances for the individual elements. Green taxes on non-recyclable rubbish seem inevitable measures for the future alongside stringent taxes on road miles and air travel. Lastly, the Eden Project in Cornwall should be mentioned here. Opened in 2001, the Eden Project is partly a green theme park and partly a socio-scientific project about education and communication focused on the major environmental issues facing the planet. Housed in giant biomes such as the Humid Tropics Biome, which is the largest conservatory in the world, the Eden Project was voted Britain's favourite building in a 2006 poll by YouGov and best expresses hopes for a sustainable future and the rise of ecolonomics – sustainable living via environmentally friendly business.

Writing in *The Times* in December 2006, Kate Muir concluded:

> Our new British religion is of course eco-worship, and like many religions, this can be conducted with extreme hypocrisy. Yet perhaps our tiny blinging, boozing, infidel country will pull itself up by its bootstraps, leading the way on emissions, organic veg, insulation and home-made windmills.

The ecological agenda has affected most people's domestic lives through recycling and green conspicuous consumption. British people are increasingly likely to be eco-friendly, but this is in a substantially different way from the past. A famous television programme of the 1970s, *The Good Life*, showed a suburban couple throwing up a wealthy bourgeois commuter life for impoverished but sustainable self-sufficient living, next door to their snobbish, socially competitive friends. Now, it is those with a green agenda who are unlikely to go without and are susceptible to indulging in a competitive lifestyle in which greener-than-thou credentials are purchased at great expense. Alongside its more serious aspects, saving the environment has become a hobby for the middle class, who may put up their own wind turbine at home, install solar panels and underfloor heating, pursue a carbon-neutral existence and own a Sub-zero Pro 48 fridge which uses less energy than a 100-watt light bulb but costs £14,000. While many people buy Fair Trade products to help other humans, and some buy organic products to protect their families (a proportion of the middle classes are eschewing supermarkets such as Tesco and Asda for farmers' 'organic box' deliveries), the expensive 'political' badge of heavy-duty environmental friendliness has become a status symbol for celebrities and the chattering classes. The green agenda runs parallel with the healthy eating campaigning that has swept Britain, imported from the USA, whose weight 'problems' still far outstrip the UK's. Britain has been dubbed the 'fat man' of Europe as it has the highest percentage of obese adults, nearing 25 per cent. Britain's 'obesity index' largely maps its financial one, with northern areas like parts of Merseyside and Tyneside labelled the 'fattest' areas (Boston in Lincolnshire took the prize with 31 per cent of adults deemed clinically obese), in stark contrast to the slimmest areas, which are all in or around London: Kensington, Westminster, Camden and Richmond. To some commentators this reveals the new class division in society between those with expensive houses, after ten years of booming property prices, and those renting; between the gym-going healthy-eating middle classes and the overdressed overweight; between the haves and the have-nots, as ever. The smoking profile of Britain has a similar shape and the government are increasingly inclined to intervene: cigarettes cost over £5 a packet at the time of writing, all packs have very large warnings covering half of one side, and there is a ban in public places from July 2007 in England, following bans already in place in the rest of the British Isles.

A further issue of the (particularly built) environment is accessibility. Though many people in Britain have been slow to recognise the special needs of the disabled, public buildings have designated parking spaces close to the entrance, theatres have signed performances, accessibility is linked to planning permission, and employers now claim that their equal opportunity policies mean that jobs are open to all people regardless of age, ethnicity, gender or disability – on all of which there is now legislation, some of it akin to positive discrimination. Despite this, disabled people are not well represented on television, and, with respect to people's misconceptions, a high-profile media figure such as the scientist Stephen Hawking (who has motor neuron disease) or the pop star Ian Dury (who had polio) can do more than

FIGURE 1.6   Alison Lapper statue on plinth in Trafalgar Square

television to raise general awareness of the difference between a 'disability', which usually relates to a specific aspect of life, and general abilities. The wider appreciation of disabled people has probably been raised greatly by the profile of the ex-Home Secretary, David Blunkett, who is blind, as well as the increasing willingness of television companies to give disabled sport more exposure. A major controversy was sparked by the decision in 2005 to place Marc Quinn's white marble statue 'Alison Lapper pregnant' on the vacant fourth plinth in Trafalgar Square alongside long-standing statues of military leaders, including Havelock and Napier, on the other plinths. The chosen subject of a naked pregnant woman with no arms and shortened legs was a brave one for London's busiest square, with the landmark of Nelson's column in the middle, but its implicit statement about gender, inclusivity and human beauty was itself a landmark for attitudes to the disabled. Overall, the campaign for responsible and fair adaptation of the natural and built environment has been seen as one of slow progress as organised groups lobby and protest on specific issues of personal or social importance against businesses whose interests are necessarily commercial.

As a final word, it can be said that while the Union Jack is seen flying at international conferences and decorating lapel badges, it is as often used as a design for underpants, a pattern for dyed hair or face-painting, and a decoration for the roof of a mini. In other words, it is an emblem of Britain's relationship to its past and will be used nostalgically, ironically, and even callously as a sign of solidarity against others. Britons have always defined themselves as an island people, whose singularity and separateness is illustrated by the channel of water dividing them from the Continent. However, the British now have an undersea tunnel that connects them with France, they are hostile to federalism but committed to joining Europe, they are soaked in influences from the USA, and are succumbing to a global culture that may leave them disunited but curiously alike. This chapter has illustrated how, in terms of place, 'Britishness' is a problematic tag for people living in the UK, and that it perhaps best serves, especially while the government urges its people to focus on citizenship over identity, as a national label for traditional values and issues that lie between the local or global concerns with which individuals are increasingly more likely to identify themselves.

Exercises

1   What different kinds of regional identity do you think there could be said to be in Britain? How many regional variations in accent can you think of?

2   Can you name any personalities or politicians who seem to you representative of a distinctive kind of Britishness? Can you say which country or region they grew up in?

3   What are the traits you associate with the British in general or the English in particular? Do you think there is any correlation between climate and culture or character, and do you think there are any dangers in promoting such beliefs?

4   Try to locate six other British cities on the map on p. 40. What do you know of each city and how do you think cultural identities might be different in each?

5   The top ten most famous Scots according to a survey commissioned by *Crabbies Green Ginger Wine* in late 2006 were:

		per cent
1	Loch Ness Monster	29
2	Robert Burns	27
3	Sean Connery	12
4	Robert the Bruce	9
5	William Wallace	7.5
6	Robbie Coltrane	6
7	Billy Connolly	4
8	Lorraine Kelly	2.5
9	Ewan McGregor	2
10	Lulu	1

Which other Scots can you easily name? Could you compile a list of who you think would be the most famous Welsh people?

 Reading

Clifford, Sue and Angela, King. *England in Particular: A Celebration of the Commonplace, the Local, the Vernacular and the Distinctive* Hodder & Stoughton, 2006. Fascinating A-Z guide to the everyday aspects of English life from allotments to rambling.

Gilbert, Francis. *Yob Nation* Portrait, 2006. Argues that the UK has become a cruel and aggressive culture from the streets to the media and government.

Kumar, Krishan. *The Making of English National Identity* Cambridge University Press, 2003. Suggests that the British have problems with self-definition because of their imperial heritage, which has repressed ordinary expressions of national identity. The final chapter is particularly helpful.

Marr, Andrew. *The Day Britain Died* Profile, 2000. Accompanies the BBC series of the same name, and suggests that while Irish, Scottish, Welsh and to a lesser extent English identities are still strong, any future prospect of a 'British' identity needs remaking as a British federation of interdependent states, supported by a written constitution. Appeared in the same year as Tom Nairn's more trenchant *After Britain* Granta, 2000.

Weight, Richard. *Patriots: National Identity in Britain 1940–2000* Pan, 2002. Near-exhaustive thematic review of post-war Britain, from shoppers to swingers.

 Cultural examples

Films

Starter for Ten (2006) dir. Tom Vaughan. A working-class student attends Bristol University in the mid 1980s.

Happy Now (2001) dir. Philippa Cousins. Welsh black comedy about murder and mistaken identity.

Ratcatcher (1999) dir. Lynne Ramsey. Vivid portrayal of life on a Scottish housing estate in the 1970s.

The Full Monty (1998) dir. Peter Cattaneo. Comical film about unemployed workers in Sheffield who become male strippers. The biggest box office attraction of the year in the UK.

Into the West (1992) dir. Mike Newell. Irish mythology, travellers and inner city life.

The Boxer (1997) dir. Jim Sheridan. Part direct and part metaphorical approach to the 'troubles' in Northern Ireland.

Local Hero (1983) dir. Bill Forsyth. Poignant film about a Scottish coastal community threatened by a multinational oil corporation.

Riff-Raff (1990) dir. Ken Loach. Social comment, set on a building site: strong regional characters.

London to Brighton (2006) dir. Paul Andrew Williams. Much lauded gritty southern drama of drugs, violence, prostitution and escape to the coast.

Books

Magnus Mills, *All Quiet on the Orient Express* (1999). Darkly comic story of English eccentricity in the Lake District by the English Kafka.

Sue Townsend, *The Queen and I* (1992). Fantasy about the Queen living on a Midlands housing estate.

R.S. Thomas, *Neb* (1985). Autobiography, written in Welsh, of Wales' most celebrated late-twentieth-century poet.

James Kelman, *How Late it Was, How Late* (1994). Booker-winning novel of Glaswegian street life.

Seamus Heaney, *North* (1975). An attempt by the Nobel-winning poet to place contemporary Northern Irish history in the context of European history and pre-history.

Nick Hornby, *How to be Good* (2001). Comic novel about the priorities and anxieties of London life in the new century.

Laurie Lee, *Cider with Rosie* (1959). Most famous and still much-loved celebration of English village life.

TV programmes

Murphy's Law. Northern Irish detective series created by well-known author Colin Bateman.

Monarch of the Glen. Spoof drama series about life on a Highlands country estate.

EastEnders, Coronation Street. Urban living in London and Manchester respectively.

Emmerdale. Previously called 'Emmerdale Farm', this is a serial about (now somewhat loosely) agricultural and village communities in England.

Pobol Y Cwm (People of the Valley). Long-running (over thirty years) Welsh-language soap.

Websites

www.statistics.gov.uk/regionaltrends39/
   The latest official UK statistics broken down by region.

www.ukvillages.co.uk
   Over 27,000 websites and online community centres for villages across Britain.

www.thisislondon.co.uk
   News and information site for the capital.

www.edinburghfestivals.co.uk
   Guide to the annual Edinburgh festival.

http://news.bbc.co.uk
> Excellent online BBC news coverage.

www.whatthepaperssay.co.uk
> Digest of regional and national British press.

www.niassembly.gov.uk/
> Northern Ireland Assembly pages.

www.londonnet.co.uk//ln/index.html
> Claims to be the best guide to London on the Web.

www.countryside-alliance.org/
> Website of the Countryside Alliance.

www.24hourmuseum.org.uk
> Vast access point to Britain's museum collections.

www.greenparty.org.uk/news
> UK's Green Party.

www.carboncalculator.com
> A British website, affiliated to the 'Global Action Plan' movement, that helps you 'Measure your share of UK carbon dioxide emissions!'

www.ordnancesurvey.co.uk
> Free map service with historical mapping of Britain.

www.spatial-literacy.org/index.php?p=familyname
> Academic site containing a surname profiler facility, free to users, that allows searches on the geography of the most frequent 25,000 surnames in Britain.

www.qwghlm.co.uk/projects/electionmap/
> Election map for Britain that is also an excellent guide to political geography.

www.icons.org.uk/theicons
> Survey of the icons of England.

www.edenproject.com/about/index.html
> Eden Project website.

Chapter 2

Education, work and leisure

Mike Storry

Timeline

600	Foundation of King's School Canterbury
1249	Foundation of Oxford University
1284	Foundation of Cambridge University
1440	Eton College founded
1803	Introduction of income tax
1902	Education Act establishes state secondary education
1936	Scheduled TV starts in England
1944	Education Act establishes free secondary education for all
1954	Independent Television Act licenses alternative broadcasters to BBC
1963	Labour Exchanges become JobCentres
1967	National Health Service (Family Planning) Act Plowden Committee recommends child-centred learning
1969	Foundation of Open University
1970	Equal Pay Act
1971	Industrial Relations Act (judiciary to arbitrate industrial disputes)
1975	Sex Discrimination Act
1975	Employment Protection Act
1976	Foundation of (private) University of Buckingham Education Act School leaving age raised to 16
1982	Channel 4 started
1990	Education (Student Loans) Act
1993	Trade Union Reform and Employment Rights Act
1994	Criminal Justice Act opposed by Ramblers' Association Sunday Trading Act allowed shopping on Sunday
1995	Rugby Union allowed professionals
1999	Bluewater shopping centre, Europe's largest, opened in Kent
2005	2012 Olympics awarded to London
2006	Age Discrimination Act allows people to work longer

Introduction

W E HAVE LINKED education, work and leisure in the title of this chapter in the belief that very often people's work is determined by the education they receive and that their leisure activities complement their work.

The timeline above picks out a number of significant historical points. From it you will see that schooling for the top echelon of British people started in AD 600, through royal patronage. Schooling for the rest came only in the eighteenth and nineteenth centuries. People had to work, and concern with the conditions thereof came only gradually and was reflected in the Factory Acts of the nineteenth century. These aimed to prevent child labour and to restrict work to ten hours a day. Today, the 'working week' generally covers 9.00 a.m. to 5.00 p.m., Monday to Friday, although few people still work those exact hours and many are now employed on 'flexitime', with unfixed times for arriving at and leaving work. Britons work the longest hours in Western Europe and attempt to express their real selves through leisure activities, both in the private space of the home and outside it. This chapter will look at the part played by education, work and leisure in forming British people's identities, and will deal with those topics in sequence.

Schools

There are about 32,000 schools in Britain with 10,100,400 pupils and 508,900 teachers. There are separate state and private systems, the latter has 2,300 schools while 164 state grammar schools survive. The school year runs from September to July and children normally start school in the September following their fifth birthday. The school day is usually from 9.00 a.m. to 3.30 or 4.00 p.m. and children are allocated places by the Local Education Authority (LEA) in the schools nearest to them, though these allocations are subject to appeal. The government has encouraged the exercise of parental choice by promoting competition among schools and adopting a policy of incentives for 'good' schools and a laissez-faire attitude to the closure of those which are becoming less popular. League tables of school exam results have been published since the early 1990s. Ofsted (Office for Standards in Education) reports are available online.

The state offers 'primary' (for ages 5–11) and 'secondary' (for ages 11–18) schooling. There are a very few 'middle' schools for children aged 10–13 and some 'special' schools for children with learning difficulties. These are the main state schools, although there are others in, for example, hospitals and youth custody centres. Pupils are permitted to leave school at 16 but a majority (2006: 73 per cent) stay on or move to Local Authority controlled Further Education (FE) or Sixth Form colleges.

The present state system evolved from a gradual move towards universal educational provision which started in the nineteenth century. Poorly funded 'board' and 'hedge' schools (the former managed by a local school board, the latter outdoors) taught pupils up to the standard leaving age of 14 years. This became 15 in the 1930s and 16 in 1976.

In 1944, R.A. Butler's Education Act introduced the '11 plus' examination. All children took this test at the end of primary school, and those who passed had their fees paid at the local grammar school. This change had significant social and cultural effects in Britain. It enabled a degree of social mobility hitherto unknown and eroded notions of those with ability coming only from higher social strata. It introduced to post-war Britain a 'meritocracy', and made a significant contribution to the affluence of the 1950s and 1960s.

On the negative side, it distanced children from their less well-educated parents. But perhaps the worst effect of the 1944 Education Act was that some people saw it as 'discarding' the 80 per cent of children who were assigned by the test to secondary-modern schools. Children were labelled as 'failures' at the age of 11 and this led to a cumulative loss of ambition, achievement and self-esteem. Many became alienated and reluctant to integrate into society. In due course, this offered fertile ground for the growth of such youth-cultural subgroups as mods, rockers and punks. Secondary-modern school pupils and teachers were demoralised by the knowledge that the most favoured students had been 'creamed off' to the grammar schools and by the fact that despite the rhetoric of 'appropriate provision', they were part of second-class educational establishments in a system of 'separate development', a sort of cultural 'apartheid'.

Partly because of the above malaise, the Labour Government, in the 1960s, endorsed a system of 'comprehensive' schools. These were co-educational (most grammar schools were single-sex) and for all abilities. Some 'comps' exchanged grammar-school-type streaming (grouping pupils according to performance) for mixed-ability teaching. Here pupils of differing capabilities shared the same classrooms in the belief that the bright would help the weak, and that improved social development would compensate for any lack of intellectual achievement. It was hoped that this would eventually lead to cohesiveness rather than competitiveness in society at large. Other comprehensive schools adopted what they saw as the best of existing educational practices, including intellectual rigour, while reducing emphasis in their curriculum on classics and sport.

In the private system, 'preparatory' schools educate children from the age of 5, prior to their entering the 'public schools' at 13. Confusingly, famous private schools like Eton and Harrow, Winchester or Stonyhurst are known as 'public schools'. (The expression 'public school' originally referred to a grammar school endowed for the public.) That system of education is now, as *Chambers Dictionary* puts it: 'for such as can afford it'. The independent school sector is disproportionately important in British life for a variety of reasons, including catchment. So, although only 7 per cent of Britain's children attend them, their alumni figure much more significantly as entrants to the universities, particularly Oxbridge (Oxford and Cambridge) and the higher echelons of British society.

State schools in Britain are non-denominational. Of the state-supported ones (known as 'faith schools'), one-third have a religious affiliation. Of these 4,600 are Anglican and 2,000 are Roman Catholic. Some Jewish schools are also state-funded. Their capital expenditure is covered by the state and their running expenses are paid by the members of their congregations. A contentious issue has been that the same financial support was not made available to Hindu or Islamic schools. This became a major issue in Bradford and other places with large Muslim populations where poor educational provision was partly blamed for riots there in June 2001. This situation changed when government developed an enthusiasm for faith schools (possibly for their social-control aspect) and funded schools from these other faiths. Even so, by 2006 there were only five funded Muslim schools in Britain and argument over proposals for a further seven.

To monitor pupils' performance, the government introduced a series of 'Standardised Assessment Tests' (SATs) – taken at age 7, 11 and 14. However, the major public exams which pupils face are those taken in individual subjects at 16 and 18 respectively: the General Certificate in Secondary Education (GCSE) and Advanced ('AS') levels. In Scotland students gain Lower and Higher Certificates. University entrance is typically based on good grades in approximately six GCSEs and three 'AS' levels. Other qualifications open to those school leavers who want to attend college are AVCEs, BTECs, HNCs, City & Guilds, RSA and GNVQs.

The school system has a reputation for quality. However a number of factors – continual reforms; the over-prescriptive National Curriculum; inspections without feedback – have produced low morale among teachers, many of whom leave the profession.

The Government is trying to address these problems through various initiatives to improve educational opportunities for children, including setting up fifteen City Technology Colleges in disadvantaged areas, plus Beacon Schools and the Leading Edge Partnership programme to share the best practice of successful schools. But spending on schools in 1999 of £2,433 per pupil in primaries, and £3,823 in secondaries, was 1 per cent below the OECD average of 12.9 per cent of all public expenditure. In 2006, amid some public scepticism, the government was promising to raise the average spend per state-secondary-school pupil to that of the independent sector i.e. from £5,000 to £8,000.

In these circumstances, unsurprisingly the independent schools sector has continued to flourish – partly because of their high academic standards. In 2003, 54 per cent of all GCSE candidates at independent schools achieved A* or A grades (national average: 16.7 per cent). At A-level 69 per cent of independent entries achieved A or B grades (national average: 44.5 per cent). Several top public schools (Dulwich College, Harrow and Shrewsbury) have 'exported' their successful ethos by setting up in the Far East, and Brighton College plans to open in Moscow.

Colleges and universities

At the official school-leaving age of 16, 73 per cent (2005/6) of pupils continue in education either in schools, Sixth Form Colleges or FE (Further Education) Colleges. The percentage entering the universities aged 18–30 is 43 per cent (government target: 50 per cent by 2010).

Besides the Open University, which is mainly part-time, there are 89 universities in Britain: 72 in England, 14 in Scotland, 2 in Wales and 2 in Northern Ireland. They have 2,175,115 students and 120,800 lecturers (2003). The standard length of undergraduate study in Britain is three years for a Bachelor of Arts or Science degree (BA/BSc), and up to seven years for 'vocational' degrees (ones linked to a specific job), like medicine, dentistry, veterinary science or architecture. Students of subjects such as civil engineering spend an intermediate year in industry (a 'sandwich' course). Many universities offer the Bachelor of Education (B.Ed) degree which is a four-year course geared towards classroom experience. The majority of primary-school teachers qualify by this route. The standard way to train to be a secondary-school teacher is to do a three-year university course in a specialist subject such as biology, history or mathematics followed by a one-year Postgraduate Certificate in Education (PGCE) which includes teaching practice.

Students on Master's courses (MA/MSc) study for at least one year and those doing Doctorates (PhDs) for upwards of three years. Students finance their studies with great difficulty. Grants were pegged at 1982 levels and abolished altogether in 1994. A system of loans was introduced in 1990/91, and in 1997 students had to pay £1,000 towards fees for the first time. Annual tuition fees of £3,000 became payable in 2006. Hence today students experience real financial hardship. Only those whose parents can afford to subsidise them are without money worries. The percentage of working-class children attending university is declining.

Oxford and Cambridge (known collectively as 'Oxbridge') are the oldest universities in Britain. Though much expanded, their student numbers are still small, compared with (say) London's 102,000. In 2005/6 Oxford had 11,225 students; Cambridge: 11,515. Other old universities are Durham and St Andrews, and they are distinguished from the so-called 'Redbrick' universities founded around the beginning of the twentieth century (for example Birmingham, Liverpool, Manchester) through their emphasis on traditional subjects. 'New' universities created in the 1960s include Lancaster, York, Keele and Sussex. In 1992 all the former polytechnics changed their names and joined the existing 44 universities.

Apart from the European campuses of several American universities, Britain has two other main universities. The Open University (2003: 158,000 students) offers a wide range of degree programmes delivered formerly by TV and radio, now by DVDs and podcasts, especially for people already engaged in full-time work. The University for Industry (UfI) is a Public Private Partnership which offers basic and technological skills, 80 per cent online, through 2,000 Learndirect centres.

Participation in higher education is still largely determined by the class one happens to be born into. For example, in Britain as a whole, currently 80 per cent of children from professional middle-class families study at university, compared with 17 per cent from the poorest homes. Moreover, at the extremes of opportunity, in 1999 in the Solihull suburb of Knowle, a population of 11,700 had 150 pupils starting degree courses, while Clifton East in Nottingham, with a population of 8,400 failed to send a single pupil to university.

The educational sector that has been most influential in raising Britain's profile abroad, the public (that is private) schools' one, has benefited from the difficulties experienced by the state sector. Some public schools have chosen to pick the best elements out of the National Curriculum. The proportion of pupils attending public/independent secondary schools has risen, as the public sector has atrophied. Independent school pupil numbers have remained fairly constant at around 630,000 at a time of declining total school rolls. Parents are eager to benefit from the fact that the private sector has always had a disproportionately high influence on British culture and society, dominating very many aspects of British public life, from Whitehall to Shire Hall, from Parliament to local constituency parties, from the Institute of Directors to local Chambers of Commerce.

Educational changes and trends

Major educational changes have been: the imposition of a national curriculum (as opposed to one agreed with local authorities and Her Majesty's Inspectors (HMIs)); the introduction of pre-GCSE examinations; and the publication of league tables of schools' performances (since abandoned in Wales and Northern Ireland). Opponents of a national curriculum felt it was closing-down room for individual initiative and saw it as sinister in its regimenting of pupils. They referred to a French Minister of Education who boasted that he knew at any hour of the day which page of which book pupils would be turning. Supporters of a national curriculum promoted it as a necessary educational reform which would ensure uniform standards in schools.

In 2007 the head of Ofsted has said that the educational system isn't working and needs fundamental reform. It currently has a 'one size fits all' approach and has to become more child-centred. Children are to be allowed to proceed at their own pace in response to teaching tailored towards them individually. This aim is very worthy but has huge resource implications and one wonders where it leaves league tables, which imply that everyone progresses at the same pace.

Reform is necessary if only because of the underachievement and disaffection of many children in school. People can still relate to George Orwell's statement in the 1930s: 'There is not one working-class boy in a thousand who does not pine for the day when he will leave school. He wants to be doing real work not wasting his time on ridiculous rubbish like history and geography' (*Road To Wigan Pier*, 1937).

Seventy years later, in 2006, journalist Neil Doyle, writing about the school he attended, made a direct link between poor schooling and disaffection leading to terrorism:

> With over 1,000 pupils on the roll in soul-destroying conditions, teaching methods that relied heavily on dictation . . . it made for perfect conditions for gangs to coalesce. . . . There's now a British Mujahideen in our midst and it's been State-nurtured and funded.
>
> (*Terror Base UK*, 2006)

Because many children in school are bored by the GCSEs they are doing, the Government is proposing to enable them to embark on apprentice-ships two days a week at 14 years of age, once 40,000 industrial placements

FIGURE 2.1   League tables mean schools 'advertise' their achievements both to pupils and prospective parents

have been found. Previous such initiatives have failed amid complaints that firms have exploited students on work-experience as unpaid labour. Ken Spours, of London University's Institute of Education said: 'In the era of league tables, it could mean schools just getting rid of their disruptive pupils – and I don't see industry falling over themselves to take them.' Some see this leading to a divisive two-tier education system where some children are denied quality education and others, with a privileged background are enabled to flower.

Constant changes have bedevileed schools. The new sixth-form curriculum's first year was chaotic. Traditionally, the lower-sixth year is one without an exam, where pupils are given space to find their feet in independent study and develop a love of a subject. Instead the AS system placed them under great pressure to perform, and they had to endure public exams three years in succession. Changes have been made however, and successful schools have now been given more flexibility. So, for example, fifty-one state schools and forty-four Independents have signed up to offer the International Baccalaureate qualification instead of AS level.

Schools matter to people because education is not just about the delivery of syllabuses. Primary schools in particular are the sites for the transmission from one generation to the next of shared culture. The culture is of the classroom, but also of the playground. Children socialise there.

The playground is a concrete jungle where children practice their games and learn, where society's folk memories and myths are recycled through chants. The song 'A Ring a Ring a roses / A pocketful of posies / Ashoo! Ashoo! / We all fall down' contains memories of the Black Death which swept Europe in the Middle Ages. Another reminder comes when, on the passing of an ambulance, children say: 'Touch your collar / Never swallow / Never catch the fever.'

In choosing a school for their children, parents worry about potential academic progress, but also about the prevalence of bullying, the development of life skills, and the kind of social, cultural and spiritual experience offered by the school. Furthermore, because schools are so important in the formation of shared cultural identity, people are interested in the way in which prominent public figures choose to educate their children. For example, Prince Charles was the first member of the royal family not to be educated by palace tutors. He was sent to Gordonstoun in Scotland. His own sons William and Harry were sent to Eton (where Tory leader David Cameron was also educated). For ordinary parents this humanised the royal family who became subject to the same anxieties and uncertainties of sending children to school as they were. Conversely, people sense hypocrisy when those who advocate state schooling in the Labour Party send their children to public schools, as when then Prime Minister Tony Blair bypassed the state system and sent his sons to the exclusive Catholic public school, Brompton Oratory.

Some parents also move, or lie about moving for the sole reason of school catchment areas, while others consider the availability of an 'old school tie' network, which may help their child to get a job and develop socially useful lifelong friendships. In Britain as elsewhere, those who have shared experiences during their formative years forge a common cultural bond which enables them to operate along co-operative and self-help lines. The most famous of such networks may be the grouping of old Etonians, Harrovians and other public schoolboys, known as 'the Establishment'. Girls' schools offering access to this network would be Roedean, Benenden or Cheltenham Ladies College. Britain traditionally works on a system of contacts among people whose business, professional, sporting and social lives produce a shared cultural milieu. This is evident in the number and social status of clubs nominally representing various interests but in practice simply enabling members to socialise. Various organisations, such as Rotary or Round Table; Cubs and Brownies; Scouts and Guides induct British children into this club mentality.

It has always been the case that pupils from single-sex schools have performed better than those at mixed ones – without the distractions of the opposite sex, so the argument goes. This has applied more to girls than to boys. Thus, in the 2004 GCSE tables seven of the top ten schools nationally

FIGURE 2.2   Roedean School, adjacent to Brighton marina, enjoys a favoured
location like most other independent schools

were girls' schools. Recently, moreover, the trend in school and university
education is that girls seem to be performing much better than boys. Various
factors have contributed to their increased pre-eminence. Today more women
in prominent jobs offer role models. Feminism has changed girls' expectations
and encouraged their ambition. A profound shift appears to be taking place
where boys are 'the weaker sex', the ones who need encouragement and the
raising of their self-esteem. This is one of the problems being addressed by
educators who argue that boys perform better at exams while the education
system has moved more towards continuous assessment.

The Labour government has appeared less doctrinaire than previous
administrations. They are prepared to support grammar schools rather than
the comprehensives which Labour introduced in the 1960s. They are also
prepared to borrow ideas from private schools and in extreme cases to allow
failing inner-city schools to be managed by private companies. However, they
are also putting less money into education than the OECD average, by a full
percentage point. In 1998 Britain was just ahead of Portugal, at second-
to-bottom in adult literacy in the OECD (Organisation for Economic
Co-operation and Development). A 2000 report by the National Skills Task
Force found that seven million adults in Britain were functionally illiterate.
This was described by Estelle Morris the Education and Skills Minister at

the time as 'quite frightening'. This perhaps explains Labour's claim to tackle 'education, education, education'.

But some of the new policies and trends are equally disturbing. For example, studying Modern Languages has always been a minority pursuit in Britain. Britons are less likely than any other Europeans to speak a second language. Since 2004 they have become even less likely. The government made it no longer compulsory for pupils to study a foreign language. Consequently, numbers of pupils studying German and French fell by 14.2 per cent and 13.2 per cent respectively to 100,000 and 230,000. University language departments are concerned at the shortage of prospective students if this trend continues. Meanwhile, by contrast, in the independent sector, Brighton College has made the study of Mandarin Chinese compulsory for all its pupils, presumably in the belief that this will lead to their ultimate advantage.

Further, recent governments, since that of Margaret Thatcher in 1979, have encouraged a shift from education to training. The word 'education' comes from the Latin *educo* meaning to lead out or develop qualities which are within. Education thus produces the fully rounded individual with a healthy mind in a healthy body (*mens sana in corpore sano*). Critics suggest that because the majority of students are still in a formative phase of their lives it is a mistake to concentrate solely on *instruction*, which implies pouring knowledge into them and ignores the stage of personal development that they have reached. Training is more to do with the supply of workers than with the personal fulfilment of the individual. Education, on the other hand, develops qualities like creativity, encourages curiosity and allows personal development. Opponents, on the other hand, say that publicly funded education should be pragmatic and does have a duty to supply society's need for skills and employers' requirements in the knowledge economy.

In 2002 apprehensions about the political apathy of the young and a 'moral crisis' in society saw the teaching of citizenship made compulsory in schools. Four years later, an Ofsted report found that the subject was being taught inadequately in most schools. Teachers felt ill-prepared and were not adhering to the curriculum laid down. They were expected to inform and enthuse pupils about, for example: legal and human rights and responsibilities; central and local government; the electoral system and voting; Britain's relations with the EU, Commonwealth and UN. Unsurprisingly Ofsted found that often such classes were 'dull, irrelevant and even counter-productive'.

University education is generally less contentious. According to figures from the OECD, in Britain in 1999 35.6 per cent of 21-year olds graduated from university. This was the highest percentage in Europe. Moreover in 2001 a report on graduate employment commissioned by the Higher

Education Funding Council found that more new UK graduates expressed satisfaction with their college courses than did their counterparts in Europe. Government figures in 2000 showed that only 17 per cent of students in the UK leave universities without a qualification, the second lowest drop-out rate in the world (after Japan).

Universities are still central to the development of future leaders of Britain. Even when the lines of political division are being redrawn, university graduates (especially from Oxbridge) still dominate the political leadership. For example, Margaret Thatcher and Tony Blair both went to Oxford and almost two-thirds of the people appointed by Tony Blair to the Labour Cabinet since 1997 were educated at Oxford or Cambridge.

Because they are seen as monolithic, institutions like the National Health Service or the educational system are always under attack. Where they are ineffectual, other means are sought of doing their jobs. In the case of education, the forums through which various skills such as 'parenting' are taught have changed. Originally they might have been taught via the family, or the church or the school. None of these institutions is still functioning as it was. TV and the Web have become the most effective mediums of instruction.

Despite sometimes rancorous debate, individuals still feel positive about their own education. A wide range of them, having had the experience of being in the school play, practising team sports like hockey or soccer, or such extra-curricular activities as chess or judo, develop and retain a shared sense of pride in their schools. Rivalry between schools is felt by children who are publicly labelled by the uniforms that most British schools make them wear. When they leave school, reports of their achievements will often indicate their schools – so, for example, members of the Oxford and Cambridge Rugby Teams have their colleges *and* schools listed thus: Carr, Kenneth: Merton; St Anthony's Comprehensive, Luton. Smith, John: Churchill; Shrewsbury School. Students will often visit their old schools and join Old Girls or Boys Associations, which meet to arrange social functions. This perhaps explains the phenomenal success of the website Friends Reunited.

Throughout their lives people who went to Eton, Harrow or Winchester schools are referred to by others as Old Etonians, Old Harrovians or Wykehamists. (Winchester School was founded in the fourteenth century by Bishop William Wykeham.) And they see themselves in this way also. Well into middle age someone will pride himself on being a *public* school boy. Professor Richard Hoggart saw himself all his life as 'a *grammar* school boy'. For Hoggart this implied someone who forever has to jump hurdles, which he places for himself, in order to retain a sense of self worth.

Even primary schools have reunions, as people feel a need to re-experience the comradeship and spirit of community of their youth. No matter how old people are, school is where they acquired their first long-term friends, developed their social personalities, and gained a deep and lasting sense of communal identity.

Employment

Education and work are linked in that an individual's success at school often determines the kind of job he or she goes on to do. The relationship is not always this straightforward, but often there is a connection between upward and downward trajectories at school and in the workplace. An important effect of the many divisions in British education – between state and private, Oxbridge and Redbrick, vocational and academic – is that the workforce experiences ideas of stratification which have been superseded in many other countries. Thus the British workforce is distinguished by its divisions rather than its cohesiveness. Remuneration replicates social division. Process or factory workers have always received (weekly) wages, while predominantly middle-class managers have received (monthly) salaries. There are still quite separate ladders of achievement in numerous workplaces and it is almost impossible for people to cross from one to another. The case of John Major, someone who did not attend university let alone Oxbridge, rising to become prime minister (1990–7), is the exception which proves the rule.

Further examples of the continuing stratified nature of Britain unfortunately abound. British company reports still append names to photos of directors while referring to technical processes beneath photos of workers. The civil service is divided into administrative, executive and clerical grades; industry into management and shop floor; banks into directors, managers, clerks and cashiers. These divisions may not be in all cases watertight, but very few people at the top of British industry have risen from the bottom and this both reflects and determines a British cultural identity based on the social and economic divisions which separate groups of people from one another.

Table 2.1 shows, respectively, the distribution of workers between different industries and the national unemployment rates in recent years. Looking at the steady reduction in unemployment in Table 2.1 it is tempting to suggest that the success of the Labour government is due to its control of this single problem. It follows that, if this trend were to reverse, Labour might be less likely to retain office.

Attitudes to work are determined culturally and work in general has always had a low cultural profile. If we 'read' British society through literature, we can see that most works of fiction for example either don't refer to work or, if they do, disparage it. In Jane Austen's novels in the early nineteenth century, people who are in trade are not quite respectable and the

TABLE 2.1   Workforce and unemployment (2001)

Workforce	%	Unemployment			
		Year	%	Year	%
Agriculture, forestry & fishing	1.3	1980	5.1	1991	8.0
Manufacturing industries	16.1	1981	8.1	1992	9.7
Construction	4.8	1982	9.5	1993	10.3
Wholesale & retail	7.0	1983	10.4	1994	9.4
Hotels & catering	5.8	1984	10.6	1995	8.0
Transport & communications	6.1	1985	10.9	1996	7.2
Banking, finance & insurance	4.1	1986	11.1	1997	5.5
Real estate/business	14.7	1987	10.0	1998	4.7
Education	7.9	1988	8.0	1999	4.3
Health & social work	10.5	1989	6.2	2000	3.8
Total no. in employment		1990	5.8	2006	5.5
Men	12,356,000				
Women	11,985,000				

Source: 'Labour Market Trends', National Statistics, Crown Copyright (2001)

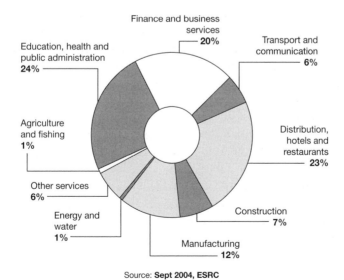

Source: **Sept 2004, ESRC**

FIGURE 2.3   Labour force by occupation

Source: ESRC (September 2004)

correct thing to do is to own land and to live off one's rents. Neither Elizabeth Bennet's Mr Darcy, nor Emma Woodhouse's Mr Knightley works for a living. Bulstrode in George Eliot's *Middlemarch* (1871–2) is a banker and thus in a profession which is not yet entirely respectable. In Dickens' novels people try to separate their public (working) selves from their private (domestic) lives in the belief that everybody wants to escape from work. Wemmick, the law clerk in *Great Expectations* (1860–1) pulls up a drawbridge when he goes back to his home where his 'aged parent' lives. Home is sacrosanct. Work is a necessary evil.

Work is rarely portrayed seriously or in detail in British films. Karel Reisz, Tony Richardson and others of the 1950s New Wave cinema were seen as daring for approaching the subject of work at all in *Saturday Night and Sunday Morning* (1960) and *Room at the Top* (1959). In fact, although there are some 'documentary' scenes from the factory floor in the former, the film concentrates on a love story. Even 'revolutionary' drama like Alan Bleasdale's lauded TV series *Boys from the Blackstuff* (1991), which shows how work is integral to a sense of both identity and culture, feels a need to portray workers as 'cheeky chappies' who avoid 'hard graft'. On the other hand, Willy Russell's popular escapist films *Letter to Brezhnev* (1985) and *Shirley Valentine* (1989) deal directly with work in and outside the home, and yet they offer their audiences a fantasy of escape from the tedium of work into romances with 'exotic' foreigners.

Unlike novels and films, TV, curiously, has produced a spate of series about work. They have accelerated beyond such hospital dramas as *Casualty* or rural veterinary practices like *All Creatures Great and Small* to include the military (*Soldiers*); firefighting (*London's Burning*) and many others. TV comedy series set in workplaces include *The Brittas Empire*, *Drop the Dead Donkey* and *Dinner Ladies*, set in a Leisure Centre, an office and a canteen respectively. Ricky Gervais' series *The Office* was an extremely popular treatment of work, relationships and office politics, while *The Thick of It* satirised office life at Labour headquarters.

A film which offers a useful snapshot of British life case-study because it did very well at the box office, and therefore may be seen to reflect popular British aspirations and values, is *Four Weddings and A Funeral* (1994). The story pursues some friends around Britain and examines their social lives in the context of the ceremonial rituals of the title. The whole is placed in the context of an Anglo-American 'special relationship', which is part shared cultural history and part wish-fulfilment designed to appeal to different agendas on both sides of the Atlantic. As in other films such as *Remains of the Day* (1994), *A Handful of Dust* (1988) or *The Shooting Party* (1984), it adds social comment to a familiar recipe of stately homes in a timeless, upstairs/downstairs England peopled with fascinating eccentrics and nameless servants. This has been called a 'Merchant Ivory' version of Britain

(from the names of the director and producer who mad‹
(1985) and *Howards End* (1992)). *Four Weddings a*
version of Britain which contains a mixture of tradir
Bohemianism, the gay community and monarchy ↿
non-threatening framework of British compromise.
lutely no mention of work. The film comes from th
of Fire (1981) and *Another Country* (1984), w
leisured Britain that they depict and steadfastly ignoɩ↿
a living. In such pointedly socially divided worlds, work persists ↿
representations as something the upper classes do not do and the woɩ↿
classes wish not to do.

To illustrate further British culture's negative representation of work,
we can look at one or two examples from the Britpop phenomenon of the
1990s. The 1995 Blur album is called *The Great Escape*. Its front cover has
a picture of someone diving from a motorboat into a beautiful Mediterranean
sea. Its back cover has the four members of the group dressed as urban
professionals huddled around a computer. Here, as with most popular
culture aimed at the country's mass population, the dominant British view
is that work is a treadmill from which people dream of escaping (Blur's other
album titles also suggest this: *Leisure, Modern Life is Rubbish, Parklife*).

FIGURE 2.4 A mixed-gender police unit integrates with the local community at a
folk festival

The possibility of a life of leisure is also a fantasy indulged in every week as the National Lottery winning numbers are announced on television and millionaires are literally 'made' overnight. It is assumed the winners will give up work without regret, but many have to be counselled by therapists to cope with (partly their wealth, but largely) their position away from the community and working-life they have known.

People establish and share identity at work through participation in such incidental 'social' aspects as car pools, coffee clubs, office sweepstakes (betting on horses), company sports clubs, and celebrations for engagements and birthdays. More people meet their future spouse through work than in any other way.

On leaving the office or the factory, there is often a shared drink with workmates and nights out to celebrate new jobs, retirements and weddings. (The latter are known as 'hen' and 'stag' nights for women and men respectively.) They take place in nightclubs, pubs or Working Men's Social Clubs. Many relationships carry on outside work and workers do jobs ('foreigners') for one another.

Despite the widespread taboo against cultural representations of work, in practice British society is constructed so much around employment that those who are cut off from it are also isolated socially. Britain was the first country to industrialise and is one of the first to have to devise programmes for coping with the problems of post-industrial and even post-agricultural society (in 1950 25 per cent of the workers in Britain still worked on the land – the figure today is under 2 per cent). It has to supply redundant workforces with wide-ranging help, from counselling to setting up small businesses, from make-work schemes to volunteering.

Unemployment and economic change

The work ethic is very strong in the UK and for a majority of the British population their identity is shaped by the notion that they *work*. However, one of the main features of the working classes in the post-Thatcher period in Britain is that a greater proportion of them than of either the middle or upper classes is *not* working. Loss of work to a class which defines itself as *working* is traumatic and will be dealt with further in Chapter 5 'Class and Politics'. It is hard for outsiders to appreciate the trauma of growing up within such a situation. Yozzer Hughes, a chief character in Alan Bleasdale's *Boys from the Blackstuff* became a cult figure with his catchphrase of 'Gizza Job', partly because so many people could empathise with him. This has also been a major theme in soap operas such as *EastEnders*.

Women in employment have fared less well than men, though there are now more women in the workforce than men. However, for a number of reasons, including prejudice and part-time working, women have often failed to gain promotion to posts of greater responsibility. The term 'glass ceiling' is applied to this consequent upper limit of women's progress in company careers. Their rate of unemployment is less than half that of men but their average pay is only 75 per cent of men's in similar occupations. However, unemployed ethnic-minority women and men are even more disadvantaged than mainstream workers, with rates of 17 per cent and 24 per cent respectively. The rate of unemployment for Muslims is estimated to be 27 per cent whereas for Christians it is under 10 per cent.

Unsurprisingly, the above climate has led to a decline in a sense of job security. According to government reports, unlike previous generations middle-aged people now do not feel secure about their financial prospects. When the chairman of a major bank predicts job losses in his industry of 20,000, others see *their* jobs as precarious, and people are cautious about spending. For example, the percentage of disposable income that people now save at 12.2 per cent is 50 per cent more than it was in the 1960s. Karl Marx's predictions about the 'casualisation of labour' appear to be coming to pass and certainly many more people are being employed on temporary or part-time contracts. Instead of seeing this as the apocalyptic end to capitalism however, some business analysts prefer to see it as following the pattern of the United States and supplying a more flexible productive base which ultimately regulates more efficiently the balance between supply and demand in the labour market.

For the last hundred years the south-east of England has been the most prosperous part of Britain and for a time in the 1980s, people there enthusiastically endorsed the concept of corporate Britain. To those in less privileged parts of the country, it seemed as though those in and around London were enabled to participate in company share purchase schemes, and supported the under-priced privatisation sales of utilities such as electricity, water and telephone companies. The majority of small shareholders (they were known as 'Sids', because of a British Gas privatisation advertising campaign with a character of that name) took their profits and sold out, in the spirit of the entrepreneurialism which was being recommended to them by government. Some did sense themselves for a time as empowered and as part of corporate Britain. Other people felt that, because the industries were owned by the country, *their* national assets were being sold to those sufficiently well off to have money to invest in them. So this was seen as yet another way of shifting money from the regions to the well-to-do south.

People on the political right argued that Britain had become a poor country because it has created a climate of dependency: its citizens lacked initiative, relied on the 'nanny' state to look after their every need and thus avoid their personal responsibilities. This hard-edged Thatcherite view led to a situation where in the interest of industrial efficiency, jobs were being axed at precisely the time when council tenants were being encouraged by the government to buy their state-owned homes ('council houses') on very good terms. Some individuals simply couldn't cope and returned their house keys to their mortgage providers. At one point in the early 1990s, homes were being repossessed at the rate of 1,000 per week, and even among the more affluent there were up to one-and-a-quarter million people in Britain with 'negative equity'. That is, the loan they had taken out from the bank was greater than the value of the house they borrowed it for. No wonder the Labour Government, with its pledge to increase employment rather than just to bolster capital, was welcomed into office in 1997.

Attitudes to work in Britain have also undoubtedly been affected by the decline in religious observance. Protestantism has had a particularly close relation to work. A belief in the moral importance of work (*laborare est orare* – to work is to pray) was especially notable in the late eighteenth century, with the growth of commerce in London, and in the early nineteenth century, with the start of the Industrial Revolution. The popularity of Daniel Defoe's *Robinson Crusoe* (1741) shows how ingrained in the culture was the idea of the 'self-employed' individual who, out of a sense of religious duty, struggled against odds to succeed. He 'justified his existence' through work. This ideology appealed to a population which until recently had been largely rural and self-employed, but who, because of the 'division of labour' was now forced to do single unsatisfying city-based jobs.

In *Religion and the Rise of Capitalism* (1926), R.H. Tawney drew attention to the link between people's religious beliefs and their relative wealth. He attributed Britain's economic well-being to the Protestant work ethic. The idea is that we are put on earth, not just to live and to eat, but to work hard (partly as descendants and inheritors of the sin of Adam and Eve (work as 'punishment')). People who believe in the sanctity of work become rich. Conversely, the more unworldly the religion the less likely the religious congregation is to become rich. The situation is undoubtedly circular – economic decline may test religious commitment, which in turn limits adherence to the work ethic. The latter is based on a religious belief, but in practice, people of all persuasions have come to believe in work as a good thing and as a defining characteristic of being British. Again, this has increased psychological and social trauma for those unable to find jobs.

If for one reason or another, both culturally ingrained commitment to work is eroded and opportunities are taken away and replaced with the mentality induced by enforced dependency upon the state, people have to find outlets elsewhere. Their energies have been channelled into leisure and this displacement has taken place in Britain progressively throughout the years of unemployment and the move to casual work. Shopping as a leisure pursuit has been encouraged because it fills people's time and is good for the economy. The graph of the decline in the number of permanent jobs, is crossed by the ascendant one of ownership of satellite TVs and DVD players, the practice of sports and other indoor and outdoor leisure pursuits.

Leisure around the home

In dealing with leisure we are concerned not just with how people occupy themselves but with the cultural significance of their hobbies and practices. This applies to group and individual activities. We may divide the leisure pursuits which British people engage in into private and public. These are crude designations, but they do offer a way in to understanding how leisure affects cultural consciousness and identity.

As mentioned in the Introduction, the dominant medium for cultural exchange in Britain is television, though for teenagers the Web is taking over. It is difficult to pinpoint the moment at which TV became a significant part of the national cultural consciousness, but many oral histories of older people refer to the novelty of watching the June 1953 Coronation of Queen Elizabeth II on TV. This they did in company with friends, relations and neighbours. The move from listening to the Football Association Cup Final on 'the wireless' (radio) to watching it on TV, marked a further important change. Particularly since the 1960s, daily consumption of TV has risen as broadcasting expanded from evenings only, to daytime, to the mornings – so-called 'breakfast TV'. TV watching is now effectively available twenty-four hours a day, especially with numerous cable and satellite stations. The average time spent watching TV is nearly three hours a day. The young and the old watch more, the middle-aged a lot less. TV is a powerful social adhesive in Britain. Following stories on TV provides people with topics of conversation, allows them to get to know one another's tastes and preferences, and enables them to explore the current social and cultural preoccupations that TV directs them towards. Workmates and friends are bonded together by their responses to the *News*, sitcoms, dramas or soaps that they have seen on TV.

It is clear that the change in the importance to their lives that people attach to TV had come about by 1974. At that time Edward Heath, Britain's prime minister, made two mistakes in devising strategic responses to the emergency of the oil crisis. In order to save electricity, he brought in a three-day working week, and he made the TV companies finish broadcasting each evening at 10.30 p.m. In other words, he prevented people from working and he interfered with their watching of television. They were not prepared to put up with either of those changes. There was widespread opposition to the government and undoubtedly the above measures were factors in Heath's loss of the General Election in 1974.

Television's place is very much in the home. So, for example, when pubs introduced large-screen TVs for specific sports events and promotions in order to increase custom, their success was limited, because pubs are places more for social interaction than for 'watching the box'. Many more people prefer to go out and attend football matches than watch them on television. They get much more of a sense of shared identity from their support for the same team. There is a 'family' atmosphere at some of the big clubs, despite the fact that there are 40,000 people present. Such large attendances indicate a wish for a shared sense of community which TV alone can't provide. In 2006, attendance at football matches was increasing and watching it on TV was declining, though events like the World Cup saw huge audiences in bars and pubs for the communal atmosphere.

However, in a country with all sorts of signs of social breakdown, from child murder and random knife attacks in the cities to rural suicides and abduction, people cling to electronic expressions of community. They watch their own society through TV dramas such as *Casualty* or *The Bill*, which offer excitement set in an everyday context, or soap operas like *Emmerdale* or *Heartbeat* which invoke an idealised rural past. Young people especially relate to soap operas. Reference was made above to *Grange Hill*, but by far the most popular soaps followed by people in the age group 14 to 25 are the Australian serials *Neighbours* and *Home & Away*. A slightly older age group watches *EastEnders* and *Coronation Street*. Given the success in numerous areas of British life of US culture, there is a surprising lack of interest in American soaps. More popular are high-adrenalin shows such as *24* and *CSI* or light dramas like *Charmed* and *Desperate Housewives*. Characters in these programmes supply viewers with topics of conversation which provide the potential glue for their own social community. Table 2.2 shows the relative popularity of TV programmes.

TABLE 2.2   Most popular soap operas/series/quizzes (2005)

	Millions
EastEnders	51.8
Emmerdale	49.7
Coronation Street	43.5
Neighbours	23.1
Who Wants To Be A Millionaire?	21.5
The Weakest Link	17.7
Deal or No Deal	15.0

Source: BARB (2005)

TABLE 2.3 Most popular magazines read by men (1980, 1990, 2000)

1980	%	1990	%	2000	%
Reader's Digest	20	Reader's Digest	14	FHM	20
Custom Car	9	What Car	7	Sky Customer	9
Do-It-Yourself	6	Classic Cars	5	Cable Guide	6
Mayfair	6	National Geographic	5	Loaded	6
Hot Car	6	Golf Monthly	4	Skyview TV Guide	6

Source: Social Focus on Men, ONS

TABLE 2.4 Readership of selected newspapers/magazines (2005)

	Thousands	% of potential readership
Sun	8,073	16.8
Daily Mail	5,427	12.7
Daily Mirror	3,884	10.4
What's On TV	3,792	7.9
Readers' Digest	3,391	7.3
Take A Break	3,383	7.5
Radio Times	2,078	4.3
Daily Telegraph	2,061	4.2
Daily Express	1,784	3.8
TV Times	1,782	3.7
BBC Gardeners' World	1,736	4.1
The Times	1,718	4.0
Auto Trader	1,617	3.4
Cosmopolitan	1,537	3.0
TV Choice	1,456	3.0
Guardian	1,158	2.5
Loaded	1,152	2.4
Private Eye	756	1.6
Big Issue	666	1.4
J17	556	2.1
What Hi-Fi?	506	1.7
Motorcycle News	467	1.0
The Economist	377	0.8
Practical Photography	305	0.7

Source: National Readership Survey (2005)

Besides television and the ever-proliferating use of the internet, the major leisure activity of many British people is their hobby. The hobbies or minority interests pursued by Britons are numerous, wide-ranging and passionately indulged in. They are part of the people's identities. Such minority activities include philately, train spotting, ferret keeping, fishing, pigeon-fancying, birdwatching, scouting, swimming, cycling, fell-running – just counting along a scale of physical activity. Most of these hobbies will have magazines to accompany them, or at the very least a newsletter. The number of browsers in high-street newsagents evidences the range and diversity of Britain's leisure interests and perspectives, as do Tables 2.3 to 2.5.

Table 2.3 shows how, over the past twenty years there has been a significant shift particularly in men's magazine reading habits, as illustrated in Table 2.4. *FHM* the lifestyle magazine, *Loaded* a 'lads' mag. and three

TABLE 2.5 Most popular types of books bought

Rank	Type	Change from five years ago
Women		
1	General fiction	Cookery
2	Romance	Romance
3	Crime/mystery	Crime/thriller/detective
4	Historical novels	English dictionaries
5	Cookery /food/drink	Puzzle/quiz books
6	History/archaeology	Gardening/indoor plants
7	Autobiography	Food/drink
8	Adventure/thriller	Historical novels
9	Science/medicine	Classics/literature
10	Psychology/social sciences	Baby & childcare
Men		
1	General fiction	Crime/thriller/detective
2	History/archaeology	English dictionary
3	Adventure/thriller	Car repair manuals
4	Autobiography	Cookery
5	Sports/games	Computer manuals
6	Science fiction/fantasy	Sports/games books
7	Sheet maps	Gardening/indoor plants
8	Crime/mystery	Sports/games instruction books
9	Business/economics	Road Atlas of GB
10	Bibles/religion	War/adventure stories

Source: Books and the Consumer 1999, Book Marketing Limited

television guides may constitute men's sole current reading, and accurately record a move from interest in active leisure and general topics towards TV watching. The magazines which sell best to women are almost exclusively gender-specific: *Take A Break* (3,383), *Woman* (1,858), *Bella* (1,943), *Woman's Own* (2,191) and *Chat* (1,480) (figures source: *The Lifestyle Pocketbook*, NTC Publications, 2001).

Reading of books, the other major domestic leisure-time activity, has held up well. Book buying, ironically, is stimulated by television. *Brideshead Revisited* (1945) and *Pride and Prejudice* (1813) and *Bleak House* (1853) sold many times more copies after their TV series than they ever did previously. Table 2.5, which covers books that people buy for themselves, is divided along gender lines and concludes this section on 'indoor' entertainments.

Public entertainment

Pubs

We will now look at some entertainments outside of the home which British people use to occupy their free time. The principal place of entertainment outside the home that people automatically think of in relation to Britain, is the public house or 'pub'. In the past, pubs have performed different social functions. Traditionally they were a male preserve. Various sociological studies have suggested that until the 1950s the British pub was a more welcoming place for a man than his home. It was familiar and cozy (small barrooms were called 'snugs'), with a fire and games such as darts and dominoes. This changed when houses in the 1950s, a period of increasing affluence, were brought up to date and made more attractive with higher standards of draughtproofing, labour-saving appliances, new furnishings and even central heating in some cases. The 1950s were a 'home-centred society'. It was then less acceptable for a woman to go into a pub on her own, than it was for a man. Some city-centre pubs specified 'men only' and many covertly discouraged single women. Today they are much more welcoming to people of both sexes but few older women will say they feel comfortable going into a pub on their own.

Among 'outside' entertainments, pubs and cinemas have been through periods of boom and bust in English social life. Cinema attendance in Britain reached its peak in 1946 with 1.6 billion cinema visits. It bottomed in 1984 with 54 million. It is currently resurgent with 176 million attendances in 2006 despite the competition of TV. A report from the Film Council said that 27 per cent of the £775 million spent on 176 million cinema visits in Britain was for humorous films. The percentages in Germany and Spain were 23 and 18.

Going out to the cinema is still a staple part of British life and appears to be on a rising trend after a long period of declining attendances. There were more than 140 million attendances in 2002 (largely thanks to *Harry Potter* and *The Lord of the Rings*), despite the competition of television. However, the majority of all cinema-going is still done by under 5 per cent of the total population, and the range of films on offer has not widened, despite the increase in the number of multiplex screens, which are owned by large multinationals and show mainly Hollywood films. So cinema attendance, as a cultural practice, has yet to regain its 1960s popularity, but can still be a cohesive social force, particularly for young people.

Pubs on the other hand, with the percentages of men and women who never drink alcohol, at 15 and 20 respectively and rising, are struggling. However, with the churches in Britain in decline, as congregations age and Sunday attendances fall, pubs are finding a new role. They fill the social vacuum created by religious decline, and perform the function of community meeting place and so are still, in the new century, very much central to British life. That this is the case is shown by the many pubs in soap operas, including 'The Vic' in *EastEnders* and 'The Rover's Return' in *Coronation Street*.

Pantomimes

At Christmas time, pantomimes form an important aspect of British cultural experience. Unknown on the Continent, they are staged in theatres, village halls and community centres of all sorts, amateur and professional. Well-known TV personalities, or even politicians often appear in them. Parents attend with children, and in a controlled dramatic environment panto-mimes offer a 'safe' form of initiation into the adult world. They contain a number of standard ingredients: cross-dressing (the 'Principal Boy' is always a woman; the 'Dame' is a man); double entendre (parents can understand lewd meanings which pass over the heads of their children); contemporary reference (current politicians, or aspects of daily life such as public transport or the NHS are guyed); ritualised audience participation, where children get to shout: 'He's behind you', or 'Oh yes it is'/'Oh no it isn't'. They very often involve reworking of myths as in *Babes in the Wood*, or *Cinderella*, where the badly treated individual gets justice and their rightful place in the world.

When London theatre was suffering during the post 11 September tourist absence in 2001, pantomime there and elsewhere in Britain was booming. Thousands of people flocked to pantos which earned millions of pounds of profit. At a time of military intervention in Afghanistan and global uncertainty, people sought out traditional family entertainment. To assuage their fears of the bogey man Osama bin Laden, a character with his name was incorporated into the year's most popular panto, *Aladdin*.

Others doing well included *Cinderella*, *Beauty and the Beast*, *Puss in Boots*, *Snow White and the Seven Dwarfs*, *Peter Pan* and *Dick Whittington*.

Theatre, ballet and opera give Britain a high cultural profile particularly with overseas tourists, even though they remain minority pursuits in Britain. They are patronised by older, well-to-do people in London and the major cities. Perhaps because the largest concentration of these cultural resources

FIGURE 2.5   The 'family-hostile' Albion Inn caters to adult customers only

is in London with its National Theatre, Royal Shakespeare Company, English National Opera and Royal Ballet, they tend to be seen as 'elitist'. However, theatres are in fact dispersed around the regions. Liverpool has The Playhouse. Manchester's Royal Exchange Theatre offers high quality drama. Leeds-based Opera North is thriving and Scottish and Welsh Opera companies are well received on their countrywide tours. Despite a difficult financial climate, several concert halls were either built or refurbished in the early 1990s including Manchester's £42 million Bridgewater Hall, Birmingham's Symphony Hall and Liverpool's Philharmonic Hall.

Some of these art forms are supported mainly by overseas tourists (London West End theatre productions such as Andrew Lloyd Webber's *Cats*, Willy Russell's *Blood Brothers*, or Agatha Christie's *The Mousetrap*), but some have a devoted local clientele. It is necessary to bear this in mind when looking at the respective 2001 attendance figures for theatre (36.7), classical concerts (11.6) and opera (6.64) (as a percentage of all adults: Target Group index BMRB, 2000). And one should be aware that, in addition to the above venues, there are an estimated 700 youth theatres catering for 53,000 participants.

Sport

The major outdoor leisure outlet in Britain is sport. People in Britain spend a great deal of their leisure time either participating in or watching it. The main sports practised in Britain during the winter are rugby and football (soccer). Rugby is controlled by the Rugby Union, soccer by the Football Association. The traditional division between lower social status professional soccer players (who need to be paid) and higher social status rugby players ('gifted amateurs') has been eroded by the Union's decision in 1995 to relax its rules to allow professional rugby clubs. Soccer is known as 'a gentlemen's game for roughs' and rugby as 'a roughs' game for gentlemen'. One of the many paradoxes of British society is that although most of the public (that is private) schools in Britain play the middle-class game of rugby as their main sport, both Eton and Harrow, Britain's most exclusive schools, still field more soccer than rugby teams. Nationwide attendances at soccer matches in the 2004/5 season totalled 25 million. This compares with the peak figure in 1954/5 of 34 million.

There are two major groups of professional clubs who play in either the Premier or the Football league. There are also two main competitions: the League Cup which is based on points, and the FA Cup which is a knockout competition. Going to a football match between major clubs such as Arsenal, Liverpool or Manchester United can be a powerful experience. Supporters of rival teams are segregated at football matches and often ritually taunt one another. For example, supporters in the Kop (a terrace at Liverpool named after a lookout hill from the Boer War: Spion Kop) used to sing: 'See them lying on the runway . . .' to Manchester United supporters – to remind them of their team's plane crash in Munich in the late 1950s. Most of the chanting is not so vicious; a milder taunt nowadays is to sing the *Monty Python* song 'Always look on the bright side of life . . .' to your rivals, when your team has just scored a goal. Much debate centres on whether football supplies a safety valve for, rather than an encouragement to violence and it is argued that aggression is harmlessly released in the above ritualised exchanges between supporters. Supporters are thought to feel a necessary sense of shared community through loyalty to their team and local pride when it wins. A measure of the seriousness with which supporters take their soccer is contained in the Liverpool manager Bill Shankly's famous remark: 'Football isn't just a matter of life and death. It's far more important than that.'

In summer, the game of cricket is played widely on village greens, as well as at the professional level, and is a genuinely popular 'grassroots' game about observance of rules, fairness and a pitting of wits and talent between equally matched teams. However, there are class associations to all British sports and in the case of cricket there is a history of contention for 'ownership' of the game. For example, many British stately homes have an adjacent cricket pitch and pavilion and over the years encounters have taken place there between 'gentlemen and players'. This again underlines the British distinction between the upper classes (gentlemen), who are leisured and admirable, and the lower (players) who work and are disparaged.

This may also be seen in rugby. Rugby league was founded as a break-away from Rugby Union famously at the George Hotel in Huddersfield in 1895. Basically the players were impoverished northern working men who wanted to be paid for giving up their precious Saturday afternoon to play a game of rugby. For the next 100 years Rugby Union remained a middle-class game, played by amateurs who could afford to do so.

Significantly, professional soccer is associated with Britain's cities while cricket, which may well be played in urban centres such as Old Trafford (Manchester), Headingley (Leeds) or Lords (London) is associated with rural Britain. So while football clubs are named 'Leeds United' or 'Manchester City', professional cricketers play for counties, such as Kent, Somerset, and Gloucestershire.

Variations occur in the terminology used to describe people watching leisure entertainments. Those who watch soccer, rugby, cinema, TV, theatre or opera are known respectively as 'crowds', 'spectators', 'audiences', 'viewers', 'theatre-goers' or 'opera-buffs'. These terms form part of a spectrum of cultural snobbery. Soccer fans are traditionally working-class and are called 'crowds', suggesting they are amorphous. Middle-class people who watch rugby are 'spectators' – they are dispassionate onlookers.

'Audiences' are more sophisticated again because they listen. 'Viewers' is a euphemism which denies the passivity of the TV 'couch potato'. 'Theatre-goer' implies some form of dynamism and the word 'buff' comes from the uniform (made of buffalo hide) worn by smart regiments.

There are many other outdoor sporting events in Britain, particularly in the summer, which attract national and international interest. However there are many more, less publicised ones, which supply the high point in individual enthusiasts' years. Surprisingly, local events can sometimes be better patronised than national ones. For example, until recent years, the 30,000 runners in Gateshead's annual Great North Run, compared with the 26,000 who took part in the London Marathon received far less publicity. The Great North Run was hardly alluded to in the national news media with their metropolitan emphasis, but the latter was hyped and televised. Impressionistically, the degree of health consciousness, fitness and dietary awareness is higher among the British young than the Americans. But young Swiss, Germans or Canadians are much more likely to swim or ride bikes than the British. There is no British equivalent to the Continental 'parcours' (outdoor fitness areas in national parks), and facilities such as the National Rowing Centre at Nottingham or the Manchester Velodrome (for cycling), are over-stretched and of no help in keeping the generality of people fit. Most exercise takes place indoors for women, and increasingly

FIGURE 2.6 Around 250 runners take part in the annual Penmaenmawr Fell Race

FIGURE 2.7   Kite buggies race on the sands at Hoylake

FIGURE 2.8   The Eureka cyclists' café is over 75 years old

for men. Health and fitness clubs or gyms have become very popular throughout the country in the 1990s (cynics say because they are dating agencies) and large numbers of people regularly attend aerobics or 'step' classes.

In a study published by the Office for National Statistics in 2001, the following sports were most popular among the four-fifths of men, randomly interviewed, who took part in at least moderate physical activity: walking (48 per cent), snooker (18 per cent), cycling (15 per cent) and swimming (13 per cent). This compares with the 10 per cent who played football. Despite this focus on fitness however, cigarette smoking among the young is again on the increase – particularly among young women.

Festivals

Arts festivals take place annually in most large cities, and smaller places like Glyndebourne and Buxton have their own opera festivals. Pop and rock festivals in particular have become a feature of youth culture. The best known are at Glastonbury and Reading. Entrance fees are relatively expensive at £85 for two or three days but they are extremely well attended with upwards of 20,000 people.

Museums

In this survey of communal leisure activities, we can also say that a traditional version of British culture is nurtured in a range of public institutions: mainly museums and art galleries. In the past it has tended to be high culture that is conserved here and they were places of obligatory pilgrimage for school-children, who in the course of their subsequent lives never returned. In recent years, this has changed. The institutions have become much more imaginative, and their collections have been partially devolved to the regions. There is a Tate gallery in Liverpool and a branch of London's National Portrait Gallery at Bodelwyddan Castle in North Wales. Instead of a single unchanging stock, museums now tend to stage more 'thematic' exhibitions, such as Liverpool Maritime Museum's slavery exhibition, or its Labour Museum which deals with the material conditions of people's lives rather than high culture. Responding to public interest, in 2001 London's Victoria and Albert Museum rearranged its collection to offer 'British Galleries'. Manchester has excellent new museums: the Lowry and Imperial War Museum North.

Holidays

Leisure was originally the preserve of the upper classes. Only they had the time and money to tramp their own grouse moors in Scotland, or sail their yachts with professional crews at Cowes. For example, the industrialist Sir Thomas Lipton was able to finance his own America's Cup yachting challenges and pay his crews in the 1930s. So when leisure became available to ordinary people through decreased working hours and paid annual leave, by and large in the 1950s, it gave social status to those benefiting from it. This soon changed, as catering for larger numbers of leisured people on a year-round basis turned into an industry. Treatment of holiday-makers became more systematic, more professional, less deferential and less status-aware.

Since the 1960s the two-week annual holiday is more likely to be spent abroad. Package holidays were introduced to Britain in the 1950s by the Russian entrepreneur Vladimir Raitz, founder of Horizon holidays. The beneficiaries became the hoteliers of France, Spain and Florida and those losing out, British seaside landladies at traditional resorts. The most pop-ular overseas holiday destinations for Britons in 2002 and the numbers going to them were: France (11.6 million), Spain (13.8 million) and the US (4.1 million). British people have become obsessed with holidaying abroad and make 42 million trips per year. David Lodge suggests in *Paradise News* (1992) that tourism is the new world religion. The Hoover company so underestimated the demand for a holiday scheme it was promoting in 1993 that it lost £200 million.

New patterns in leisure

Gambling

Betting on the sport of the rich, horse racing has always been practised by the working rather than the middle class, whose puritanism in regard to gambling has been tempered only by government-sponsored Premium Bonds and the National Lottery. The latter has become a major national talking point in Britain, which was the last country in Europe to introduce one, in November 1994. As a social and cultural phenomenon it is especially interest-ing. It generates comment in the media, between politicians and among people in general. It has brought a whole new clientele into gambling. Tickets are sold through newsagents and Post Offices – where everybody goes – whereas other forms of gambling such as horse racing are contained within betting shops where passers-by may not even see in through the windows and where the family is virtually excluded. Many people, once a year will place a bet on the Grand National or the Derby, but with the Lottery and its sequel 'Instants' scratch cards, everyone has a 'flutter' (a bet) week by week. Online betting has become a major industry.

The National Lottery has become an important social and cultural phenomenon. Its revenues, at £65 million per week are well above initial estimates of £14–35 million, and nine out of ten adults are claimed to buy tickets on occasions. It is clearly a financial success. This is especially striking since the bookmakers Ladbrokes have likened the chance of winning the jackpot to that of Elvis landing a UFO (Unidentified Flying Object) on the Loch Ness Monster. The odds are about 14 million to 1. George Orwell, writing in 1948 imagined it with quite uncanny accuracy:

> The Lottery, with its weekly pay-out of enormous prizes was the one public event to which the proles [workers] paid serious attention. It was probable that there were some millions of proles for whom the Lottery was the principal if not the only reason for remaining alive. It was their delight, their folly, their anodyne, their intellectual stimulant. Where the Lottery was concerned even people who could barely read and write seemed capable of intricate calculations and staggering feats of memory.
>
> (Orwell, *1984*, p. 71)

It is tempting to say that TV programmes like *Deal or No Deal* or the Lottery itself are really about the possibility of social change. The latter certainly has caused social upheaval and division. Predictably some people have not been able to cope with huge winnings. Many legal cases have centred on breaches of trust among workmates, within families and between friends.

The weekly TV programme on Saturday nights where the draw is made has 12 million viewers for its mixture of orchestrated hype and celebration of greed. The proceeds are devoted to 'good causes', many of which are associated with heritage or 'high' culture like Sadlers Wells ballet or the Royal Opera Company. It has introduced the word 'rollover' (un-won prizes carried forward) into the dictionary. It has increased the number of what were previously [football] 'pools winners' (in its first year it produced more than 100 millionaires) and so raised their profiles as social and cultural phenomena.

A number of lobbies have predictably come out against the Lottery. Church leaders, directors of charities helping the poor, other charities whose revenues have fallen and the companies who previously received the money gambled on football, via their weekly 'pools coupons'. They raise the following main objections: people are spending money they can't afford; revenues are being diverted from the poor to the rich; the state is encouraging gambling; less money is going to charity overall.

Public acceptance of the Lottery and people's enthusiastic identification of themselves as prepared to take a risk may, however, represent a sea-change in Britain's attitudes to gambling, entrepreneurialism and the new rich. In much British middle-class culture and entertainment – from the novel to plays to TV sitcoms, the most reviled characters have been the nouveau riche, whether as individuals or as a class. Mrs Malaprop, Josiah Bounderby and Hyacinth Bucket are examples of people whose wealth and pretension exceed their level of cultural attainment, sensitivity and good manners. A series like *Fawlty Towers* probes the interrelationships between class, snobbery, deference, respectability, good manners, money and service, in the crucible of a home-cum-'guest house'.

A lot of the criticism of the Lottery is based on the fear that one class will be subsidising another's pleasures. A major complaint about the disbursement of funds is that places of entertainment for the rich have benefited. What irks many people is that winning the Lottery goes against their idea of 'natural justice', as defined by the middle classes, in terms of the work ethic we discussed earlier: 'unearned' money is frowned upon. Also, when someone with a criminal record won several million pounds, the *Daily Telegraph* expressed its readers' sense of outrage that such 'undeserved' luck should happen. But the paper itself is caught in the bind of accepting and promoting such aspects of capitalism as free enterprise and entre-preneurialism yet not liking one of the inevitable consequences.

Shopping

The growth of consumerism has made a great impact on people's leisure lives. Esther Rantzen's TV programme *That's Life* (1973–94) represented a major turning point in Britain. It helped the development of a consumer culture. Hitherto corporate Britain could afford to ignore disgruntled customers. But Rantzen held up such arrogance to ridicule and 'empowered' the wronged consumers. A shift occurred in the relative balance of power. Now the consumer is king. Redress is demanded and forthcoming. Trading Standards Officers are feared. America's litigious consumer culture has spread to Britain where customers can sue McDonalds for spilling coffee over them or making them fat.

Because of this apparent liberation of the common man via spending, shopping has become one of Britain's major leisure pastimes. Many shops, particularly supermarkets and high-street stores, are open seven days a week. This has had a significant impact on many people's lives. The work-life balance of those in the retail industry has obviously been adversely affected, as their low wages entail them working longer hours. For others, Sunday has become a day for shopping, like any other, and the demise of the traditional work pattern where even low-paid workers were off on Sundays has meant that fewer people are guaranteed the 'community' time on Sunday which might originally have been spent in church, but which is now spent shopping, pursuing leisure activities or watching football on TV.

Trends in entertainment

There is now a noticeable preference by young people for inanimate over animate sources of entertainment. This is evident not just in the decline of such live arts as theatre or home pastimes like card playing or in the preference of nightclubs with DJs over live gigs. Technophiliac 'Generation X' (from Douglas Coupland's 1991 novel of that name) often prefer things to people: cash machines to bank cashiers [US: tellers]; computers to socialising; cyber cafes to coffee houses; virtual reality to reality; the internet and technological gizmos such as ipods, mobile phones and answering machines, to live individuals. Nor do people just prefer TV and cinema to live entertainment. Within electronic media they prefer cartoons to 'real' representations of people. Technology has proved that it can deliver the 'real world' yet people want less 'real' images than are contained in traditional representation. They prefer their TV adverts to contain animated characters rather than real ones.

Another notable change in the pattern of people's leisure is a move away from socialising at home to frequenting public places of entertainment: 'fun pubs', multiplexes (containing cinemas, bowling allies, fruit machines and nightclubs). There are regional variations, but generally the fact that British socialising took place in the pub or club made it difficult for new people to integrate into post-war British society. Asians in particular preferred to socialise at home, and this exacerbated cultural differences and separated people. In time however, as in so many aspects of culture referred to elsewhere (body piercing, casual clothing, rap music, use of marijuana),while young mainstream people adopted immigrants' practices, young people from minority backgrounds joined the move to socialise outside the home. So young people of all ethnic origins now mix in places of public entertainment. McDonalds has had a universalising impact here. Their premises, balloons, party poppers and so on are supplied free of charge for children's parties, and draw in all comers. Operators of multiplex cinemas, bowling allies and nightclubs (many of them multinationals, such as Time-Warner) benefit from this groundwork and cater to a young population brought up on 'canned' culture and dedicated to Britain's consumer society. Most Britons are unaware that the owner of the greatest number of pubs in Britain (4,867) is the Japanese company Nomura – or that the following famous British brands are now foreign-owned: Walkers Crisps and HP Sauce (American), Thomas Cook and Rolls Royce (German), Rowntree (Swiss), Hamleys Toys (Icelandic).

The older generation meanwhile, which saves 13 per cent of its disposable income (v. the national average of 4 per cent) continues to opt for home entertainment. Eighty-four per cent of British households have video or DVD recorders and are catered for by an estimated 2,000 video shops – supplying a market which didn't exist thirty years ago, and which has expanded with DVD-by-post services.

Irish pubs

Lastly in this section on leisure, a revealing debate has been taking place about the introduction of Irish pubs into the British high street. This trend, a 'simple' commercial phenomenon, is seen to have all sorts of other implications. Irish pubs are financially successful, but people ask: 'what are they saying about Britain? Do they suggest it is a soulless place which needs an infusion of Celtic culture?' CAMRA, the Campaign for Real Ale resists the trend as part of a commercialising of the English institution of the pub – a dilution of authentic English values. Others are unhappy about the ideological implications of this raising of the profile of a 'minority' culture in the war for hearts and minds in relation to an Ulster political settlement. Others again are concerned that national identity is being exploited for purely commercial ends. Some see the trend as just one more illustration of a postmodern phenomenon which uses elements of the past and elsewhere as a vocabulary with which to write the new Britain. In that respect Irishness has only a surface significance – it could as easily be an American influence like McDonalds, or a Japanese one like Karaoke – and they suggest that the trend should be welcomed as more evidence of tolerant multicultural Britain.

However, perhaps the most significant thing is that the forum in which this nationalistic venture is being played out – the high street – is a more democratic one than parliament, whose legislation cramps and controls people. (The post-war Labour administration, which produced 1,000 pages of legislation per year was seen as 'interventionist'. The present government produces 3,000 pages per year.) People want to liberate themselves through culture and feel that cultural change can't be legislated. They suspect that laissez-faire capitalism will produce stampedes of commercial developers to out-of-town shopping centres or a situation where all high streets have more or less the same shops: Halfords, Boots, Marks & Spencer. In other words, a homogenising commercial process will take place which will ultimately dilute rather than enrich culture and cultural identity. In order to counter these forces they have only the cultural practices listed above. By exercising individual choice, they can wrest control over their lives away from commercial or government agencies.

Conclusion

To sum up this chapter: the cultural ambience is not neutral, it is a plane on which warring factions contend. Education, work and leisure are defining aspects of British cultural identity. Schools place a distinctive stamp on their pupils – a past pupil will be defined both in society at large *and* by the individual him- or herself as a *grammar school* boy or girl, or more specifically as a product of Shrewsbury School or King Street primary. This pattern is repeated in the work arena when society labels people 'owned' by particular industries or by the state as: a *Ford* worker, a *civil* servant. People acknowledge these descriptions of themselves, because they also define themselves by their schools and their work functions. The rhetorical question 'How do you do?', on being introduced to people, is very shortly followed by 'What do you do?' and soon thereafter by 'Where did you go to school?'. So education and work are significant defining aspects of identity. As we have seen further, people will always try to take control of their lives and define their own identities through the exercise of individual choice in their leisure activities. And finally we have highlighted a number of debates which arise in relation to these issues.

 Exercises

1   Reading checklist:
- Why are public schools so called?
- What is the origin of the word 'education'?
- What is the difference between wages and salaries?
- Are average female earnings the same as those of males?
- What are 'hen' and 'stag' nights?
- What is the Protestant ethic?
- What is a 'glass ceiling'?
- What is a wireless?
- Where is the Kop?
- How are soccer and cricket teams differently named?
- When is the Sabbath?
- What is a Merchant Ivory representation of Britain?
- Who plays the Principal Boy in a pantomime?
- What is CAMRA?
- Which was the last country in Europe to have a National Lottery?

2   What kinds of schools are more likely to be portrayed in films? Why is this? You might consider viewing on video films such as *Kes*, *The Belles of St Trinians*, *Another Country*. How do these representations differ from the school in (say) *Dead Poets' Society* or *The History Boys*?

3   Why are portrayals of work so rare in British novels/plays? Is American writing more likely to deal with work? Are British cultural forms more or less escapist than American ones?

4   Discussion questions:

- What is the effect on individual identity of pupils attending state or private schools?
- Does education always involve the imposition on one group in society of the values of another?
- Is it healthy or unhealthy to watch soap operas?
- How is unemployment related to identity?
- Does self employment confer more dignity on workers?
- The chapter refers to the presence in Britain of McDonalds. Are overseas influences in a culture to be welcomed or resisted?
- Should the state fund culture? If so, should it aim to encourage high or popular culture? If not, why not?
- How important are tradition and traditional ways in a culture?

Reading

Giles, J. and T. Middleton. *Writing Englishness 1900–1950* Routledge, 1996. A very useful sourcebook of traditional material relating to the construction of the concept of Englishness.

Marwick, A. *A Society At Odds With Itself* Penguin, 1996. Updated historical account which plays on John Major's goal of 'a society at one with itself'.

Room, Adrian. *An A to Z of British Life* OUP, 1992. A mine of information. Comprehensive and well illustrated, a useful reference source.

Storey, John. *An Introductory Guide to Cultural Theory and Popular Culture* Harvester, 1993. A very accessible book set in a British context.

Cultural examples

Films

How to Get Ahead in Advertising (1989) dir. Bruce Robinson. Satire on the advertising and marketing professions.

Educating Rita (1983) dir. Lewis Gilbert. A working-class woman, unfulfilled by life at home with her husband, tries an Open University English course and develops a strong relationship with her tutor.

Clockwork Mice (1995) dir. Jean Vadim. Gentle drama about a young teacher starting at a Special Needs School, his relationships with pupils and staff, and his attempt to involve the children in a cross-country running club.

Another Country (1984) dir. Marek Kanievska. Speculative drama about the claustrophobic public-school life of two future British spies, Guy Burgess and Donald MacLean.

The Browning Version (1995) dir. Mike Figgis. Remake of the Terence Rattigan play about a boarding-school teacher's realisation that he and his wife have led empty, unloving lives.

Books

Muriel Spark, *The Prime of Miss Jean Brodie* (1961). Powerful story of the effects of education on susceptible young people.

David Lodge, *Changing Places* (1975). Deals with insights into human nature gained by academics from Britain and America who exchange jobs, houses, educational experiences and much more.

Linda La Plante, *The Governor* (1995–6). Drama about a woman whose working environment is a prison, where she is the governor.

Bill Bryson, *Notes from a Small Island* (1996). Idiosyncratic but informed view of Britain offered by an at-the-time resident American journalist with experience of British work and leisure.

TV programmes

Boys from the Blackstuff. Sympathetic portrayal of unemployed people who work on the side, and their encounters with officialdom. Written by Alan Bleasdale.

Porterhouse Blue. Series set in Cambridge academe with David Jason and Ian Richardson – from the novel by Tom Sharpe.

Drop the Dead Donkey. Award-winning weekly comedy series set in a newspaper office. Written by Andy Hamilton.

As Seen on TV. Comedy programme of very talented comedienne, Victoria Wood. Includes sketches, stand-up, piano songs.

The Royle Family. Written by Caroline Aherne and starring Ricky Tomlinson. A couch-potato Salford family watch TV, eat, drink and entertain. Has won numerous awards.

The Navigators. Ken Loach drama about privatised railway maintenance workers. Mocks the jargon and short cuts of the enterprise culture.

The Office. Ricky Gervais' acclaimed sitcom portrays the trials of everyday white-collar life.

 Websites

www.nc.uk.net/
Official site of the National Curriculum, with information about what attainment levels are required in each of the subject areas.

www.knowhere.co.uk
This is an informative youth and leisure-oriented site – the antidote to Tourist Information.

www.Football365.co.uk
>   Lots of facts here for the football-obsessed.

www.its-behind-you.com
>   Gives an account of the evolution of pantomime through commedia dell'arte, mystery plays and Elizabethan masques.

www.efestivals.co.uk
>   an online agency containing information and booking for many UK festivals.

www.liv.ac.uk/IPM/
>   Institute of Popular Music at Liverpool University. Has collections and sound clips.

www.leagueofgentlemen.co.uk
>   Website devoted to the cult television programme. Has a scrapbook and downloads from the first and second series.

www.youtube.co.uk
>   Snapshot of people's private lives – demolishing sheds, playing guitars, etc.

Chapter 3

Gender, sex and the family

Roberta Garrett

Timeline

1831 —— Infant Custody Act

1848 —— Factory Act

1861 —— Abolition of death penalty for sodomy

1882 —— Married Women's Property Act

1928 —— Vote for women over 21

1967 —— Abortion made legal

1969 —— Divorce Reform Act (divorce by mutual consent)

1975 —— Sex Discrimination Act

1987 —— Clause 28

1993 —— Child Support Agency

2000 —— Age of gay consent lowered to 16

2003 —— Employment Equality (Sexual Orientation) Regulations

2004 —— Civil Partnership Act

Introduction

SINCE THE INDUSTRIAL REVOLUTION, rapidly changing employment patterns coupled with demographic and social movements have challenged the beliefs, laws and customs governing notions of family and gender. As the timeline indicates, there has been a long series of legal reforms affecting sexual behaviour, kinship structures and the social status of women.

On the one hand, these reforms were the result of progressive, humanitarian social movements such as feminism, which, in less than 200 years, have secured rights of guardianship, property ownership, political representation and reproductive control for British women. On the other hand, protective legislation – such as the 1848 Factory Act limiting women and children to a ten-hour working day – countered the exploitation of women workers in the newly developing manufacturing industries primarily in order to ensure their allegiance to motherhood and wifely duties. In this sense, nineteenth-century parliamentary reforms went hand-in-hand with a gradual acceptance of the state's right to directly intervene in and regulate the domestic sphere. During the 1960s and 1970s 'permissive' legislation such as the legalisation of abortion, the introduction of the no-fault divorce and the decriminalisation of homosexuality have reversed this trend, reflecting the higher priority awarded to personal choice and freedom as opposed to public morality and duty.

In the twenty-first century, there will undoubtedly be further contentious reforms in legislation concerning sexual discrimination, abortion, divorce and sexual practice. All of these affect, and are in turn affected by, social attitudes and cultural activities. Their strongest impact, however, will be perceived in terms of the British family unit and so, when looking at trends in attitudes towards gender and sex, it is here that we must begin.

The family unit

At present, there are factors pulling in opposite directions in terms of the size of the British population. While the average lifespan has increased in

FIGURE 3.1 Changing attitudes to motherhood are evident in Damien Hirst's 'Virgin Mother', a 35 feet tall, 13½ ton bronze statue revealing the insides of a pregnant woman

the UK, British fertility rates have until recently been steadily declining since the population boom of the immediate post-war years. Birth rates per woman were at 1.79 in 1995, the highest since 1992 but significantly below the baby boom rates in the 1960s, which peaked at 2.95 in 1964. A higher number of couples do not have children, however, and those that do generally have smaller families than their parents. This is largely attributed to both improvements in female education and career prospects and greater social acceptance of contraception. The majority of women work outside of the home both before and after having children, regardless of marital status – contributing to one argument that Britain's long hours and overtime culture has led to a work-life imbalance that is 'destroying the family' – and childbearing is frequently postponed until the late 20s or early 30s (the average age of mothers at childbirth is now nearly 29). Consequently, the often-quoted 'average' British family with 2.4 children has now dwindled to nearer 1.7: a trend which reflects the overall decline in the proportion of 'conventional' family units (2.4 people is actually now the average house-hold size, compared with 2.9 in 1971). Only about a quarter of contem-porary British households fall into the 'two adults plus dependent children' nuclear model, and this figure includes not only married couples, but the increasing number of long-term cohabitees (who may decide not to marry for personal and ideological reasons, but also for financial ones as the average 'white' wedding costs nearly £20,000). Cohabiting is on the increase but the law still needs to catch up; at present, cohabitees with dependants cannot seek maintenance for themselves if they part, only for children from their partner. This is almost certainly an unsustainable situation as Eng-land and Wales have between them around four million people cohabiting in 2007, an increase of 67 per cent in ten years, and 40 per cent have children.

Household sizes vary between ethnic groups: Muslim, Hindu and Sikh households being highest at around an average of 3.5, while Christian, Jewish and Buddhist were lowest at 2.3 with the highest proportion, 30 per cent, being single occupancy households. Perhaps one of the most signifi-cant shifts over the last few decades has been in attitudes towards marriage, which, though still popular (around 75 per cent of people marry at least once) is less so in the last twenty years than at any previous time in British history: according to the Office for National Statistics there were 308,600 marriages in the UK in 2003 and 270,700 in 2004, a slight upturn on 2001 (249,221), the nadir of a downward trend since the peak of 480,300 in 1972. The decline in registered marriages has also been mirrored by high levels of marital breakdown over the last thirty years, such that if current trends continue some 60 per cent of men between 25 and 40 will be single or divorced bachelors in 2010. Four in every ten British marriages currently ends in divorce, making UK rates the highest in Europe, and by 2025 divorces could even outnumber marriages. As a result of these changes, the number of single-parent families (90 per cent of which are headed by women) has risen dramatically, comprising one in five of all family units and generating the latest in a long line of perceived threats to the fabric of British family life. It is also feared by some that this number will increase as childbirth out of wedlock rises: in 2004, 42 per cent of births took place outside of marriage (the figure for Europe as a whole was 33 per cent), and a Conservative Party report two years later found that cohabiting parents were statistically six times more likely than married ones to part before their child reached the age of 5 (one in two separating, compared with one in twelve married couples). It is also true that women are more likely to seek divorce than their husbands: of divorces filed in England and Wales in 2003, 69 per cent of them were at the wife's behest. Other figures also suggest the traditional family image promoted in the post-war era is no longer a norm as values and patterns of behaviour change: as examples, in 2007 a quarter of women now marry men younger than themselves (whereas accepted thinking is that a man should marry a woman half his age plus seven years), while 38 per cent of women and a quarter of all men under aged 20 to 24 live with their parents and males between 25 and 64 are twice as likely to live on their own as they were in the 1980s.

If the statistics indicate a rapid decline in allegiance to the traditional family unit, and the latest reports say that by 2012 half of all babies will be born to unmarried mothers, these figures need to be balanced against other interrelated changes in life experience and cultural norms. For example, while the liberalisation of the divorce laws and the (albeit limited) possibility of female economic independence has undoubtedly done much to make divorce a realistic option for greater numbers of discontented married people, the extended life expectancy of both partners is also an important contributory factor. A couple who marry in their 20s are now committing themselves to stay together for the next fifty or so years, whereas a century ago, when people rarely lived beyond their mid-40s, a lifelong marriage would have covered only thirty years. When these differences are taken into account, it appears that the length of the average marriage has stayed fairly constant over the last century, settling at around fifteen to twenty years before either death or divorce. However, the number of children affected by divorce is at an all-time high and more than half of couples divorcing have at least one child under 16: 153,500 children under 16 years in England and Wales went through their parents' divorce in 2003, when there were 166,700 divorces.

Ethnicity is also an important factor in accounting for different British family structures. For example, many Vietnamese and Bengali families still retain an extended family structure, while a higher than average proportion of Afro-Caribbean families are mother-led. In addition to this, the relatively low proportion of 'traditional' British families does not reflect the symbolic or ideological importance of the conventional family unit, which remains strong despite its minority status. The two-parent, patriarchal family continues to be regarded by many as the most important of all social institutions, bearing the brunt of responsibility for producing well-adjusted, law-abiding citizens. And although the Conservatives have tried to assume the role of 'the party of family values', the family tends to occupy an elevated position within the rhetoric of all major political parties. Public discussion of the family is generally concerned with the best means of defending it and ensuring its continuation, as opposed to whether other forms of socialisation – such as communal child-rearing – might prove to be a healthier or more practical model for most people. In short, the overall desirability or legitimacy of the institution itself is rarely questioned, at least within mainstream political debate.

But as with any social institution, notions of what constitutes a healthy, normal family unit vary according to contemporary cultural practices and social concerns. In the 1970s, the 'teenage bride' became the subject of much moral concern, whereas such debates since the 1990s have instead focused on the growing numbers of teenage pregnancies and single mothers. It would seem that, whether young women are for or against marriage, their marital status constitutes an ongoing cause of anxiety (the insistence on and resistance to the use of Ms instead of Mrs and Miss illustrates this). In this sense, shifting conceptions of gender identity and, in particular, women's greater participation in public as opposed to domestic life, has been a key factor in generating fears about the collapse of the family throughout the last two centuries. In a similar manner, notions of the family are closely linked with debates over national identity and cultural cohesion; at all points of the political spectrum, commitment to 'the family' is frequently invoked as a source of national unity.

In attempting to understand the symbolic importance of the contemporary nuclear model, it is useful to examine its historical development. This is usually traced to the late Victorian period, when, as religious influence declined, the family took up the mantle of moral guardianship. It was expected to provide both moral guidance and social stability, or as early twentieth-century social anthropologists put it, to function as a 'Nursery of Citizenship'. Despite being more of a cosmopolitan dynasty than a cosy nuclear group, the British Royal Family swiftly came to symbolise the ideal British family unit. Even today, the Queen is sometimes referred to as 'the mother of the commonwealth', just as England, the imperial centre, was once viewed as 'the mother country'. The ideological importance of the Royal Family goes some way towards explaining why the acrimonious partings and occasional scandals blighting the present House of Windsor are a cause of such consternation within the UK, especially in relation to the ostracisation of Princess Diana, the life of her orphaned children, and Prince Charles' marriage to Camilla Parker-Bowles. The younger generation, led by Diana's children, Prince William and Prince Harry, may usher in a new era of royal relations with the public, and a lot will depend on their family life as they grow older. William was widely tipped to marry his long-standing girlfriend, Kate Middleton, however, the prospect of their scrutiny under the media spotlight appears to have dashed that relationship.

Given this weight of expectations, it is not surprising that the family, as an institution, seems always to be in crisis. Nevertheless, while fears of its erosion are often exaggerated and vary according to cultural context, there is no doubt that the last twenty years have witnessed a particularly turbulent period of change in family structure and gender roles. To consider these transformations in more detail, this chapter will next examine the changing status of British women and then move on to look more broadly at attitudes towards marriage, parenting and sexuality.

Gender and British institutions

Despite the strength and longevity of the British women's movement, many traditional British institutions remain remarkably male-dominated, although this is slowly beginning to change. We can start to examine both institutionalised sexism and the attempts to challenge it, by looking at predominantly male institutions such as the political and legal systems and the Church of England. The culture of Westminster is often likened to that of a boy's public school. Not only are there very few female Members of Parliament (less than one in ten) but the House of Commons thrives on an atmosphere of masculine combat. Heckling, jeering and the routine exchange of insults are so much part of the daily proceedings that the then Prime Minister Tony Blair, who sought actively to promote women within the Cabinet, repeatedly discussed the possibility of a ban on name-calling and a new emphasis on 'mature' debate (at the time of writing, only a very few insulting words, such as 'liar', are not allowed, and so not heard, in the House).

But, for aspiring female members, the macho culture of Westminster is a minor problem compared to that of getting elected, or even selected to stand, in the first place. Not surprisingly, local constituency executives nominate the candidate with the best chance of getting elected, which, given the age-old prejudices of both sexes, is less likely to be a woman. Of course, there are always notable exceptions. Margaret Thatcher's eleven-year reign proved that a female leader could be quite as confrontational and bloody-minded as any man. During her years in office, Thatcher was frequently described as both 'the best man for the job' and 'the iron lady', perhaps indicating the degree of unease and confusion produced by the presence of a female leader in a traditional male enclave (the 'TV classic' satirical puppet show *Spitting Image* emphasised this by always showing her using a men's toilet). As it made her the first female British prime minister, Thatcher's election was of symbolic importance, although it may be noted that the overall number of female MPs fell during her term in office and that she herself was outspoken in her opposition to women's rights.

Of the major political parties, Labour has the strongest commitment to and historical identification with inclusivity. Since 1997, when a raft of new female MPs entered parliament (Blair's Babes), Labour have aimed to counter discrimination by promoting a high number of women to power-positions within the party (such as the shadow cabinet). Additionally, they have devised all-women electoral shortlists for some constituencies. These policies have aroused much controversy, for while many think it necessary to take positive action to achieve equal political representation, others have argued that the policies undermine the achievements of the women they favour. Furthermore, New Labour's pro-feminist sympathies have never guaranteed the largest share of the female vote. In fact, the Conservative Party's endorsement of strong law-and-order policies, combined with a commitment to traditional family values appeals to a higher proportion of (particularly older) female voters.

The British legal system is one of the country's oldest, most traditionalist institutions. As such, it is often accused of gender bias in terms of proceedings, sentences and professional opportunities. Although women are now entering the legal profession in ever increasing numbers (half of all British law students are female), they are less likely to reach the top of their profession, more often becoming solicitors than higher ranked and (generally) better paid barristers. There are few female QCs (senior barristers, called Queen's Counsels) and even fewer female judges. It is therefore less surprising that the judiciary has come in for particularly harsh condemnation regarding its attitudes towards sexual assaults and other forms of violence against women. British judges have been accused of letting rapists off lightly and apportioning an inexcusable degree of blame to female victims. Indeed, one of the main reasons that so few sexual assaults are reported in the UK is that women feel anxious that they, and not their attacker, will be made morally, if not legally, culpable for the crime. This fear is exacerbated by well-publicised comments made by prominent members of the judiciary concerning the clothing-style and sexual history of victims.

Another contentious issue has been that of domestic violence. Again, the judiciary have been condemned for showing leniency towards men who perpetrate it, but have little sympathy with women who retaliate. In response, women's groups have mounted lengthy campaigns for the release of women convicted of killing violent, abusive husbands arguing that even in cases in which the death was premeditated, years of persistent abuse amounted to provocation, and thus could not be regarded as cold-blooded murder.

On 11 November 1992 the General Synod of the Church of England voted in favour of the ordination of women priests. This decision was the result of over a century of struggle on the part of women's rights campaigners, and ended a lengthy and divisive battle within the church. The initial demand for female ordination began in the late nineteenth century as part of the first wave of the British feminist movement. As a result of this pressure, the Church of England created the somewhat ambiguous order of 'deaconess' which entitled women to preside over certain rituals, but was not regarded as part of the holy triumvirate of bishops, priests and deacons. The Church of England did not permit women deacons until as late as 1987, by which time Anglican churchwomen in Canada and the US had been taking the priesthood for around ten years. In this respect, the Church of England was somewhat out of kilter with other branches of the Anglican Church and indeed, the British public at large, 80 per cent of whom had been in favour of the ordination of women for some time. The fiercest clerical opposition to female ordination came, not surprisingly, from the Church's influential Anglo-Catholic wing, many of whom either renounced the priesthood altogether or converted to Catholicism when the decision was announced. Since the vote was taken many hundreds of women have been ordained in Britain. English and Church Census figures show that half of priests ordained in recent years have been women: there were 1,262 serving women priests in 2002.

Women and employment

Probably the most important factor in the transformation of British gender identities has been the long-term and seemingly irreversible trend towards female participation in the paid labour force.

Women continued to enter the labour force in ever increasing numbers throughout the twentieth century, but many fears have been voiced about changing gender roles and a perceived deterioration of family life. Women's paid employment may be an accepted fact of modern life, but it is still regarded by many as an undesirable one. In the first half of the twentieth century, government policy reflected the widely held view that the female population constituted a reserve labour force, only to be drawn on in times of dire necessity. During the First World War, the vast numbers of women who were encouraged to enter the labour force had to fight bitterly to achieve the same wage as their male counterparts, a privilege which was granted to women workers during the Second World War, in which, for the first time, state-run nurseries were also provided. But, like the previous generation of women war workers, they were expected to relinquish both their jobs and their state childcare facilities, during peacetime. The immediate post-war period saw a forceful reassertion of traditional roles; women were enticed back into the home as sociologists and psychologists warned of the dangers of maternal deprivation caused by the working mother's absence. Fears concerning the welfare of so-called 'latchkey kids' (those who had no mother to greet them from school) reinforced the notion that children could not be properly cared for without a home-based mother,

FIGURE 3.2 (a) The role women played in the war was not acknowledged until the unveiling of this memorial near the Cenotaph in 2005

FIGURE 3.2 (b) The annual Poppy Appeal (helps support war survivors who fought for Britain)

heightening public hostility towards such women. But in spite of these attitudes, women's participation in paid employment rose dramatically in the late 1950s and has continued to increase in every decade since. Shifts in patterns of employment, particularly the expansion of secretarial, administrative and clerical occupations in the 1960s and 1970s, and the rapid growth of the service sector in the 1980s, opened up new areas of female employment. Between 1971 and 2005 the labour market grew from 25.5 million to 30 million, but this growth contained only 0.2 million men compared with 4.3 million women. On the other hand, within the 25 per cent of labour force employees who were on part-time contracts there were five women for every two men.

Coupled with the demise of heavy industry, and a subsequent drop in the male-dominated areas of unskilled manual work, for the first time ever, the balance has tipped towards an almost evenly divided male and female British labour force. Moreover, there is a marked difference in the composition of the female labour force: in the first half of the century the majority of working women were either young and single or middle-aged with grown children, whereas the greatest increase in the 1970s and 1980s has been amongst those with partners and dependants. But these statistics can be misleading: British women are still far from achieving equality in the workplace. Despite the legacy of hard-won women's rights legislation, such as the Equal Pay (1970) and Sex Discrimination Acts (1975), women are still earning less than men, and according to Eurostat the pay gap stood well above the European average at 22 per cent in 2006. In practice, equal-pay legislation is difficult to enforce and discrimination hard to prove. Women are still much more likely to be discriminated against on grounds of age or physical attractiveness, although clearly, employers are no longer able to openly specify gender in a job description. The affix 'man' – as in postman, salesman, fireman – has either been replaced by 'person' (salesperson) or dropped completely (firefighter).

It is also the case that a small number of women are now working in previously male-dominated areas, but sex segregation persists. Female employees tend to be heavily concentrated in non-unionised, unskilled areas of work, with an overwhelming majority (81 per cent) working in service industries (e.g. as cleaners, waitresses, bar and hotel staff). The catering industry, for example, relies largely on part-time and casual labour; precisely the kind of low-paid, low-status, 'pink collar' occupations, which women with small children and limited childcare assistance are often forced into accepting. But even predominantly female-skilled occupations – such as secretarial or administrative work – tend to command less pay and status by virtue of their 'feminine' associations. Probably the most serious example is that of British nurses, who earn considerably less than those in most other parts of Western Europe, chiefly because nursing is still viewed in this country more as an extension of woman's natural 'caring' role than as a skilled profession. In addition, there is little evidence to suggest that women's increased participation in the labour force has been accompanied by a corresponding shift in domestic responsibilities. Working women continue to do the majority of housework, child-rearing, and caring for elderly relatives. Surprisingly, this rule applies even in situations where women are the primary earners. Studies of areas of high male unemployment, such as Wearside in the post-industrial North East, show a rise in stay-at-home husbands and working wives. But they also indicate that while husbands are prepared to perform 'light' domestic duties (such as shopping and cooking) they still draw the line at cleaning and other 'menial' domestic tasks (in May 1999, a survey by the Office for National Statistics reported that on average men spend 45 minutes a day on cooking and routine housework, compared to women's 138 minutes). In short, traditional gender identities persist and role reversal was regarded as temporary and pragmatic.

As we might expect, female employment opportunities are also heavily influenced by other factors, such as region, class and race. For example, although a higher than average number of Afro-Caribbean women go on to further education, levels of unemployment within this ethnic grouping are significantly greater than amongst their white female counterparts.

Predictably, the greatest career gains have been made by white, middle-class, university educated women, who are now beginning to make significant inroads into previously male-dominated professions such as law and medicine. But even they fare badly in private industry, and despite the much-touted success of a handful of British female entrepreneurs comparatively few British businesses are currently owned by women.

All in all, employment opportunities for British women certainly exceed those of previous generations, but they are still far from equal with those of British men. Nevertheless, if the reality of women's employment opportunity is not as rosy as it is often assumed to be, this does not diminish its impact in terms of cultural representation and notions of female identity. British advertising and television are now beginning to represent women in a much wider spectrum of roles than just girlfriend, wife or mother. In recent years there has been an abundance of television programmes featuring women in traditionally male or 'high-powered' professional jobs. These can be seen as presenting new role models or as adding a new twist to well-worn fictional formulas such as the police procedural or hospital drama series.

Perhaps as a result of these images, young women now have far greater expectations than ever before. A recent study of British teenage girls revealed that many now confidently expect to have both a successful career and a family, although given present working conditions, they are unlikely to achieve both these aims.

Marriage and divorce

Prior to the implementation of the 1969 Divorce Reform Act, a legal separation required a guilty party. Adultery was by far the most frequently cited reason and the 'wronged' wife or husband had to provide evidence that an affair had taken place. Not surprisingly, this emphasis on moral culpability heightened any existing bitterness between parties, as lurid details were dragged out in court. In fact, when divorce became available through mutual agreement (albeit after a five-, and later, two-year separation) the majority of British private detective agencies went out of business as a result. From that point onwards divorce rates have soared, causing many to argue for stricter divorce laws.

This view was widely endorsed by the Conservative government in the early 1990s, who launched a 'moral crusade' popularly known as the 'back to basics' campaign. This initiative implored the public to stand firm in their commitment to marriage and family life, but was discredited by the disclosure of a string of sex scandals involving prominent MPs. From then on the phrase 'back to basics' became almost synonymous with sexual hypocrisy and corruption.

Those who uphold the sanctity of marriage view Britain's one-in-three divorce rate as an indictment of its commitment-shy national culture: divorced people are sometimes castigated as selfish and fickle, putting their needs above those of their children. On the other hand, while few regard it positively, many argue that it indicates a more realistic, tolerant attitude towards the breakdown of relationships and breakup of couples. From whichever viewpoint, it is clear that while a high percentage of the population continue to marry – and of Britain's seventeen million families seven out of ten were still headed by a married couple in 2005 – people's expectations of what this entails are vastly different from those of their parents.

Until the late nineteenth century, British women, unlike those in Islamic or Hindu societies, were required to relinquish all property rights upon marriage. Divorce was virtually unheard of amongst anyone except the upper classes. Nevertheless, it was still more easily accessible to men, who had only to establish that adultery had taken place. A wife needed proof of adultery plus desertion, bigamy, incest or cruelty to divorce her husband. It was not until 1923 that women and men could bring a divorce suit on the same grounds, and women were denied a share of their ex-husband's income until as late as the mid 1960s. Given that many had no independent means of support, divorce was clearly not an attractive or realistic prospect for large numbers of women. Even today, a woman's credit rating usually drops following a divorce while the reverse is true for her ex-husband. But in spite of this disparity by far the majority of divorces are instigated by women, who are also much less likely to marry again. In part, the higher divorce rate is therefore an inevitable consequence of women's increased financial autonomy, but it also corresponds to more general shifts in the structure of the family and the relative importance attached to the heterosexual couple.

At least until the mid-twentieth century, the dominant form of family structure was extended rather than nuclear, with parents and even grandparents, uncles and aunts living in close proximity to their grown-up children. It was also considered normal for women and men to inhabit quite different worlds in terms of both work and social activities. Due to the increased geographical and social mobility of the population, this often romanticised family unit has gradually declined in numbers and is now found for most people mainly in soap operas based in traditional working-class communities: Albert Square in 'cockney' soap *EastEnders* is a good example.

One consequence of the decline of the extended family has been the emergence of stronger adult friendship networks based on neighbourhood, educational establishment, leisure pursuit or some other shared interest. Another has been the emergence of a more 'companionable' idea of marriage based on equality, and finding a partner who may also be a best friend and soulmate. Within the contemporary companionate model,

FIGURE 3.3 Communities and families support each other, but as more people eat out, some people fear the 'family meal' is less common

mutual respect, emotional fulfilment and shared 'quality-time' have, at least in theory, replaced the old model which assumed separate spheres and female dependence.

But if higher expectations and better alternatives have done much to increase the divorce rate, the financial incentives to marry are also not what they used to be. Over the last fifteen years, tax relief for married couples has been gradually reduced. Meanwhile, unemployed married people are disqualified from certain state benefits if their partners are in work. This also applies to cohabitees, but clearly it is rather more difficult for the state to establish their domestic arrangements. As approximately one child in three is now born out of wedlock, several proposals have been put forward to further extend the legal rights of long-term cohabitees, though plans for one-year no-fault divorces met with stiff opposition.

Parenting

Compared with other European countries, Britain could hardly be regarded as a child-orientated society. There has undoubtedly been a rejection of the often harsh child-rearing methods favoured in the UK a century ago, but children are still not generally welcomed or adequately catered for in public places such as pubs and restaurants. More serious perhaps is the fact that British nursery provision is the poorest in Europe, with only half of pre-school-age children able to obtain a place. Yet, at the same time, the family is revered and the popular media is dominated by debates about the falling standard of British parenting. We can begin to consider this paradox by

FIGURE 3.4   Ice skating at Christmas is a communal and family activity

focusing on two particularly contentious issues: firstly, the increase in single-parent households and secondly, children's exposure to violence both within the family and as depicted in forms of popular entertainment.

For many years, arguments have been put forward to maintain that Britain's high proportion of single-parent families is due to an over-generous state-benefit system encouraging young, single mothers to 'marry the state' and embark on a 'benefit career', while some politicians have suggested that in some cases teenage girls were becoming pregnant chiefly in order to secure scarce local-authority housing. At the heart of this issue was not only the assumption that many young women preferred not to work, but the fear that rather than becoming single mothers through male abandonment – and thus becoming worthy recipients of state support – young women were actually choosing to live without men, in communities of single mothers. In response to these suggestions, groups such as the Association of Single Parents swiftly pointed out that although many single parents relied on state subsidies, this resulted from difficulties in finding a decent enough job to cover childcare expenses, rather than a disinclination to work. In addition to this, it was revealed that two-thirds of lone parents had become so through divorce or separation rather than choice, and that far from enjoying a high standard of living at the taxpayers expense, as many as 75 per cent were surviving below the official poverty line. Due to these and other criticisms, plans to cut benefit for single parents were shelved. But for fifteen years, up to 2007, an even more explosive parenting debate raged over the establishment of the Child Support Agency (part of the Department for Work and Pensions).

This government-funded body was set up to fix maintenance payments and pursue absent fathers after the discovery that fewer than one in three were supporting their children. The agency soon came under fire for fixing payment rates at an unrealistically high level, often destroying amicable agreements in the process. Critics also argued that the agency was more concerned with raising the payments of those who were already contributing rather than finding those who were not. The furore intensified after the occurrence of two well-publicised suicide cases, in which financial stress caused by the agency's demands was thought to be a contributory factor. Eventually, a House of Commons Select Committee was formed to review the workings of the agency. Stricter guidelines were introduced to ensure that fathers were left with sufficient funds to live on and, as was often the case, support second families.

While the single parent and the Child Support Agency controversies highlighted the financial responsibilities attached to being a parent, there has also been a growing awareness of the widespread extent of child abuse and the long-term psychological effects on its victims. This has led to much debate concerning the difference between legitimate expressions of parental authority and malicious ill-treatment. For example, many thought that a poster campaign run by the Royal Society for the Prevention of Children, went too far in emphasising the damaging effects of verbal as physical abuse. Questions have also been raised as to how far the state entitled to intervene in family life, leaving the social services to tread a dangerous path between accusations of unnecessary and disruptive interference and negligence.

The most serious debates about British parenting arose in 1993, after 2-year-old James Bulger was abducted from a shopping centre in Bootle, Merseyside and murdered by two 11-year-old boys. Not surprisingly, the horrifying case caused a national outcry and much attention was given to seeking an explanation for the boys' behaviour. While a good deal of blame was apportioned to the two boys' parents, questions were also raised as to what extent the murder reflected a rising tide of British violence and how far this could be traced to the corrosive influence of violent, American 'video nasty' imports. It was suggested that the children's behaviour had been influenced by a horror film – *Child's Play* – which the pair were alleged to have watched shortly before the murder. In this respect, the Bulger case rekindled a much older debate about popular entertainment and British crime rates, centring on the wide availability of violent American videos and their moral 'contamination' of the nation's youth. As there has never been any substantial evidence to suggest that behaviour is dictated or even strongly influenced by viewing habits (despite numerous studies) other commentators looked closer to home for causes. A study authorised in the wake of the Bulger case by the Commission on Children and Violence found that the key determinants linking young, violent offenders were parental abuse and poverty rather than excessive exposure to television or cinema violence. The case has remained high profile and the release from prison of the two boys in 2001 was met with howls of protest from, among others, the family and friends of James Bulger. The vehemence of the reaction from sections of the community has meant that the boys will have to be given new identities and police protection once they return into society. The painful national reactions to the case were revived in 2002 when two girls were murdered in a quiet Cambridgeshire village, Soham, a town whose name for many years will simply be associated with the brutal killings by a man who had been previously accused of rape and sex with underage girls, but who had nonetheless been appointed as a caretaker at the girls' school. Concerns over the appointment of adults to positions of authority and influence over children have since remained very high on the national agenda alongside the issue of paedophilia. The Labour government was repeatedly under pressure to increase its published list of 'sex offenders' as many parents demanded the right to know if paedophiles were living in their area. The issue was brought to a head in 2001, when many ex-offenders were attacked in their homes and the assaults spread to the extent that a paediatrician was attacked by a

...tood the meaning of the word. Subsequently,
...e satirical Channel 4 mock news-programme
...debate over media representations of paedo-
...he show as an attack on glib 'investigative'
...onalised issues such as paedophilia and titillated
...i reactionary quarters, especially the *Daily Mail*,
...ramme's maker, Chris Morris, be prosecuted.
...ocused on what is currently the most controversial
...British morality, it met with almost hysterical
...ss, charities, politicians, and also sections of the
...ne Office Minister, Beverley Hughes, was compelled
...mme on national radio, even though she had to admit
she in... 2005, Hughes went on to take over from Margaret
Hodge in a new ... created by the prime minister to assuage some of the
growing fears over the young: 'Minister for Children'. Despite this,
government support for new families is not great: £250 is invested at birth
(£500 for low-income families) for collection when the child is 18, and
weekly child benefit is £17.45 for the first child (£11.70 for subsequent
children). This does not compare favourably with schemes elsewhere in
Europe and is one of the reasons why the Labour government under Tony
Blair has been thought to pay little more than lip service to the British
family.

Sexuality and identity

The British are famed for both their prurience and prudery, creating a stereotype of sexual reserve which, though exploited within many British cultural
forms (Merchant Ivory 'heritage' cinema, for example) probably derives
less from contemporary cultural attitudes than from England's former role
in the global imposition of repressive middle-class norms and values. It is
certainly true that British censorship laws are still stricter than many other
European states, and that it is one of the few countries in which a government minister will be forced to resign over a minor sex scandal. But in other
respects attitudes are fairly liberal. The shift towards so-called 'permissiveness' is associated with 'swinging London', the explosion of British youth
culture and the legalisation of homosexuality, abortion, birth control
and divorce reform in the 1960s. The Obscene Publications trial of 1960,
in which it was finally decided that D.H. Lawrence's sexually explicit
but critically acclaimed novel, *Lady Chatterley's Lover*, would be made
available to the British public, is generally regarded as something of a
watershed, dividing prudish 'Victorian' Britain from permissive, contemporary Britain.

However, while the majority of permissive legislative reforms date from the 1960s (when registered marriages actually increased) the social effect of this legislation was not really felt until the 1970s and even 1980s, by which time, permissiveness had begun to acquire a pejorative meaning, denoting the collapse of moral authority and the traditional family unit. Aside from concerns about single mothers, absentee fathers and rising divorce rates, the backlash against permissiveness was given a new impetus by the Aids crisis, with much attention focused on the British gay community.

Britain's first official Aids-related death, that of Terrence Higgins, occurred in 1982 and led to the establishment of what remains Britain's biggest Aids/HIV education and advice service, the Terrence Higgins Trust. The British Government, however, was much slower to respond to the crisis. This reluctance was not only due to its disinclination to mount costly HIV-prevention campaigns, but also related to the problems of censorship which preventative education created. Addressing the problem of HIV transmission necessitated the acknowledgement of a range of sexual practices and an extent of extra and premarital sexual activities which a 'family orientated' administration did not want to be seen to endorse. Only when the hetero-sexual risk factor became very apparent did the Department of Health launch a full scale, £5 million television, cinema, poster and house-to-house leafleting campaign in 1987. Although the Health Department's ubiquitous slogan was 'Aids: don't die of ignorance', preventative education tended to be both oblique and alarmist, stressing promiscuity as a central factor despite over-whelming medical evidence that viral transmission was related to particular sexual practices rather than sheer number of partners. Sexually transmitted diseases are slightly on the increase and Britain has the highest rate of teenage pregnancies in Europe, but most British people remain monogamous according to a 2006 national study published in the medical journal *The Lancet*.

The early years of the Aids crisis produced a wave of anti-gay hysteria, exacerbated by the popular press, who were quick to wrongly identify Aids as an exclusively homosexual 'plague'. Many British newspapers actually went so far as to support such draconian measures as the recriminalisation of sodomy or the forced quarantine of those suffering from the disease. British rates of infection have not reached these initial predictions and in the first years of the twenty-first century Aids has been backgrounded, not least because sex has become the essential ingredient of any marketing campaign. Surveys continue to indicate that while 'safe' sexual practices have been widely adopted within the gay community since the mid 1980s, the majority of heterosexuals do not regard themselves as significantly at risk, despite the fact that new cases of HIV reached a high of 3,500 in 2000. Furthermore, the climate of homophobia created by the initial burst of Aids scare-stories did much to undermine growing acceptance of the gay community. In Britain, it has never been illegal to actually be a homosexual, only to participate in homosexual acts, while lesbianism has not been recognised by the law, supposedly because Queen Victoria refused to acknowledge its existence.

Following the 1967 Sexual Offences Act, which decriminalised homosexual activities in England (extended to Scotland in 1980 and Northern Ireland in 1979), a lively gay and lesbian subculture flourished in urban areas of England in the late 1970s and 1980s. Soho, for example, famous for its gay-owned shops, pubs, clubs and cafes, has become one of London's biggest nightlife attractions. Moreover, the widespread media adoption of the word 'gay' a term denoting positive self-identification, as opposed to 'homosexual' or more pejorative terms, suggested a growing acknowledgement of gay identity as an alternative lifestyle choice, rather than just a sexual preference. The growing acceptance of gay lifestyles has been apparent on television, from the first 'lesbian-kiss' broadcast in *Brookside*, through the huge popularity of the drama serial *Queer as Folk*, to the winning of the second series of *Big Brother* by a gay man in 2001. More importantly, in September 2001 the first ceremonies for gay couples were begun in London, which started a civil register of gay partnerships. Though the 'pacts' had no legal status they were made formally at a ceremony conducted by an approved Greater London authority officer. Gay rights groups hoped that eventually the ceremonies, after wider recognition, would lead to legislation that conferred on homosexual couples the same legal rights as married people, and this was largely achieved by the Civil Partnerships Act of 2004 which came into effect in 2005 and saw almost 20,000 couples entering partnerships in the first year (high-profile individuals included Sir Elton John and the actor Sir Anthony Sher). Though there are as yet no questions in the Census covering sexual orientation the figure for the lesbian, gay and bisexual population is estimated to be placed at around 6 per cent of the population.

There remains at least one major area of concern, however: an addition to the Local Government Bill of 1987 inserting the notorious Clause (a.k.a. Section) 28. This amendment stipulated that local governments could not 'Promote homosexuality or publish material for the promotion of homosexuality' or 'promote the teaching in any maintained school of the acceptability of homosexuality as a pretended family relationship by the publication of such material or otherwise.'

The Act was eventually passed, but rather than silencing the gay community, it had the effect of mobilising and reaffirming British gay identity. The annual Gay Pride march – always the biggest, though generally one of the least publicised, demonstrations in the capital – recorded a much higher than usual attendance in the year following the introduction of the clause, and the organisers of what is now called the Gay Pride Mardi Gras in Finsbury Park, which concludes the march from Hyde Park, now aim to make London the gay capital of the world, in which they are supported by the tourist industry, less concerned with gay rights than with attracting the 'pink' pound. Ranging from 'professional' pressure groups such as Stonewall to more militant organisations such as Act Up (Aids Coalition to Unleash Power) and Outrage (who sometimes adopt the term 'queer' to distinguish themselves from more moderate, assimilationist gay groups) there has been a resurgence of British gay activism since the late 1980s. Two specific issues, that of the age of gay consent, and that of the forced exposure or 'outing' of homosexuals and lesbians, have commanded particularly high levels of public interest and will be examined in turn.

Initiatives to bring the gay age of consent (which was 21) in line with that applied to heterosexuals (16), was part of a broader gay equality package drafted by the Stonewall group, and inspired by the European Union's social charter commitment to ending all forms of discrimination. An uneasy compromise was reached in February 1993 when the homosexual age of consent was changed to 18 but it was finally lowered to 16 in November 2000. At the other end of the spectrum, groups such as the Faggots Rooting Out Closet Sexuality Group (F.R.O.C.S.) adopted the more controversial tactic of outing allegedly gay public figures – specifically those perceived to have lent their support to discriminatory practices. Outing is often associated with the exposure of pop stars and media celebrities, but in Britain (if not in the US), gay outing groups tend to target more establishment figures, such as eminent clergymen or Members of Parliament. This has to be distinguished from the routine exposure of gay media celebrities more commonly practised by the tabloid press, who are also, ironically, almost unanimous in their opposition to 'political' outing.

British attitudes towards homosexuality and lesbianism have to be considered in relation to the overall political climate. The Aids crisis increased prejudice, but current attitudes appear to be much more tolerant than before. Amongst younger age groups in particular, the distinctions between gay and straight culture are more blurred than ever. Gay male dress codes have been widely adopted by heterosexual men and gay clubs are now more mixed in terms of both gender and sexual orientation.

If gender roles are learnt first and foremost within the family, they are reinforced or challenged in our choice of social activities and leisure pursuits. Indeed, if the family is less central to most people's lives today, these may provide a greater source of identification. One of the clearest indications of the collapse of polarised gender identities is the slow decline of exclusively male or female British institutions such as the Women's Institute or the Working Men's Club. Although it is often dismissed as a backward-looking, traditionalist organisation, the Women's Institute (WI), was formed in 1915 with the intention of informing and broadening the horizons of housewives, many of whom, at that time, received little or no conventional education.

In fact, many of the institute's early philanthropic patrons, such as the first chairperson, Lady Denman, were inspired by the first-wave feminist movement. But as women's educational and career opportunities have increased, the Institute has come to be associated with one particular aspect of its work: the appreciation and preservation of traditional 'feminine' crafts such as cookery and needlepoint. Clearly, as the majority of women now work, not only do they have less time to devote to pursuing home-based crafts, but these have become less important as an indication of gender identity. Consequently, membership has fallen from 500,000 in its heyday in the late 1950s and early 1960s to the contemporary figure of 272,000. The WI is still involved in raising awareness of contemporary women's health issues, such as breast cancer, or environmental risks to children, but as membership is largely drawn from the over-50s age group and the institute has little appeal for younger women it looks set to fade away in time. Its only recent high-profile moment came when the Prime Minister Tony Blair was given a slow handclap in 2000 by a WI meeting because he used the occasion to discuss general policy issues which the largely conservative gathering believed were not addressed to them but to members of the press in attendance. That the WI remains a 'national institution' was shown by its affectionate parody in 2006 as the centre of the comedy series *Jam and Jerusalem*.

Like the Women's Institute, the formation of Working Men's Clubs harks back to a period in which male identity (particularly that of working-class men) was primarily constituted through the kinds of manual trades and blue-collar occupations which have receded in the post-war period. With an annual membership of 350,000 around the country, Working Men's Clubs are still popular. But most have evolved into mixed social clubs and are now only tenuously linked to the workplace. Very few still exclude women from the premises, although they are barred from participating in organisational responsibilities in many more, and, like the WI, the clubs now appeal to older people in the main. Amongst the under-25 age group, leisure activities are becoming virtually indistinguishable. Pubs, still the most popular of all British social environments, are no longer male-dominated territories, although many women still do not feel comfortable visiting one alone.

The health and fitness culture which has flourished in Britain over the last fifteen years has also opened up a new range of cross-gender leisure activities. Women are still less likely to compete in team sports and tend to favour fitness classes, but activities such as running, swimming and weight training are becoming increasingly popular with both sexes. The gym, once a strictly male domain, is now frequented by almost equal numbers of men and women. Furthermore, while it is often maintained that women's participation in fitness activities is motivated by vanity and men's by health concerns, there is much evidence to suggest that British men, especially 'metrosexuals', are becoming increasingly preoccupied with appearance and body-shape. This can be understood as part of a more general shift in perceptions of British male identity. British men have often been characterised, perhaps unfairly, as badly dressed and proudly indifferent to common standards of style, taste and personal grooming, but the expansion and diversification of the menswear retailing industry, coupled with a growth in men's grooming products, has revolutionised attitudes towards British masculinity.

At other times such images may have carried distinctly gay connotations, but their contemporary appeal is ambivalently cross-gender. Male bodies were more crudely objectified in the new women's porn magazines, and male strippers became a regular feature of the hen party or girl's night out. It is not surprising that British men are now beginning to develop the kinds of body-image disorders, such as anorexia and bulimia which were once confined to women. As a result of these developments, British men have finally been cajoled into spending a greater proportion of their leisure time engaged in that most 'feminine' of activities, shopping, which now takes up a fair proportion of leisure time for both sexes, augmenting more traditional male activities, such as Saturday afternoon football.

Conclusion

Today, the British population comprises roughly 51 per cent females and 49 per cent males. However, more boys than girls are born each year and the higher numbers of women are heavily concentrated in the over-60 age group and do not reflect the gendered composition of the population as a whole. Recent studies also suggest that male life expectancy is catching up (it is currently about five years lower) and that over the century this imbalance is likely to be reversed in favour of men. Such predictions may be altered if all parents in the future are allowed, as some argue they should be, the right to choose the sex of their children. Either way, the gender composition of the population will undoubtedly affect attitudes towards age, marriage, children, and women in paid employment.

However, the overall picture which emerges at present is one in which gender roles are becoming somewhat more flexible and the two-parent, patriarchal family is gradually becoming less dominant. This has produced a variety of responses. Right-wing politicians and many prominent Church leaders tend to blame permissive legislation and the new social movements of the 1960s and 1970s (such as feminism and gay liberation) for the decline in traditional family life and conventional gender roles. From this perspective, the nuclear family unit is evoked as a symbol of social cohesion, and its break-up is regarded as the root cause of many contemporary social ills, from vandalism to drug addiction. Yet fears about the future of the family cross traditional party lines, and while the more conservative sectors of society tend to blame liberal reforms, others have argued that if permissiveness weakened the family, it was Mrs Thatcher's right-wing revolution that really poisoned it and Labour governments have since done nothing to improve it. The rampant individualism and consumer greed associated with the 1980s economic boom, and their legacy in subsequent decades are, in this version, responsible for undermining the moral values thought necessary to sustain family life.

Lastly, we must consider whether the decline of the traditional family has actually led to a more atomised, alienated society. There is also evidence to suggest that new, more flexible family structures and systems of community support are beginning to take its place. Single mothers, for example, often rely heavily on one another for both childcare assistance and emotional support. Similarly, while children of divorced parents are generally regarded as disadvantaged, it has also been suggested that many actually benefit from drawing on a wider support network of two families. It is also important to recognise the new range of identities which the decay of the traditional British family has opened up. For women in particular, the decline of the traditional family unit clearly coincides with greater social freedom and status, and increased financial autonomy.

 Exercises

1   What is the difference between a nuclear and extended family? Do you know or can you think of other kinship structures? How do family structures vary according to (a) class, (b) ethnic background? Which, if any, is most commonly represented in popular television and film?

2   What is the meaning of the following popular phrases: 'Victorian values'; 'Family wage'; 'White wedding'; 'Lie back and think of England'? How did they originate, and in what ways might they be specific to British culture?

3   The British blockbuster film, *Four Weddings and a Funeral* featured three traditional English and one Scottish wedding. What do you think are the staple ingredients of a British Wedding? What is the significance of each?

4   In recent years there has been much debate about non-sexist language. Can you think of gender-neutral alternatives for the following occupational titles: Seaman; Craftsman; Fisherman; Postman? Do you think it is important to adopt non-sexist language, or is it just political correctness?

5   Do you think 'outing' is a fair practice? Under what circumstances? Consider arguments for and against.

Reading

Barlow, A. *et al. Cohabitation, Marriage and the Law: Social Change and Legal Reform in the 21st Century* Hart, 2005. Examines the present state and future of cohabitation in Britain.

Jeffrey-Poulter, S. *Peers, Queers and Commons: The Struggle for Gay Law Reform from 1950 to the Present* Routledge, 1991. An examination of the British legal and political system in relation to its treatment of homosexuals and lesbians.

McRae, S. *Changing Britain: Families and Households in the 1990s* Oxford University Press, 1999. Overview of the place of women and the family in modern British life.

Wilson, F. *Organisational Behaviour and Gender* McGraw-Hill, 1995. An industrially based sociological and statistical analysis of employment discrimination against women in Britain.

Zweiniger-Bargielowska, I. *Women in Twentieth-century Britain: Social, Cultural and Political Change* Longman, 2001. An analysis of women's lives, work, culture and citizenship through the twentieth century, looking at changing British attitudes towards motherhood, marriage and work.

Cultural examples

Films

Four Weddings and a Funeral (1994) dir. Mike Newell. Courtship and marriage rituals amongst the English middle-class.

School for Seduction (2004) dir. Sue Heel. Comedy about an Italian who comes to Newcastle to teach a group of Geordie girls the art of romance.

Me Without You (2001) dir. Sandra Goldbacher. Charts the relationship between two teenage girls as they progress through their student days into maturity.

Casino Royale (2006) dir Martin Campbell. Twenty-first James Bond movie, starring Daniel Craig and featuring Judi Dench as a female 'M' who patronises Bond for his unreconstructed sexism.

Morvern Callar (2002) dir. Lynne Ramsey. Samantha Morton plays the Scottish adolescent coming to terms with the death of her boyfriend. Based on Alan Warner's novel.

The Queen (2006) dir. Stephen Frears. Dramatic portrait study of the Queen, and her relationship with Tony Blair, in the period after Lady Diana's death.

Books

Rachel Cusk, *The Country Life* (1998). Poignant, well-written story of a woman who leaves her husband and home in London to live in the country.

Alan Hollingshurst, *The Line of Beauty* (2004). Booker-Prize winning story of British life in the 1980s among the sex and drugs Tory elite.

Nick Hornby, *How to be Good* (2001). Very popular social comedy centring on a modern couple attempting to save their marriage.

Mark Haddon, *The Curious Incident of the Dog in the Night-time* (2003). The world, and in particular the separation of his parents, seen through the eyes of an autistic child.

TV programmes

Absolutely Fabulous. Classic comedy depicting the outrageous antics of two 1960s-generation women as they reach middle-age.

Men Behaving Badly. Post-feminist situation-comedy exploring traditional and contemporary ideas of masculinity.

Prime Suspect. Highly acclaimed police procedural series (occasional one-offs, up to a final episode 2006) centred on a female detective and exploring sexism in the British police force.

My Family. Popular situation comedy featuring an 'average' British family.

 # Websites

www.theory.org.uk/ctr-que1.htm
    Site devoted to explaining and exploring queer theory.

www.disgruntledhousewife.com/
    Humorous and irreverent pro-feminist site on how to conduct a male-female relationship.

http://uk.gay.com/
    Guide to UK gay culture and campaigning.

www.nationalarchives.gov.uk/partnerprojects/outthere/
    The National Archives are a very useful resource, and now include an archive of gay and lesbian history links.

www.familymatters.org.uk/
    Website of the Family Matters Institute, a pro-family Christian community group.

www.direct.gov.uk/RightsAndResponsibilities/fs/en
    Government's rights and responsibilities website, containing a detailed section on 'Marriage, Cohabitation, Civil Partnerships and Divorce' among other subjects.

www.statistics.gov.uk/downloads/theme_social/Social_Trends36/Social_Trends_36.pdf
    Official guide to Social Trends 2006.

http://epp.eurostat.ec.europa.eu/portal/page?_pageid=1090,30070682,1090_33076576&_dad=portal&_schema=PORTAL
    Eurostat website with wide and varied statistical information about Europe.

Chapter 4

Youth culture and style

Jo Croft

Timeline

Age

16 —— Leave school
Sex legal in UK except in Northern Ireland
Buy cigarettes
Average age at which virginity is lost for both sexes
Marry with parental consent

17 —— Drive a car
Sex legal in Northern Ireland

18 —— Buy alcohol
Watch adult films
Marry without parental consent
Vote

29 —— Average first marriage age for women

31 —— Average first marriage age for men

41 —— Average divorce age for women

43 —— Average divorce age for men

60 —— Retirement age for women

65 —— *– from 2010* Retirement age for women
Retirement age for men

76 —— Average age of death for men

81 —— Average age of death for women

Introduction

WHEN WE ATTEMPT TO describe somebody else, or when we are required to describe ourselves (on an official form, for example) age almost always seems to be a crucial component to such descriptions. Age shapes and sets limits upon the way we live our lives in a way that we take for granted. As the timeline shows, age dictates such things as when we can leave school, when we can legally have sex (either homosexual or hetero-sexual), when we can drive, when we can marry, when we can join the army, when we can drink alcohol, when we can retire and when we can vote. In an obvious sense, age is a 'fact' we cannot alter because it literally describes how long we have been alive: however much advertising campaigns for beauty products, vitamins or health foods might try to convince us otherwise, it is something which fixes our position in society as much as, and often more than, other factors such as race, gender or class.

Nevertheless, once we begin to consider the different ways in which age underpins the identity of any given individual, it emerges as a category which is far from being simply a biological given. The social effects of age have implications far beyond the explicit classification of how old someone is. Age, consequently, is an aspect of identity which powerfully reflects the particular character of life in any national culture and we can learn a lot about a nation's values and cultural practices by paying attention to the significance it attaches to certain life stages. It is worth noting, for example, that – unlike the United States and many European countries – Britain had no specific legislation governing 'age discrimination' until an Act was passed in 2006.

As the timeline demonstrates, the official landmarks of age in Britain seem to become fewer and further apart once you reach the age of 18, though there is a slight reversal of this trend during old age (driving licences, for instance, have to be reapplied for when you reach the age of 70). In any case, the period between the ages of 11 and 21 is a time when life is most punctuated by changes in status – when the rules about what you can do and where you can go are shifting most dramatically. Therefore, in terms of understanding British cultural identities, the age groups that fall broadly within the category of 'youth' offer some of the most interesting insights – not least because British institutions seem to subject young people to such close scrutiny. It is almost as if young people in this country are – consciously or unconsciously – regarded as guarantors of not just the nation's future but its soul, for whenever anxieties surface about moral or social decline, the first target for concern is youth. For example, Robert Stevens in his book *University to Uni*, says:

> Britain has for its teenage generation the worst crime rate in Europe and the worst statistics for unmarried pregnancies, drugs and alcohol. Under-eighteens' pregnancies are twice the rate in Germany, three times the rate in France and five times the rate in the Netherlands. England leads Europe in the use of both cocaine and cannabis by young people. English girls now drink more than boys and five times as much as girls in France. England also has the worst illiteracy rate.
>
> (Methuen, 2005, p. 65)

Britain is a nation which seems to attach particular importance to 'tradition'. 'Britishness' in both the upper class and the working class tends to be characterised by an adherence to 'old values', and it could be argued that the British see themselves, and are perhaps viewed by the rest of the world, as having an 'old' (established, traditional, or even ancient) culture. In consequence, it might also be claimed that, precisely because of this British conservatism, young people are regarded as both threatening and vulnerable. One of the issues which will be explored in this chapter is the extent to which British notions of social stability are explicitly associated with the stability of relationships between generations. A claim, after all, might be made that the massive changes in people's lifestyles in post-war Britain have been felt most acutely in terms of 'age relations'. 'The generation gap', juvenile delinquency, loss of community, the fragmentation of the nuclear family and disappearance of the extended family: all these much-debated social phenomena seem in one way or another to be associated with a perceived deterioration in relationships between different age groups.

Along with the rest of Europe, Britain will soon have to cope with some drastic changes in the age distribution of its population. Over the next twenty years, the average age will increase considerably. By the year 2025 the number of pensioners is predicted by a European Commission report to rise by 43 per cent. Meanwhile the working population is set to decline and the number of young people under 20 will also fall. Additionally, along with many other European countries (France, Holland, Denmark), Britain's birth rate has fallen over the past twenty-five years, so that now it is not sufficient to maintain the current level of population and in the Western EU countries as a whole immigration needs to be in the region of seven million people a year to retain current levels.

The changes expressed in these figures will have profound implications. At the simplest level, when a declining workforce has to support more people it can easily lead to intergenerational tensions. Also, as the proportion of people in retirement grows, the strain on state social and health services grows. The effect of these additional expenses will be to lower people's spending power which will in turn threaten industries which produce or sell goods. The decline in the numbers of young people may also disrupt the housing market and have an influence on pension provision. Such changes and their likely implications will probably add to the importance attached to youth and its conduct.

It could perhaps be argued that in earlier epochs of British history less emphasis was placed upon youth as a time of crisis because there was less legislation governed by age, and hence fewer official turning points or transitions in a person's life. Age, in other words is a component of identity which is very much tied to cultural factors such as the education system, health or marriage practices. This is probably most acutely exemplified by British attitudes towards children in the nineteenth century: the Victorian era was a time of great sentimentality and also great cruelty towards children, when the infant mortality rate was much higher than now, and when mass poverty meant that children had to 'earn their keep' in working-class families.

In this chapter, while other aspects of age in Britain will be touched upon, the focus will be on late childhood, adolescence and youth culture, because it is in these fast-changing periods of life that British people absorb and challenge accepted cultural identities. It is also here that the direction of present and future British identities can be apprehended, as a range of new ideas and beliefs are added to those associated with the traditional social values attaching to work, class and the family: the staple ingredients sustaining cultural identity for older British citizens.

Youth, teenagers and adolescents

At first glance, the terms 'adolescent', 'teenager' and 'youth' seem to mean exactly the same thing: they all refer to young people who are not children, and yet who are also not quite adults. However, there is also a sense in which these words suggest different forms of identity, different groupings of the British population. For example, 'youth' is generally used to refer to young people operating in the public sphere, as part of a social group, and most typically it is associated with boys rather than girls. We talk about 'youth clubs', 'youth training schemes', 'youth unemployment' and of course, 'youth culture'. 'Adolescence', on the other hand, is a term which is more likely to be used in connection with an individual's identity – to refer to a private, psychic realm of experience, as in such common expressions as 'adolescent angst', 'adolescent diary' or 'adolescent crisis'. The term 'teenager' first emerged in the 1950s when young people were newly identified as a distinct group of consumers, and since then it has typically been associated with certain kinds of products or markets: for example 'teenage fashion', 'teenage magazines' and 'teen pop idols'. With respect to gender, we should note that the expressions 'teenage pregnancy' and 'gang of youths' suggest that 'teenage' is feminine and 'youth' is masculine. More recently, the term 'tweenager' has been coined to describe 11- and 12-year-olds who aspire to the lifestyle of their older siblings, and nowadays have the pocket money to do so. While they shop for the fashions aimed at teenagers, another term, 'kidult', has arisen to describe adults who dress in the style of a younger generation. Both terms are predominantly applied to females rather than males, and there is also concern expressed about the way even younger children adopt adult habits too early, with 6-year-olds attending make-up parties and 7-year-olds wearing crop tops and fake tattoos. Fashion is clearly no longer restricted by any age limits, with pre-teens shopping for themselves at Gap, Tammy Girl, Children's Next and Miss Selfridge, their tastes dictated by pop bands such as Sugababes and Destiny's Child as well as magazines such as *Girl Style*, *Mizz* and *Sugar*.

The three fundamental natural events – birth, procreation and death – offer the most succinct summary of the human lifecycle. However universal these events may be though, there are inevitably massive differences in the ways that they are experienced by people from one culture or community to the next. In the contemporary context of Western capitalist societies, patterns and levels of 'consumption' best illustrate some of these differences. Whenever statistics are sought on the details of people's lives (to answer the question 'How do people live?'), the most plentiful and perhaps scrupulous sources of information are provided by market research. In other words, the way in which money is spent and the kinds of things that people choose to buy tell us quite a lot about the identities of British people, and cultural formation is partly reflected in modes of consumption. The British may not be a 'nation of shopkeepers', but, as a capitalist nation of consumers, 'we are what we buy'.

In order to gauge how age shapes patterns of behaviour, it is important to read between the lines of facts and reports which detail how people spend their money and their time at different stages of their lives. The term 'lifestyle' itself seems to have become inextricably linked to the notion of choices over spending. The phrases 'lifestyle politics', or 'lifestyle magazines' therefore tend to be used (often derogatively) to refer to middle-class pre-occupations with 'consumer choice', and Britain today, where the phrase 'everyone is middle class now' is increasingly common if still inaccurate, seems to be overwhelmingly characterised as a 'consumer culture'. In this context, the typical British teenager is viewed as the consumer 'par excellence', and is seen by some, often older commentators, as a 'fashion victim' driven by larger forces then personal expression. But others see the teenager as a supple negotiator of the minefields both of contemporary style trends and of technology. Knowing the price of a 'Big Mac' from McDonalds is sometimes the limit of an older person's familiarity with youth culture, which is more often about empowerment than victimisation.

Famously, the 'teenager' is considered to have been an invention or symptom of shifting consumer markets in the 1950s, both in Europe and in America. Many studies of British youth that have been carried out since then have focused, in one way or another, upon the way young people characterise themselves through the clothes they wear, the music they listen to, the films they watch and the places they go. When Richard Hoggart wrote (rather apocalyptically) about the state of the nation's youth in his well-known book *The Uses of Literacy* (1957), he summoned up an image of the British teenager being almost literally consumed by a 'Mass Culture' which in turn was linked to the saturating effects of 'Americanisation'.

More recently, social commentators have argued that it is precisely through their role as consumers of popular culture that British young people express themselves most powerfully and creatively, not least because they feel excluded by the more traditional realms of the arts. There is a widening gap between the officially sanctioned practices of 'high art' and the forms of self-expression and creativity that young people choose to explore in their everyday lives. An acute example of this is young people's use of graffiti in the UK, an art form initially borrowed from the inner-city subcultures of black Americans. From the mid 1980s onwards, complex, brightly coloured designs produced with spray-paints became a common sight on 'spare' bits of wall in many towns and cities, especially along railway tracks and under motorway bridges. Typically, these motifs would be based around a single word, name or phrase, with obscure connotations, and an important element of the appeal of graffiti within British youth culture is that you have to know *how* to read its messages, and above all to recognise the 'signature' of the artist. For many young people, the explicit association between British graffiti and urban America seems to imbue this art form with the power to 'glamorise' mundane environments such as housing estates or shopping malls – to make these spaces both more exotic and more hard-edged. Perhaps this accounts, then, for the particular prominence of the graffiti scene in new

FIGURE 4.1   Graffiti of the school of 'Banksy' has increased house values

towns such as Crawley, just south of London, where (generally) white working-class youths became minor celebrities and where police would search teenagers for incriminating spray cans.

In the following sections, we will focus on the way that British young people spend their money and their time, both when 'going out' and when 'staying in'.

Going out: 'dressing up and dressing down'

It may be simplistic to characterise British youth cultures in terms of fashion styles. Nevertheless, dress codes are obviously crucial keys to understanding how the lines are drawn between different identities in Britain. After all, the way that we dress can serve either to confirm or to subvert various facets of our identities, such as our gender, race, class and age. Clothes also reflect our perceptions of the historical epoch in which we live – how we relate to the cultural mood of the day. The postmodern pre-occupations of the last decades of the twentieth century, for example, are linked to nostalgia, pastiche and what might be better described as kinds of 'fusion' or as cultural hybridity (mixing different styles of fashion, music or anything else). Contemporary fashions conspicuously play upon these cultural themes, and styles from every previous decade have resurfaced to evoke the spirit (or *zeitgeist*) of contemporary Britain. 'Now' is in many ways a recycling of previous *zeitgeists* but with new, modern twists.

One way of thinking about different subcultural groupings within young British fashion is in terms of class identities. Subcultures such as punks, hippies, crusties, bikers and Goths have tended – in one way or another – to challenge the traditional values of smart and respectable dress. On the other hand, mods, soul boys (and girls), teds, skinheads and home-boys have usually emphasised a 'sharper' style of dress, though of course in diverse ways. This opposition between 'smart' and 'scruffy' clothes bears some relation to class allegiances insofar as dress codes which place greater value on clothes 'looking new' are more often adopted by working-class young people, while scruffier 'bohemian' styles are more likely to have middle-class wearers. But often, subcultural styles of dress confront and confound mainstream expectations about people's position in the social structure, especially in the cities.

The above is too simplistic a formula to apply to all UK youth sub-cultures, especially as these styles in themselves are not necessarily mutually exclusive, and most young people, in any case, are likely to draw on a range of possible influences. The enormous increase in the student population, for instance, is bound to affect the class delineations of subcultural style, as many more working-class young people enter a terrain which had previously been a middle-class preserve.

As Dick Hebdige points out in his book *Subculture: the Meaning of Style*, black subcultures have been a central factor in the formation of many white working-class subcultural styles such as that of mods (short for moderns). Both Afro-Caribbean and Afro-American influences have been critical in shaping British youth culture since the 1950s, not least because more and more young people in this country are growing up in multi-ethnic, cross-cultural environments. In the late 1970s and 1980s, the Afro-Caribbean Rastafarian style influenced both black and white youth subcultural fashion, with red, green and gold Ethiopian colours commonly featuring on T-shirts, hats, badges and jackets. Today, more than ever, black subcultural styles tend to lead the way in British street fashion, especially those derived from the Afro-American rap scene: the 'home-boy' look of very baggy jeans, big hooded jackets and baseball caps is almost ubiquitous among teenage boys, especially the under 16s. 'Clubwear' styles (for example tight lycra, shiny fabrics and bright colours) also seem to be influenced strongly by black street fashions. Perhaps most significantly, Asian youth culture in Britain seems to draw very much on Afro-American and Afro-Caribbean subcultural styles (as in the music of Apache Indian). The influence of the European club scene has also affected British styles, as clubs in the UK often try to recreate the atmosphere of Ibiza or Ayia Napa, and European bands have by now eroded the deep-seated British aversion to pop music from the Continent, previously denigrated as Europop. Identifications and cultural allegiances in Britain are now much more complex, in other words, than is suggested by traditional models of assimilation.

When considering what people wear, we need also to think about where they go, as the two are usually connected. The pub remains the stalwart of British socialising, and fears about youth drinking have grown (in 2006, though figures are lower for women, over two-fifths of young men aged 16 to 24 exceeded four units at least one night a week, and one-fifth exceeded eight). So, it is perhaps not surprising that UK pubs seem to be becoming more overtly geared towards a youth clientele, as increasing numbers of them, and particularly pub-chains, introduce competitions, quizzes and games areas. Nevertheless, pubs still have a unique status in British culture as places where people of different ages and, to a lesser extent, different classes, are likely to socialise together, particularly with the introduction of sports screens to show live football matches. British soap operas such as *Coronation Street* and *EastEnders* have long played on the pub's function as a place where lots of different kinds of people could plausibly meet up. This, in turn, has led to complaints from TV monitoring groups that soap operas might encourage viewers to drink more alcohol, because characters are so often portrayed having a drink in their 'local'.

Since the 1990s, clubs as much as pubs are the focus of many young people's social lives. The growth of the 'rave' scene in Britain (which began with 'Acid House' parties in the late 1980s) has meant that dancing has again become a central activity, as it had been in the 'dance halls' of the 1950s and early 1960s, and the discos of the 1970s. In contrast to these earlier dance scenes though, alcohol has tended to be a peripheral element of contemporary UK dance culture. Instead, rave puts much more emphasis on taking drugs such as 'Ecstasy', the effects of which tend to be cancelled out by alcohol. People dancing constantly for several hours are more likely to drink fluids, especially bottled water, to avoid dehydration and to restore energy levels; and traditional drink companies have also remarketed themselves to appeal to a new generation and a variety of lifestyles: Lucozade Energy, Lucozade Sport, Lucozade Low Calorie and Lucozade Solstis.

Significantly, though, raves were one of the key targets of the Criminal Justice Act (1994), and this no doubt partly accounts for the decrease in their popularity now, their place increasingly being taken by big ('legitimate') clubs such as Cream (Liverpool) and The Ministry of Sound (London). More than anything, however, these shifts in the popularity of different venues reflect the fast-moving, changeable nature of British youth culture: new scenes or styles quickly transmute from 'subculture' to 'mainstream' trends, and with equal rapidity they also fade from favour or disappear altogether. This ebb and flow in subcultural activity informs most young people's cultural identities in one way or another, but this is by no means to suggest that everybody's lives follow the same patterns. For instance, even though clubs and parties might well represent a central (and glamorous) social activity in 1990s' Britain, many young people on a 'night out' will still often 'start the proceedings' by visiting a pub. The more traditional activity of 'pub crawls' – on which lots of different pubs are visited in one evening – also persists in Britain, particularly among students, and groups of 'laddish young men' (such as the members of a rugby team or the groom and his mates on a 'stag' party).

Traditional features of pubs such as bar billiards have now been superseded by CD or video juke boxes, and wide-screen televisions tuned to MTV or Sky Sports. And yet, whether or not loud music is played in pubs, most of them still retain the same function, especially in the countryside where pubs are not vying for clientele in the way they are in the cities. The pub remains *the* primary leisure institution for white British culture but is generally much less popular among Afro-Caribbeans and Asians. It could be argued that pubs are bound up with British ideas of 'rites of passage', insofar as a young person's 'first legal drink in a pub' is often treated as a landmark. Growing concern about under-age drinking has meant that more attention is paid to young pub customers providing proof that they are over 18, and the major companies that run pubs have introduced their own ID cards. It is perhaps not surprising therefore that, since the late 1970s, increased emphasis has been put on 18th birthday celebrations, rather than 21st birthdays.

In large cities, especially northern ones such as Liverpool, Manchester or Newcastle, there is a long-standing ritual which revolves around 'going out on the town' on Friday and Saturday nights. Snaking queues form as hundreds of people gather around the pubs, clubs and wine bars – young women often dressed extremely glamorously in thin-strapped, backless evening dresses, gauzy tunics or very short skirts, and young men in more casual (but nevertheless immaculate) shirts and trousers. In the context of 'a night out on the town', the stereotype of the British love of queuing acquires another significance. The more popular clubs, for instance, sometimes hire 'queue spotters' who look out for particularly stylishly dressed 'punters' – the best dressed may well be allowed to go to the front of the queue, while those guilty of certain 'fashion crimes' (for example wearing white socks or the 'wrong' kind of shoes) may not be allowed in at all. Like the film lines curling around corners in the heyday of cinema-going, these queues of clubbers function as a kind of social scene, a place to meet your friends, to flirt, or compete with your peers. Young people also might end their evening in another queue, waiting to buy chips or a kebab, or standing in line for a taxi.

This kind of weekend spectacle is not often regarded as being part of any specific subculture, apart from what might be broadly described as 'clubbing', and yet it is still governed by a distinct set of codes – for example, in many cities, Friday night is girls' and boys' night out but Saturday night is for couples. One of the most striking aspects of these weekly events is the disregard most of the young people appear to have for the weather – the rule seems to be that jackets or coats are not worn even on freezing winter nights (this is also a question of money as it is a luxury to buy an impressive coat or jacket which will only be 'checked', hung away, at the club). Perhaps most noticeable, though, is the fact that men and women tend to go out not with boyfriends or girlfriends, but with their 'mates' of the same sex. For women especially, this seems to be an important element in the way they choose to dress – the flamboyance and overtly sexual nature of the outfits that many young women wear are apparently in some way legitimated by the fact that they are dressing up 'for fun', rather than explicitly to attract men. Indeed, it is often said that women on these occasions are 'dressing up' for other women, that an integral part of the ritual is be identified as part of a female subculture and to gain the approval of other members of that social group. None of these so-called 'rules' or codes of dress is clear-cut however.

Staying in: young people and the media

On average, people in Britain spend more time watching the television or video every day than their counterparts in any other European country, though the amount is decreasing as those with Broadband spend more time online. These days, after talking about the weather, it is accurate to say that television programmes provide a favourite topic of conversation for British people (according to market research, 46 per cent of the UK population discuss TV programmes with their friends or family). In many ways, television seems to be at the hub of 'the British way of life', offering a structure and rhythm around which many people shape their leisure time. Nowadays, the success or disappointment of major national holidays such as those at Christmas and Easter is far less likely to be talked about in terms of the quality of church services than the quality of programmes on television. Now, in fact, there is a mood of nostalgia about the 'good old days' of family viewing on television, especially in connection with Christmastime, and weekend nights are crammed with 'Top Ten' shows and compilation pro-grammes about the past. In the 1950s through to the 1970s, there was actually a regular programme broadcast from a theatre in Leeds called 'The Good Old Days' which simulated a night out at the music hall in Edwardian England (complete with audiences in fancy dress Edwardian clothes, singing along with the performers). Today, equivalent viewing slots are more likely to show archive footage of old TV shows, and now there are many satellite TV stations such as 'UK Gold' which are entirely devoted to reruns of 'classic' British programmes. So, whereas thirty years ago older people might sentimentally reminisce about 'happier' times when the family would make their own entertainment – singing songs around the piano or playing charades, people these days are more likely to recall nostalgically 'the golden age of television' during the late 1960s and early 1970s – a time when adults and children could supposedly sit together to watch favourite programmes (such as *The Morecambe and Wise Show* or *The Generation Game*), comfortable in the knowledge that it would all be 'good clean fun': the resurgence of the current BBC top programme, *Doctor Who*, is a prime example of this as children encounter the sci-fi show for the first time and adults revisit an old favourite.

A traditional British Christmas has been characterised (or caricatured) through images of the family, ranging across three generations, sitting in front of the television after Christmas dinner, watching the Queen's Speech at 3 p.m. and then a rerun of a film such as *The Sound of Music* or *The Wizard of Oz*. It is important not to underestimate the status of these televisual myths in relation to the attitudes British people themselves express about national identity, and as a corollary of this, it is often the case that anxieties about social decline are most readily articulated in terms of 'falling standards' and 'dumbing-down' on television. The concept of 'family viewing' is a central stake in debates about the role of the BBC, a public-owned institution known to the country as 'auntie' (suggesting its cosy, nanny-like persona). In an attempt to recapture the 'all-round' entertainment of twenty or thirty years ago, in addition to *Doctor Who* the BBC now has nostalgic TV shows such as *The New Generation Game* and panel shows on TV's history which celebrate television's 'good old days'.

Young people nowadays watch more television than preceding generations. However, as far as television programmers and advertisers are concerned 'youth audiences' are potentially the most elusive segment of the population in this country, for although television may play an influential role in the identities of British young people, they generally spend less time watching television than people over 25 or under 12 (that the older generation are expected to stay in explains the prevalence of nostalgia shows on Saturday nights). British youth, implicitly, are less likely than any other section of the population to be seen as inhabitants of the domestic environment. In response to this, there has been a growing movement towards 'Youth Television' in Britain, which aims to 'catch' young people either before or after they go out socialising. Youth Television was famously pioneered in the 1980s by the cockney TV producer Janet Street Porter and sometimes satirically referred to as 'Yoof TV'. The kinds of programme that fall into this category tend to have a fast-moving magazine format with young, fashionably dressed presenters, often speaking in 'non-standard' English.

Other television programmes are broadcast later at night, working on the assumption that they will be watched by young people returning from a night out. Another way of interpreting 'youth television' though, is to argue that it is watched in a different way: less as a central activity than as a backdrop – more akin, say, to having the radio turned on than watching a film at the cinema. This is reflected in the success of reality TV shows in the new century, especially those that can also be 'watched' on the internet twenty-four hours a day, such as *Big Brother*. The rise in reality TV, in its general public and minor celebrity versions, has been perceived in numerous ways, from 'dumbing-down' to the fulfilment of Andy Warhol's prediction that 'in the future everyone will be famous for fifteen minutes', but its main effect has been to place 'ordinary' people on television, and so to encourage young viewers (participants are rarely over 35) to make assessments of themselves and their peers in relation to a set of 'real personalities' they might themselves easily know or even be. Students are also notoriously likely to celebrate kitsch shows broadcast during the day, and will make a hit of programmes intended for a wholly different audience. The late-afternoon schedules are also currently stocked with innumerable quiz shows, such as *Fifteen-to-One*, *Countdown* and *The Weakest Link*, which can appeal to anyone wishing to unwind from the day, and arguably reflect the traditional British love of games.

However, whereas youth television seems to anticipate (or fantasise about) an audience which is caught up with the demands of a hectic social life, other activities such as computer games (which now generate more profits than films), reading, or listening to music suggest a more solitary vision of the teenager at home. Uncommunicative teenagers playing with their Gameboys or listening to their Walkmans acutely exemplify this. Recent years have seen the emergence of a whole new range of concerns about the state of the nation's youth which focus upon the dangers of children and adolescents inhabiting private fantasy worlds, accessed through computers. Jokes and anecdotes are commonplace about the technology 'generation gap', whereby children are deemed to be more adept than their parents at operating machines like videos and computers (many TV adverts play on this discrepancy). However, the internet has rendered such jokes a little more sinister, in that they suggest a loss of parental control. Above all, fears seem to centre upon the fact that the internet enables children to communicate not only with other children but also with adults, without supervision, leaving them open to 'grooming', which has now become a legal offence. The much-publicised emergence of chatrooms has created a mood of pessimism about what might otherwise have been greeted more optimistically as a communication system which encourages the breakdown of many traditional boundaries, including those between different ages and generations. In terms of computer games, 'shoot-em-ups' and strategy games have acquired a cultish popularity, particularly with teenage boys. Unlike much internet communication, playing these games, unless online, involves no human interaction, and so is an activity which seems to provoke different anxieties in some adults because it is deemed to be antisocial and introspective, plunging the player into a fantasy world.

Aesthetically and thematically, computer games have a close relationship to comics and magazines. Since the mid 1980s, comics – especially 'graphic novels' – have spawned a whole subcultural scene, and most British towns now have a specialist comics shop (Forbidden Planet, for instance, is a nationwide chain of shops). Virgin Megastores, which principally serve as music and DVD outlets, also sell comics and magazines aimed at this cultish readership, thus suggesting further subcultural cross-overs between computer games, music, movies and comics. However, when people in Britain talk about 'teenage magazines', they are most likely to be referring to publications aimed at girls – for example magazines such as *Sugar*, *Bliss* and *Cosmogirl!*. This is significant in that adolescent femininity in the UK tends to be associated – more than any other aspect of youth culture – with stereotypical consumerism. While things have definitely moved on since the days when British teenage girls were represented almost solely in terms of 'teenybopper' culture – screaming at popstars, or gazing at posters on their bedroom walls, it is still the case that young women are more explicitly identified as a 'market', even one enfranchised with 'girlpower', rather than as a series of subcultures. Surveys about how much money is spent on clothing and footwear in the UK actually tell a very different story. For instance, around 6 per cent more clothes and shoes are bought by young men than by young women in the same over-15 age group. The point to make here, perhaps, is that the cultural activities of British young women are interpreted less positively, in that women are more likely to be stereotyped as passive consumers (of clothes and popstars) than as creative participants in a subcultural scene.

Many parents tend to expect their children to buy and enjoy the same activities and styles as they did. Shifts, as with music and youth fashion, are almost always perceived negatively by older generations. In the 1970s, *Jackie* was by far the highest selling magazine for teenage girls, selling an average of 605,947 copies per week in 1976. More recently, this pole position has been taken up by magazines like *Mizz* and *Shout*, which had a readership of 520,000 in 2006, selling primarily as a lifestyle magazine. Comparing the content of *Jackie* in the 1970s, with *Shout*, creates some sense of the kinds of changes that have taken place in the lives of British teenage girls over the last thirty years. The most notable, and perhaps optimistic difference is that teenage girls today seem to be far less exclusively associated with a private, domestic space (the adolescent girl, in her bedroom, dreaming about love). *Jackie* by and large used to be concerned with 'romance', whereas contemporary teenage girls' magazines focus much more on actual, often sexual, relationships (most are dominated by their 'problem pages' where readers' questions are answered). The magazines use the same terminology that their readership does, considering attractive girls 'honeys', boys 'hotties', and a whole raft of phrases meaning fashionable: 'chung', 'mint', 'buff', 'phat', 'nang', 'lush'. Far more attention is also now paid to music and fashion, which can be interpreted in a number of ways. These preoccupations would seem to confirm the idea that the British adolescent girl's identity is almost wholly shaped by her status as a consumer. However, it could also be argued that these features imply that young women now participate more actively in the public domain – they are no longer 'stuck in their bedrooms'. Above all, perhaps, the images of British young women offered by contemporary teenage magazines suggest cultural identities which are far from straightforward insofar as they often negotiate conflicting concerns between sexual relationships and autonomy.

Another concern for the older generation is young women's hedonistic lifestyle, driven by increasing levels of financial independence. The consequence is that some hotels and restaurants refuse to accept bookings from all-female parties, where once they would have thought twice about all-male groups. Some pubs now ban 'hen' parties and, reportedly, holiday companies claim that Britain's new wave of ladettes, young women with a love of binge drinking and brazen behaviour, are exceeding the antics of male 'yobs' in terms of noise, abuse and violence. Another recent cultural phenomenon is 'excessorexia': supposedly, because of the aspirational character of life in the twenty-first century, one in five people in Britain are thought to be obsessed with wanting more than they already have. A phenomenon which may be related is the 'Quarter life' crisis, a tendency for young fast-living urban professionals to suffer a mid-life crisis twenty-five years too soon.

Overall, the crucial point to make about youth culture is its speed of change and its difference from more mainstream representations of British identity, whether those of children at school or adults at work. Youth identities are more commonly associated with pleasure and leisure, but they are crossed by other crucial factors in cultural positioning discussed in this book: gender, ethnicity, region and class.

Sex and drugs and rock 'n' roll

It is both clichéd and true to say that the lives of young people in the UK in the post-war era have been characterised on the basis of the rather unholy trinity of 'Sex and Drugs and Rock 'n' Roll'. This concluding section will therefore focus on these three aspects because they are associated more closely and apprehensively with British youth culture than any others.

Although the poet Philip Larkin suggested that 'Sex began in 1963 . . .', anxieties about the sexual mores of the younger generation certainly preceded the so-called sexual revolution of the 1960s. Nevertheless, sex is undoubtedly a realm of contemporary British life where the mythical 'generation gap' is felt particularly keenly, and this is no doubt exacerbated by a perceived difference between what is sexually common now and what was acceptable forty years ago. Nostalgia is now expressed with peculiar intensity in relation to notions of childhood innocence, whereby today's children and teenagers are regarded as both more vulnerable and as more sexually 'knowing'.

Whereas a hundred years ago, fears were rife about the social dangers of adolescent masturbation, since the 1970s the key areas of concern surrounding British young people have been: the role of sex education, the availability of contraception, HIV, teenage pregnancy, sexual abuse, and homosexuality. In Britain's increasingly secular climate on the other hand, the issue of 'sex before marriage' or cohabitation is no longer hotly contested, and 70 per cent of women now cohabit before marriage.

More than anything, carnal knowledge seems to be the central stake in debates about young people's sexuality. Since the 1980s, for instance, UK campaigns and initiatives such as 'Childline' and 'Kidscape' have increased public awareness of childhood sexual abuse. The fact that these issues are now more openly discussed has sometimes been taken as an indication that the British nation is being overwhelmed by an epidemic of paedophilia. However, this is not the case, and it is probably much more accurate to say that British people are now less inclined to draw a veil of silence over these kinds of problems. Social Services policy, as well as the less official influences of magazine problem pages and TV shows have been key factors in bringing about this shift. Changing attitudes towards child sexual abuse in the United States have also been extremely influential in the UK, especially with the increasing popularity here of American talk shows.

Until the 1980s, the general perception in Britain had been that sex would inevitably be subject to fewer and fewer restrictions for each subsequent generation. However, concern over HIV and Aids has obviously put paid to this vision of an unstoppable machine of sexual liberation, and this has been compounded by wider knowledge about sexually transmitted infections such as chlamydia, which by 2010 may affect one in five women between the ages of 16 and 24 and, if untreated, can cause infertility. It could even be argued that many young people today have more restricted sex lives than their parents had as teenagers. It may be the case that British young people have less sex with fewer partners than teenagers did in the 1970s and early 1980s, the heyday of the contraceptive pill. Certainly there are more fears about sex, and unwanted pregnancy no longer necessarily represents the worst possible scenario for sexually active teenagers. Campaigns to educate people about 'safer sex' have meant an increased openness about referring to sexual practices which fall outside the scope of 'straight sex' (for example, dressing up or using 'sex toys'), and the idea of conventional sex as being the only kind has ceased to dominate. Glossy media representations of sex are far more likely nowadays to play on fetishistic imagery (made by designer Gareth Pugh and worn at clubs like Torture Garden in Brixton), and where earlier advertising used to appeal to men almost exclusively along the lines of 'buy the car, get the girl', marketing often now seeks to associate products with erotic experimentation. As if, perhaps, to distract attention away from the fact that sex is now more circumscribed by risks, contemporary British youth culture seems to place a premium upon the idea of imaginative sexual practices, and is perhaps less ready to equate 'experience' (that is of penetrative sex) with sexual pleasure and knowledge. Though more experimental, the current generation in the new century are in fact less promiscuous and more monogamous than their parents' generation.

Sex, for British young people today is double-edged. Talking about sex, listening to other people talking about sex, reading about sex and even watching sex on the television or online has become progressively easier. In a sense though, actually having sex is becoming more complicated, not least for teenagers. In 1996, controversy erupted about the content of magazines aimed at teenage girls in the UK after a Tory backbench MP, Peter Luff, made an unsuccessful attempt to introduce a 'Periodical Protection Bill'. Luff's main objection to magazines such as *Bliss* was that they encourage young girls to be obsessed with sex because they deal with sexual issues too explicitly. What is most telling about the debates which surrounded Luff's crusade, is the polarisation of the arguments. For some people, childhood is in danger of becoming entirely eroded, while for others, young people can never know too much.

Drugs are another area of life where the 'generation gap' appears to be wide. In post-war Britain, youth subcultures have always been associated with the use of particular (usually illegal) drugs: mods with amphetamines ('speed'), hippies with cannabis ('dope', 'pot', 'blow', etc.) and LSD ('acid'), ravers and clubbers with 'Ecstasy'. Today though, drug use has become fairly mainstream among the UK youth population, and it is estimated that more than 50 per cent of young people will have tried at least one illegal drug by the time they are 18 (while more than half of all students say they are regular users of cannabis, according to the Office for National Statistics in 2001, 30 per cent of all 15-year-olds in England have tried the drug). The drugs scene has now been characterised, rather ambiguously, as being about 'recreational drug use', rather than as a small alienated enclave of drug addicts, as in the past. This is a shift indicated by the increasing calls to legalise soft drugs.

Now that Thatcher's generation of children – born between 1979 and 1990 – have come to maturity, an apolitical consumerism appears to have taken hold of British youth for an earlier generation raised on CND marches and anti-Vietnam protests, hippie love-ins followed by punk-rock anarchism. However, the young in Britain seem yet again to fulfil their role as 'sophisticated' consumers who make discriminating choices from, in this case, a whole menu of intoxicating substances. Value for money influences the decisions young people make about using drugs, judging a pint of lager against, say, the psychoactive clout of an LSD blotter. The high-energy fizz drink has for many become the staple beverage alongside bottled water, but with the added attraction that drinks such as Red Bull serve as mixers for vodka, the popularity of which is witnessed by the high number of vodka bars, with names like Revolution, that have sprung up in British cities.

Set against this image of British youth as adept 'recreational' users of drugs, are the media portrayals of young people either as hapless victims or as crazed addicts. Such representations do not offer an accurate overall perspective. In the 1980s there was a huge increase in heroin use among British working-class youth, especially in urban areas, and this was often the target of sensationalist news stories. Although there has been no drastic change in the numbers of people using heroin in the UK since the 1980s, media attention has almost completely shifted towards other drugs: in the early 1990s, concern was focused upon the possibility of a cocaine epidemic, and numerous stories were run in the press and on TV about crack-related crime in the United States; since then the spotlight has shifted once again to Ecstasy prompted by a number of media-led moral panics in the mid 1990s, based around the widely publicised deaths of teenagers using the drug. Though less than six people a year on average have died in Britain from Ecstasy use (that is less than 1 per cent of alcohol-related deaths of young people), national publicity focused on this drug in particular at the turn of the century (even though, for example, in 2000, 20 per cent of pupils excluded from schools were suspended for drinking alcohol on the premises). Since which time, the pendulum of concern has swung again towards alcohol, particularly since the relaxing of the licensing laws in 2005 so pubs could serve beyond 11.00 p.m., and the rise of nightly 'binge-drinking' by the young (one in four deaths of young men aged between 15 and 29 is alcohol-related).

One of the most commonly expressed concerns is that British parents no longer 'know what their children are doing', and the relative novelty of Ecstasy and other designer drugs has seemed to exacerbate older people's sense of estrangement. However commonplace drugs may be within the social lives of many young people in this country, they are seen as both alien and threatening to much of the British population over 40, even those who were teenagers in the 1960s. Most British youth subcultures have been aligned, at some stage, with a particular type of music. Consequently, as delineations, cross-overs and fusions between different styles of pop music have become ever more complicated, so too have the criteria distinguishing one subcultural scene from another. Rock 'n' roll music certainly no longer is (if it ever was) a single unifying symbol of youth rebellion. At one level, it is almost as if British pop music has become so diverse that the differences between music scenes now seem to be blurred and indistinct. The 'tribalism' of the 1960s and 1970s, whereby musical taste was often inextricably bound to much broader allegiances, seems to be fading in the 1990s. Music nevertheless still plays a critical part in the construction of identities for British youth, but in more fluid ways. In 1978, British 15-year-olds may well have used musical taste as a means of declaring themselves to be punks or mods. Today, 15-year-olds are probably more likely to say that they like particular bands of different stripes than to use music to ascribe a specific subcultural identity to themselves, and the proliferation of music styles,

FIGURE 4.2 Drug graffiti near the historic city of Chester shows how far the drugs culture has permeated teenage Britain

FIGURE 4.3   A street band contrasts traditional instruments with contemporary style

giving rise to new forms means that musical fashions are changing more quickly than in the past.

The 'serious' end of popular music in the twenty-first century has become far more diffuse, though bands such as Radiohead and Coldplay manage to play songs that would have fitted into airplay lists in the 1970s and still be enormously successful. Now that the first rock stars, for example Bob Dylan, Paul McCartney and Mick Jagger, have turned 60, there is an increasing tendency to see rock as both 'over', in the sense that 'rock bands' are to an extent passé, and have in some sense 'won' the battle over popular music: to have become a part of the mainstream, such that even the Prime Minister, Tony Blair, used to be in a band. The music scene more generally has diversified into a battery of trends, such as alternative country, trance, ambient, garage, trip hop, the new acoustic movement, and so on, though the most common word on the scene continues to be 'fusion', suggesting again that old categories such as 'rock' are fast becoming outdated.

There does also seem to be a definite shift in Britain since the 1990s away from the oppositional youth subcultures of the previous three decades, and mainstream British pop has leant heavily towards manufactured, choreographed bands of pretty dancing singers who espouse a distinctly upbeat, celebratory view of teenage life, with many temporary 'stars' created by popular television shows where the public vote for the winner.

Conclusion

To conclude, we will look briefly at two aspects of culture which are in many ways opposed to each other: fashion and New Age culture (you will find out more about the New Age in relation to religion in Chapter 7). Both are associated with youth, but both also in fact stretch across the generations and provide intriguing case studies for analysing the production and consumption of contemporary British identities.

Fashion for young people focuses on 'street style' in Britain, emphasising flexibility, eclecticism, originality and, above all, the refusal of most stylish British teenagers to be 'slaves' to the dictates of the catwalk or the high-street fashion chains. While the newsagents in this country are filled with row after row of women's magazines giving the latest tips about 'what's in this season', the British seem to maintain a rather ambivalent attitude to the very concept of 'fashion'. There is a sense, of course, in which this ambivalence can be linked to British conservatism or reserve – to the nation's reputed resistance to anything new. However, there is another, equally important, strand to the way in which many British people seem to approach fashion, which is the almost mythical 'eccentricity' of the British (or perhaps more precisely the English). In fact, the most famous of British designers – Vivienne Westwood, Katherine Hamnett and Paul Smith are often characterised specifically in terms of their eccentricity and their lack of conformity with the broader trends of the global fashion industry. There is even a clothes company called 'English Eccentrics'. 'Reserve' and 'eccentricity' are attributes which are famously associated with 'the British character', and as qualities – albeit stereotypical ones – they possess a particular resonance in relation to British fashion, not least because they seem almost to cancel each other out. 'Classic' British clothing, of course is characterised by muted colours (especially brown, navy blue and green), sensible/comfortable tailoring, fabrics such as wool or corduroy, and the obligatory, 'understated' string of pearls for women. Above all, perhaps, this style of dress is associated with an upper-class lifestyle of 'hunting, shooting and fishing', readily mythologised through media representations of the Royal Family striding over moors, walking dogs and so on. It is probably not surprising then, that these kinds of clothes tend to conjure up conservative, non-urban identities (and often Conservative with a capital 'C'), though they are far from being the exclusive preserve of the aristocratic, landowning echelons of British society. Rather, the 'wax jacket and brogues' way of dressing seems to be identified with what we might call an 'aspirational lifestyle' (cf. 'young fogies', *Country Life*, Marks and Spencer, etc. – shops for women like Laura Ashley). Perhaps most significantly, this 'classic' style of British dress has been readily exported and is almost certainly more popular with young people abroad than it is with their British contemporaries.

Often, the way people dress in Britain is explicitly informed by distinctions of social class, and yet certain articles of clothing have much more ambiguous class connotations. The 'cloth cap' for instance (which is typically made of woollen cloth, in a small check pattern) is associated both with traditional working-class men (especially in northern Working Men's Clubs) and with upper-class gentlemen (especially out shooting, etc.). In a far more specific and self-conscious way, clothes such as Burberry raincoats, and even 'deerstalker' hats have crossed certain cultural divides insofar as they were adopted in the late 1980s and early 1990s as part of black street fashion – a gesture which seemed at the time both to mock the complacency of white 'Home Counties' style, and to challenge the monopoly of designer sportswear in black Afro-Caribbean fashion itself. In a way, this tendency within British fashion to play with or parody familiar images of British tradition represents a central element in the dress codes of several youth subcultures in this country: for example Teddy boys, Wigan soul, skinheads and punk.

In the last few decades the 'Doc Marten' boot or 'DM' has probably exemplified the shifting, playful moods of British fashion more than any other single item of clothing. Skinheads in the late 1960s adopted DMs as part of a dress code which seemed to be an exaggerated version of the clothes worn by manual labourers (drainpipe Levis, Ben Sherman check shirts and braces). A particular brand of work boots therefore acquired a significance far beyond the bounds of their initial function, and by the late 1970s the divisions and subdivisions between different subcultures such as punks and rudeboys were marked out not only by haircuts and music but by the way people wore their DMs (the number of holes, the colour, customised versions). As part of a more general impetus among feminists in the early 1980s to reject the trappings of a 'stereotypical' femininity, DMs became more and more popular with young women, especially students, who tended to adopt a kind of 'proletarian' look of baggily practical clothes – overalls and donkey jackets – as a gesture of rebellion against both sexism and the materialistic excesses of the decade. Now, the Doc Marten boot seems to have entered yet another phase, having been adopted, briefly, by the catwalks of international fashion houses at the beginning of the 1990s. The omnipresence of the DM in high-street chains of shoe shops has robbed it of much of its potency as a symbol of non-conformity and nowadays it's as likely to be worn to school by a middle-class 11-year-old (or by a schoolteacher for that matter) as it is to be worn by an 'indie' musician or an anarchic art student. You can now buy velvet or silver or brocade Doc Martens but somehow they seem to have lost the power to shock, acquiring instead the more dubious accolade of a British 'design classic', which of course is readily exportable and hence less likely to be popular in Britain. At the other end of the spectrum are Jimmy Choo shoes, founded in a workshop in Hackney in London, but now bought in bulk by stars such as Cameron Diaz and Jennifer Lopez.

Mainstream street looks are today probably most influenced by idolised figures from pop or sport. The latter are particularly important to boys, for whom the media are always keen to identify role models or hero-types. There have been countless newspaper articles from the late 1990s onwards speaking out about the downturn in boys' fortunes generally, and their lack of positive role models in particular. Much of this concern is based on statistics such as the following: boys are five times more likely to commit suicide than girls, and four times more likely to be addicted to drugs or alcohol; boys are nine times more likely to be sleeping rough; girls out-perform boys at every level of education and now outnumber boys at university by a ratio of three to two. The concern over such figures has grown, and the causes of boys' disaffection has been variously diagnosed as a general 'crisis of masculinity', as poorer communication skills and an inability to express feelings, a macho culture that is anti-education, the lack of male teachers in primary schools, and a new 'postfeminist' imbalance between perceptions of girls and boys, reflected in assessment patterns that favour assignments over exams. The social results are supposedly football thuggery, an increase in violent crime, the spread of drugs, and more playground bullying, but there is no consensus over the way to give boys more confidence and a sense of purpose. A related concern is that over the phenomenon of 'dumbing-down', a general accusation made by older generations against the shift towards a post-literate visual culture, in which theoretical abstractions and analytical complexities appear less and less in the media. The argument seems to hinge upon whether one considers aspects of culture, from news reporting to summer movie blockbusters, to be more accessible and inclusive than they were, losing their overly didactic and 'improving' elements, or increasingly crass and simplistic. The phenomenon that encapsulates this trend is that of 'chavs' and Anti-Social Behaviour Orders (ASBOs). While all the British football team 'WAGs' (wives and girlfriends) at the 2006 World Cup were taken to be frontline celebrity chavs, the king and queen of chav lifestyles are said to be the Beckhams, who serve as laudable role models but attract opprobrium for flaunting money rather than style and for supposedly cheapening designer labels by their patronage. These are considered by the tabloid papers to be the high-end moneyed chavs who are only generally to be found in wealthy areas of the country such as the South East or Cheshire. The street equivalent is the Burberry-wearing aspirational but uneducated members of the working class, epitomised for many by the Scouse footballer Wayne Rooney's socialite fiancée, Colleen McLoughlin, who became the face of fashion for supermarket chain ASDA in 2006 and has by 2007 eclipsed Victoria Beckham as the highest profile nouveau riche celebrity. Chavs inhabit a strange hinterland between fashion victimhood and council-estate aliena- tion, and for some youths on the edge of society, the acquisition of ASBOs became a badge of honour, a sign of rebellion and toughness. The orders are often linked in the media with the phenomenon of 'hoodies': youths who keep their identity safe from eyes and CCTV cameras by wearing tops with hoods, and who are often therefore assumed to be criminally inclined.

Finally, we need to note how youth culture can become softened and anaesthetised, but also transformed and diffused. It has now become a kind of truism that more or less every town or even village in Britain is bound to have a troupe of Goths and a resident punk, a figure as much a part of the repertoire of stock British types as the bowler-hatted city gent. Like most myths though, this scenario of 'a punk in every high street' represents only a very partial truth, one which fails to register the complex differ- ences between particular communities and the constant mutations in the ways different subcultures identify themselves. Elements of punk can be found in various British subcultures, the most notable probably being New Age travellers. Crucially though, the style of clothes worn by many New Age travellers draws very heavily on a hippy aesthetic – ethnic clothes, beads and bangles. New Age hairstyles similarly seem to draw on a range of cultural references such as dreadlocks (Rastafarianism), bright hair dye (punk), shaved (skinhead), mohican (Native American/Hari Krishna/punk), and shaggy, matted long hair (hippy). Any subcultural identity can of course be dissected into its component parts of 'key' motifs and symbols, but the example of New Age subculture in Britain today also acutely demonstrates how problematic such checklists of cultural identities can be, not least because contemporary British cultural identities seem to be so enmeshed and hybrid – often self-consciously playing with or parodying the styles they adopt. New Age subculture was perhaps the most recent indication of an extra-social trend that did not react or rebel from within mainstream culture but sought a mode of life outside society, and has consequently been portrayed negatively and ignorantly in most media. People tend to get lumped together according to very superficial criteria, and what is interesting about the phenomenon of New Agers is that certain marginalised elements of the population which may have previously formed far more distinct groupings such as hippies, travellers, political activists, the urban homeless, and young unemployed people from both urban and rural communities, came to be bracketed together, albeit in an impressionistic way. In fact, the very vagueness of the boundaries which surrounds this subculture suggest that the label of 'New Age traveller' is more likely to be invoked as a derogatory/ disapproving term to describe scruffy youths or homeless people, while the

FIGURE 4.4 New Age dancers perform at a party

styles have been taken over by festival-goers and weekend-hippies. In 2001, the Archbishop of Westminster, leader of 4.1 million Roman Catholics in England and Wales, declared that Christianity 'has almost been vanquished' in Britain and that people now increasingly gained their 'glimpses of the transcendent' in music, green issues and especially New Age movements. Indeed, New Age culture seems to combine spirituality with green politics and music in a way that speaks to the young and the young-at-heart in a more positive way than any other movement since that of the hippies in the 1960s.

Though many people who identify with New Age lifestyles may originally come from urban areas, there are several reasons why the sub-culture is generally associated with more rural areas. The many new commercially run festivals that have packaged previous events incorporate countercultural behaviour into the consumer mainstream once more. The festival circuit and celebrity camping with state-of-the-art facilities attracts the likes of model Kate Moss and her musician boyfriend Pete Doherty, or Gwyneth Paltrow, married to Coldplay's Chris Martin, and her daughter Apple. Similarly, the protest movements of the 1990s have been sanitised into widespread concerns for the environment and the country's Green Belts, but activity is mostly limited to charitable work and lobbying rather than sit-ins and militant road protests.

In this chapter overall, we have seen how Britain's youth since the 1950s continues to generate a varied range of subcultures, most of which in the 'noughties' seem uninterested in political stands or in politicians but believe in self-expression and consumer power. This proliferation of styles and trends means that the images and assumptions of their parents' generation can no longer be applied to the way teenagers and youths see themselves today, though the liberal principles of parents mean that the young are also less alienated than previous generations.

Exercises

1   How important do you think age is within British culture? Would you say that the differences between age groups are becoming more or less distinct?

2   What kinds of music do you associate with the following British youth subcultures? Name specific bands/artists where possible:
    - Hippies
    - Goths
    - Skinheads
    - Rudeboys
    - Bikers
    - Rastas.

3   Why do you think Britain has produced such distinct subcultural styles and groupings? What, if anything, does this tell us about British culture as a whole?

4   What do the following phrases mean? Comment upon the possible insights they offer into British attitudes towards age, and the question of whether it is possible to avoid 'ageism'.
    - 'Mutton dressed as lamb'
    - 'Put out to pasture'
    - 'Trying to teach your grandmother to suck eggs'
    - 'Toyboy'
    - 'One foot in the grave'
    - 'Whippersnapper'
    - 'Wet behind the ears'
    - 'Darby and Joan'
    - 'Long in the tooth'
    - 'Cradle snatcher'
    - 'Pushing up the daisies'.

5   How do you think attitudes towards sex and drugs are changing?

6   To what extent do you think that young people have more in common with the youth of other nations and cultures, than with older people from their own country?

📖 Reading

Bennett, Andy and Keith Kahn-Harris (eds). *After Subculture: Critical Studies in Contemporary Youth Culture* Macmillan, 2004. Seeks to take the debate about youth styles beyond the notion of subcultures.

Griffin, Christine. *Representations of Youth: The Study of Youth and Adolescence in Britain and America* Polity: Blackwell, 1993. Academic analysis of youth and its influences across the Atlantic.

Hebdige, Dick. *Subculture: The Meaning of Style* Routledge, 1979. Still influential review of youth and alternative culture.

Thornton, Sarah. *Club Cultures: Youth, Media, Music* Polity: Blackwell, 1995. An exploration of subcultures across the main areas of youth activity and performance.

Cultural examples

Films

This is England (2006) dir. Shane Meadows. 1980s Britain seen through the eyes of youth, and particularly a group of skinheads in a coastal town. Concerns subculture, gang rivalry and racism.

The Football Factory (2003) dir. Nick Love. Adaptation of John King novel about masculinity and the end of empire focusing on warring tribes of football fans.

Human Traffic (1999) dir. Justin Kerrigan. A day in the life of hardcore clubbers in Cardiff.

My Beautiful Laundrette (1985) dir. Stephen Frears. Urban realist film, with touches of magic realism, looking at sexuality and racism in the 1980s 'Enterprise culture'. Focuses on the relationship between two youths – one Asian, one white working class.

Quadrophenia (1979) dir. Frank Roddam. Authentic 1960s, London-and-Brighton film about mod culture, featuring Sting and based on album by The Who.

Jubilee (1977), dir. Derek Jarman. Anarchic, decadent depiction of punk subcultures in Thatcher's Britain.

Books

Matthew David Scott, *Playing Mercy* (2004). Britain's first chav novel, about a family ruled by designer brands.

Irvine Welsh, *Trainspotting* (1993). Grim, darkly humorous novel about heroin subculture in Edinburgh. Made into a film in 1996.

Colin MacInnes, *Absolute Beginners* (1959). Cult novel about swinging teenage life in London. Also made into a film in the 1980s.

Richard Allen, *Skinhead* (1970). Teen-novel about violent youth subculture.

Maude Casey, *Over the Water* (1990). Teenage novel about the problems of growing up as a second generation Irish immigrant girl in the UK.

Hanif Kureishi, *The Buddha of Suburbia* (1990). Growing up in and around London, in the 1970s, between different ethnic cultures.

TV programmes

See www.bbc.co.uk/cult/ for the BBC's guide to its cult programmes.

BBC's children's programming is covered at CBBC and Cbeebies:
   www.bbc.co.uk/cbeebies/
   www.bbc.co.uk/cbbc/

 Websites

www.youngbritsatart.co.uk/
   National art competition in 2006 that invited students aged 11–16 from schools in England, Scotland and Wales to depict how they see themselves in contemporary Britain.

www.theoldie.co.uk/
   Highly regarded reactionary magazine aimed at those not obsessed by 'yoof' culture.

http://news.bbc.co.uk/1/hi/magazine/4074004.stm
   A lexicon of teen speak.

www.pennyblackmusic.co.uk/GenSitePages/NewHP.aspx
   The Penny Black Music record shop's site provides in-depth knowledge and obscure information.

www.theory.org.uk/
   Ultra cool social studies and cultural theory site.

www.byc.org.uk/
   British Youth Council official site for finding out about UK youth culture and activities.

www.myspace.com/
   Unofficial best site for finding out about British youth culture.

www.confused.co.uk
   Hip online spinoff from *Dazed & Confused* magazine.

Chapter 5

Class and politics

Frank McDonough

Timeline

1911	House of Lords Reform Act
1924	First Labour Government
1940	Churchill PM
1945	General Election: Labour elected
1948	National Health Service
1951	General Election: Conservatives elected
1955	General Election: Eden PM
1956	Suez Crisis
1959	Gaitskill failed reform Clause Four General Election: Macmillan PM Third consecutive Tory victory
1964	Labour victory
1967	Devaluation of the pound
1973	Britain joined EEC
1979	'Winter of Discontent' General Election: Thatcher PM
1981	Urban riots
1982	Falklands War
1990	Poll Tax riots Thatcher ousted from office
1992	Fourth consecutive Tory victory
1994	Police Act
1997	Labour leader Tony Blair elected PM
2001	Second consecutive Labour victory
2005	Third consecutive Labour victory

Introduction

IT WAS ONCE COMMONPLACE to portray Britain as a class-ridden society. Class was a staple part of the British way of life. Each class had unique characteristics. The upper class had stately homes, aristocratic backgrounds and posh accents; the middle class, semi-detached houses, suits and bowler hats; the working class, common accents, fish and chips and council flats. This produced a society divided between 'Us' (the workers) and 'Them' (the rich and the bosses). Pubs always had a 'public bar' and a 'lounge'. Even railway carriages were divided into First, Second and Third class compartments.

In recent years, many writers have begun to speak of the 'decline of class' in British society. The term 'classless society' has become commonplace. And in modern day consumer society everyone is deemed to be middle class. The credit for this transformation is mostly given to Mrs Thatcher, Prime Minister from 1979 to 1990. Accordingly, many political commentators have suggested that the 'Thatcher Revolution' removed class from the political landscape, by shifting power through government reforms away from the Establishment, the bureaucrats and the trade unions to individual consumers and the free market. Many of Mrs Thatcher's reforms were delivered in the rhetoric of 'empowerment of the people'. Parents were encouraged to become school governors and take control of their schools as teachers faced the imposition of a National Curriculum to ensure that children in both state and private schools received a core course of study. The Community Charge (Poll Tax), which was later replaced by Council Tax, was designed to recoup money for local amenities more evenly across the total adult population. It was also promoted to make local authorities more accountable to local people, but revenue-raising limits were effectively imposed by the Treasury. Privatisation ended up turning public utilities like gas, electricity, telephone and water into private monopolies. Nevertheless a large number of commentators have argued that the Establishment (monarchy, Church of England, Oxbridge and the BBC) no longer exists. The middle-class bureaucrat is made to work much harder, often implementing reforms which are designed to 'get government off the backs of the people'. The working class has retreated from collective action towards domestic pleasures. The only

ve working-class unity today is the purchase of a weekly
ticket. Even the railways now only have two classes: First

hatcher seemingly blew class off the face of British society.
view Britain as a socially fragmented society, with life
he individual, his or her family, and the idea of a better
wnership and consumer goods. And under Tony Blair,
, there has simply been more of the same, but with a
socialist twist of equal opportunities for all, including measures that favour
the disadvantaged. But pronouncing the death of class is premature. A recent
wide-ranging survey of public opinion found 90 per cent of people still
placing themselves in a particular class; 73 per cent agreed that class was
still an integral part of British society; and 52 per cent thought there were
still sharp class divisions. Thus, class may have become culturally and politically invisible, yet it remains an integral part of British society. Britain seems
to have a love of stratification and hierarchy.

One unchanging aspect of a British person's class position is accent. The
words an individual speaks immediately reveal her or his class. A study of
British accents during the 1970s found that a posh voice sounding like
a BBC newsreader, usually spoken by a person from the south-east of England, was viewed as the most attractive voice. Most respondents said this
accent sounded 'educated', 'soft' and 'mellifluous'. The accents placed at
the bottom in this survey, on the other hand, were regional city accents: Liverpool (Scouse), Birmingham (Brummie), Newcastle (Geordie) and London
(cockney). These accents were seen as 'harsh', 'common' and 'ugly'. No great
prejudice was expressed against well-spoken Scottish and Irish accents.
However, a similar survey of British accents in the US turned these results
upside down and placed Scouse and cockney as the most attractive and BBC
English as the least. This suggests British attitudes towards accent are, to a
large extent, based on ingrained class prejudice. Can it be mere coincidence
that British people reserve their most negative comments for accents
associated with areas containing large groups of working-class people?

In recent years, however, young upper middle-class people in London,
have begun to adopt fake cockney accents (estuary English), in order to
disguise their class origins. This is another sign of class becoming invisible.
However, the 1995 pop song 'Common People' by Pulp puts forward the
view that though a middle-class person may 'want to live like common
people' and 'sleep with common people' they can never appreciate the reality
of a working-class life.

In the power stakes, however, if you want to get ahead in Britain
then you would be well-advised to lose a regional accent. An example of the
importance of accent to upward mobility is Mandi Norwood, appointed
editor of *Cosmopolitan* magazine at the age of 31. When she began her career

in journalism she had a Geordie accent. Her London friends advised her to drop it, if she wanted to get on. In a couple of years she admitted to 'speaking like Lady Di'. From that point on, her career went swiftly upward. Even more significantly, a survey of recruitment managers of major corporations found that, although the majority of them knew it was wrong to discriminate against people because of a regional accent, they did. Despite all the talk of a classless society, it is still possible to divide British society into three broad classes – upper, middle and working – even though the nature and composition of each class have undergone change.

The upper class

The traditional upper class was always closely associated with the aristocracy. They lived in stately homes and had their character shaped on the playing fields of Eton. They were an hereditary élite whose wealth and position were based on property and title. These were both used to gain substantial political privileges. For example, the House of Lords, an unelected second chamber, had a veto over House of Commons legislation until 1911. However, during much of this century the power and position of the aristocracy has been steadily weakened. As long ago as the 1930s Noel Coward commented that the 'Stately Homes of England' were 'rather in the lurch'. By the 1960s the aristocracy were lampooned by Harold Wilson, the Labour Leader as the 'Grouse Moor tendency'. The House of Lords was further slimmed down by the Blair government. Peers were invited to choose from among their number, those who were to continue in office. Other 'life peers' were appointed and effectively the Upper House became an advisory body to the Commons rather than its master. Hence, over time the aristocracy have been gradually replaced by a new upper class of businessmen who emerged with 'gentlemanly characteristics' and settled in London and the South East. These 'gentlemanly capitalists' have come to dominate the financial and political heart of British society. By the 1980s Denis Healey, a leading Labour politician was able to suggest Mrs Thatcher had transferred power from the 'aristocracy to estate agents'.

Wealth, however, can never replace 'breeding'. The *Sunday Times* publishes an annual 'Rich List' showing whose wealth is rising, falling or static. This gives a snapshot of both how rich the country is (the thousandth richest person on the list was worth £166 million) and how wealth and power are shifting. Most of the 2001 top ten had family wealth (Duke of Westminster, Lord Sainsbury, Sir Adrian and John Swire). The remainder were mostly self-made business people. That is even more marked in the 2006 list, where only the Duke of Westminster and Hans Rausing retain their top-ten places. A surprising number of landed aristocrats still feature further down the list among sports personalities, pop stars and other 'mavericks'.

TABLE 5.1 The *Sunday Times* 'Rich List', 2006

1	Lakshmi Mittal	£14,881m	Steel
2	Roman Abramovich	£10,800m	Oil, industry and football
3	The Duke of Westminster	£6,600m	Property
4	Hans Rausing and family	£4,950m	Food packaging
5	Philip and Tina Green	£4,900m	Retailing
6	Leonard Blavatnik	£4,670m	Industry
7	Sri and Gopi Hinduja	£3,600m	Industry and finance
8	David and Simon Reuben	£3,250m	Property
9	Sir Richard Branson	£3,065m	Transport and mobile phones
10	John Fredriksen	£2,856m	Shipping

Hence, most writers would put wealthy families involved in the control of major banks, insurance companies, pension funds and stocks in the City of London at the core of the modern upper class. These families still pass on wealth from generation to generation and enjoy a dominant position in society. But the nature of the modern upper class is very complex. Most vast family businesses are becoming increasingly global and are run by a highly paid managerial élite, often dubbed 'City Fat Cats'. The modern upper class is not as visible as the former owners of the stately homes of England who sought to impose standards and demanded deference. The new upper class is much more culturally invisible. Highly paid managers, PR people and the Conservative Party now represent their interests. It has been shown that a numerically small number of powerful families wield enormous power over the business life of the City of London. The Conservative Party has increasingly become the party of this City business élite, and downplays its past association with the monarchy, the Church of England and aristocracy. Many of Mrs Thatcher's reforms in the 1980s, including sharp reductions in the highest rates of personal and company tax, the removal of exchange controls, City de-regulation, the expansion of the private sector through privatisation and the weakening of trade unions have clearly benefited the business élite. The result is an upper class which has never been more wealthy. A recent study, for example, showed the top 1 per cent of wealth owners possessing 21 per cent of the nation's total wealth. Tony Blair's Labour government, with its 'Third Way', unlike previous Labour administrations, was at least as friendly to business and the upper class as was its Tory predecessor.

Thus, the modern upper class is still based on individuals with a common background and close social contacts. Power is still kept in the family. For example, 45 per cent of bank directors with a listing in *Who's Who* could boast a father with a previous entry. Moreover, 75 per cent of bank directors attended fee-paying public schools and 50 per cent had been to Oxford or Cambridge. Furthermore, a study of the top 250 companies in Britain recently revealed multiple directorships in the hands of a few wealthy families.

Hence, the upper class is largely made up of wealthy families. It is not exceptionally large. In 2006, for example, 43,500 people (less than 0.1 per cent of the population), held 7 per cent of the nation's wealth – or £740,000 each – while the wealthiest 10 per cent in Britain owned 50 per cent of all marketable property. Yet the numerical smallness of the upper class only serves to add to its exclusivity. It is a self-selecting élite, closed to outsiders – and money cannot buy someone into it. Networking is much more important. Contacts occur so frequently within the upper class because of their common background. The first point of entry is family background. The second is a public-school education, privately funded by parents. The ethos of British fee-paying public schools such as Eton, Harrow and Rugby, is geared towards lifelong friendship. At boarding schools, pupils live with each other during school terms. This allows the development of extremely close social friendships between pupils and their families. This is followed by an Oxford or Cambridge education which expands the networking process still further. It is quite remarkable to note that, though public-school pupils account for only 5 per cent of the total school population, they take over 50 per cent of Oxbridge places. A public school and Oxbridge education, therefore, moulds an integrated élite.

However, the question of whether the upper class acts in unison is extremely difficult to answer. There are clearly powerful families who wield power in the City of London, and have influence over both the Conservative and Labour Parties. Yet the increasingly competitive nature of business suggests that conflicts of interest are likely to develop between elements within this ruling group. Equally, the close networking ethos of the upper-class business élite is able to make life difficult for the 'new rich' such as Richard Branson (owner of the Virgin group of record label, airline, radio station, Cola), Alan Sugar (business tycoon behind Amstrad and chairman of Tottenham Hotspur) and Anita Roddick (creator of the Body Shop). These brilliant entrepreneurs, who have truly gone from 'rags to riches' are still considered 'outsiders' within the upper class. This partly explains why Richard Branson decided to withdraw his Virgin group from the stock market because he feared its independence was being compromised by powerful City groups. The turn of the new century spawned a rash of dotcom millionaires, People like Martha Lane-Fox and Brent Hoberman became rich overnight through the stock-market flotation of their company Lastminute.com. A year later they were relatively poor (£25 million) as the bubble burst and Lastminute.com joined 'the 90 per cent club' of those companies which lost most of their value.

For all the talk of an 'enterprise culture' much of British business is dominated by companies set up well over a hundred years ago. Upper-class families who own these companies have enormous power over investment, markets, companies and shareholders. The fate of any 'self-made' business person ultimately lies in their hands. Hence, the upper class may be small in size but its members occupy positions of leadership in the major businesses in Britain. The upper class uses its wealth to confer social advantages and to retain a privileged position for its future generations. The closeness of the upper class ensures over-representation by this group in all the key positions in society. For example 59 per cent of today's Conservative MPs attended a fee-paying public school (down from 65 per cent in 1987). Equally, many of its members have made accommodations with the ruling Labour administration. Thus, the upper class can be seen to be a relatively closed, coherent and self-recruiting élite. It may have become an invisible élite in cultural terms but its underlying power and influence have never been stronger.

The middle class

In recent times, it has become fashionable to be a middle-class hero. This was not so in the 1960s. In those days, the lifestyle of the middle class was derided in pop songs such as 'Semi-Detached Suburban Mr Jones' by Manfred Mann and 'Matthew and Son' by Cat Stevens. These songs suggest a suburban middle-class lifestyle is boring and repetitive. In the 1970s prejudice against a conformist life continued. The popular comedy show *The Fall and Rise of Reginald Perrin* portrayed the dull life of a middle-class executive who takes the same route from his semi-detached house to work each day. At work, Reggie grows tired of life with equally dull people, at home he despairs of his boring relatives whose idea of fun is to drink prune wine and visit a safari park at the weekend. To break free of this middle-class Alcatraz, Reggie Perrin fakes his own suicide and disappears.

In the 1980s, however, Reggie Perrin came back from the dead to find the boring middle-class lifestyle he escaped had become, of all things – fashionable. Everyone aspired to own a dull semi-detached house in the suburbs and go to work in a dull job in the City. A middle-class hero suddenly became something to be. The coffee morning became the 'in thing'. Everyone wanted Gold Blend coffee at these events. Indeed a sequence of advertisements featuring the burgeoning romance of a couple whose close relationship blossoms over several cups of coffee became extraordinarily popular – so much so that the last advert featuring the 'Gold Blend Couple' drew a larger audience than popular soap operas such as *EastEnders* and *Coronation Street*.

Even so, it is difficult to pigeonhole the middle class neatly. Much definition of the middle class still revolves around the differences in their employment situations. A common assumption these days is that the middle class is extremely fragmented. However, there is general agreement that most middle-class people fall into one of four broad categories. The first are the higher professionals – doctors, lawyers, architects, accountants and business executives. They may lack the power and wealth of the upper class but they are certainly a distinct group. Higher professionals value education, training and independence. They have all been to university and in most cases have postgraduate and professional qualifications. They have generous pensions, holidays, expenses, sick pay and considerable freedom within their own job. It is quite noticeable that family members of this group tend to follow their parents into a professional career. For example, 64 per cent of the sons of higher professionals end up in similar jobs, while only 2 per cent end up in a manual job. This low level of downward mobility suggests a high level of shared values concerning hard work and educational attainment which are passed on from generation to generation.

However, this higher professional group is not a completely closed élite. In 1996, for example, 28.3 per cent of male professionals were the sons of manual workers. Even so, one recent study showed that 34.5 per cent of top professionals had a father from a similar background. There are clearly difficulties for a working-class person finding 'room at the top', to quote the title of a well-known 1957 novel. Indeed, the novel's leading character, Joe Lampton, shows the difficulties an upwardly mobile member of the working class faces when entering the world of the upper-middle class. Joe Lampton is portrayed as a ruthless opportunist who marries upward to a life of boredom and soul-destroying disillusionment – the underlying moral being that working-class people who wish to rise can only do so by acquiring the moral scruples of vipers. Oddly enough, this powerful image of educated working-class people 'selling out' and feeling ill at ease 'above their station' has acted as an effective weapon to prevent talented members of the working classes ever wanting to find any 'room at the top'. This may explain why only 6.5 per cent of top professionals had fathers with semi-skilled or unskilled manual backgrounds. Indeed, in many of the top professions the proportion of those whose father came from a manual background is exceptionally low. Hence, the medical profession, merchant banking and the judiciary remain largely Joe Lampton-free-zones.

The second major group in the middle class are salaried professionals (sometimes known as the 'salariat'). This group includes university and college lecturers, school teachers, local government officials, civil servants and social workers. They too have all attended university, and often have postgraduate and professional qualifications. In most cases, they have modest pensions and some freedom over their own job. Yet they have nowhere near the same level of salary autonomy enjoyed by higher professionals.

The largest group in the middle class are routine white-collar workers. A great deal of white-collar work takes place at a desk and is heavily supervised. It is very much a nine-to-five job with little freedom. Clerical work is now becoming female-dominated. In 1911, for example, 21 per cent of clerks were women. Today the figure is 78 per cent. Some clerical jobs such as a secretary or a telephone operator are almost totally held by women, though work in call centres is more evenly divided between men and women, and many of the latter now work part-time. Oddly enough, 50 per cent of clerical workers now view themselves as part of the working class. However, there is little evidence of clerical workers flocking to join old working-class bastions such as trade unions. They do not exhibit an 'Us' and 'Them' view of themselves and their employers. In general, lower middle-class employees use their jobs to improve the quality of their lives through consumer goods, foreign holidays and entertainment.

The final group in the middle class are the self-employed. They became the 'stars' of the 1980s in cultural terms. These small businessmen and shop-keepers have more control over their working lives than clerical workers. They view themselves as middle class. Yet they work exceptionally long hours, have no career structure and must finance their own pensions. In many cases, they earn less than a routine clerical worker.

The working class

Oddly enough, it is the working class, at the bottom of the social pile, who have been most closely examined as a class. More ink has been spilled about them than any other group in British society. They have been portrayed in novels, plays, films and TV documentaries. Endless sociological surveys on working-class life and numerous government reports have been produced. Unfortunately, most of these studies have been conducted by members of the middle class. For example, George Orwell in *The Road To Wigan Pier* (1937) views the plight of the unemployed working class of the 1930s through the eyes of a bourgeois intellectual. Many films contain the idea that 'it's grim up north' for a member of the working class. (*Private Eye* parodies this with a cartoon series 'It's Grim up North London'.) Even the TV series *Our Friends in the North* (1996), produced as part of a 1990s 'acceleration of nostalgia' for the 1960s, repeats many of the old stereotypes about traditional working-class life in the north, as do *The Royle Family* and *Shameless*. Richard Hoggart, an eminent writer on working-class life has been accused of being over-critical of the life his education had allowed him to escape. Hence, what we know of the working class is more often than not what the middle class think about them.

In the 1950s, there was a traditional picture of typical, usually male, members of the working class. Such people left school without any qualifications to find a job as a manual worker. They had a regional accent, a trade-union membership card and lived in a close-knit community of 'two-up-two-down' terraced houses owned by a landlord or the council. They enjoyed a pint 'down the local pub', a bet, and a trip to the football match. The chip shop was the central aspect of local cuisine and the Sunday roast dinner was a national ritual. They always voted Labour and enjoyed a shared experience. Of course, the working-class woman was depicted as a wife who always stayed at home to look after the kids with very few leisure activities, except perhaps the Bingo. The working class saw themselves as 'Us' and the middle and upper classes as 'Them'.

Even in the 1950s it was already being suggested that this traditional picture of working-class life was undergoing change. The sweeping victories of the Conservatives in general elections in this period led many writers to speculate whether improved wages, living conditions, education, welfare and consumer goods had led the working class to no longer feel part of the 'lower orders'. It was even suggested that as workers became more affluent they ceased to feel a close affinity towards the Labour Party. The idea that a classless – You Never Had it So Good – consumer society had emerged was widespread. It seemed as though the working classes were looking forward to their next consumer purchase and not some grand socialist revolution. Many books, novels and films reflected the idea of a new working class emerging. *Saturday Night and Sunday Morning* (1960) which examined the life of an affluent worker within a traditional working-class community in the late 1950s is a prime example. The film portrays the life of Arthur Seaton, a young lathe-operator from Nottingham who, though highly paid, is dissatisfied with the parochial attitudes and restricted cultural activities of the working class. He proclaims with rugged individualism: 'I'm Me, and nobody else; and whatever people say I am, that's what I'm not, because they don't know a bloody thing about me.' This rugged individualism leads Arthur to have contempt for his new-found affluence which is mostly spent on drink, women and fishing. Significantly, he is indifferent to politics.

A flood of studies appeared in the 1950s and 1960s to examine whether affluent workers had ceased to feel close class solidarity. The most prominent example was a detailed study of Ford car workers. This showed affluent workers had grasped the idea of a better life through consumer goods and spent a great deal of time on 'domestic pleasures'. Yet these studies concluded that in cultural terms the majority of affluent workers did not aspire to be middle-class. They still saw being a member of a trade union and voting Labour as extremely important expressions of their class-identity. Even so, these affluent workers placed a better life for their family as a greater priority than the struggles of the Labour movement. This tends to indicate that the advent of a consumer society and improved standards of living were already leading to a more individualistic approach to politics among the working class before the 1980s, and that has certainly continued into the new millennium.

It is, however, the years since Mrs Thatcher came to power in 1979 which have reopened the debate over the 'embourgeoisement' of the working class. Previous assumptions about the working class are being discussed once again. The Thatcher years are being viewed as a period of cultural transformation which has produced an increasingly fragmented working class. There are few who would doubt that the working class has changed. The crux of the traditional picture of working-class life suggests a shared experience. In 1979 male manual workers formed a majority of the work-force and most belonged to trade unions. Today nearly 50 per cent of the present workforce is female or a member of an ethnic minority. The membership of trade unions has fallen from 13 million to less than 7 million today (of which 39 per cent are female). In the 1970s trade unions were seen as having the power to bring down governments. Yet this power has been all but extinguished by successive trade-union reforms during the 1980s. Trade-union leaders who enjoyed national fame in the 1960s and 1970s are now unknown figures. In the 2001 General Election, Arthur Scargill, President for life of the National Miners' Union stood against the official Labour candidate Shaun Woodward, former Conservative MP and member of the wealthy Sainsbury family in the working-class constituency of Wigan. He was trounced. This shows how rapidly Britain has changed since the union heyday of the 1970s and 1980s. Many former steel, coal mining and dock areas have become industrial wastelands. Many have even been turned into industrial museums. In 2000 there were 76 unions representing only 6.8 million workers. Membership figures for some of the largest unions are given in Table 5.2.

However, the greatest division within the working class is the gap between the employed and unemployed. The living standards of those in full-time jobs have improved, but the plight of the unemployed has worsened. For a start, unemployment has increased rapidly. From 1951 to 1979, un-employment never rose above 1.5 million. Under the Tories from 1979 to 1997 it was as high as 3.5 million and rarely below 2 million. A great many male unskilled workers fell down a black hole of despair with no job, little hope and no future. They became walking museum exhibits.

These changes led to talk of the development of an 'underclass' in Britain which is cut off from the consumer society and is poor and politically apathetic. The divide between rich and poor is growing, and those in the bottom 10 per cent are stuck in poverty. According to the Office for National

TABLE 5.2 Membership of selected major unions in 2001 (compared with 1994)

	2001 (000s)	1994 (000s)
Amalgamated Engineering and Electrical Union	727	835
UNIFI (formerly Banking, Insurance and Finance Union	171	141
General, Municipal and Boilermakers' Union	694	835
Graphical, Paper and Media Union	201	224
Manufacturing, Science, Finance	416	516
National Association of Schoolmasters, Union of Women Teachers	184	138
National Union of Teachers	201	169
Transport and General Workers' Union	872	949
Union of Construction, Allied Trades and Technicians	123	136
Union of Shop, Distributive and Allied Workers	310	299
UNISON (formed by merger of NALGO, NUPE & COHSE*)	1,300	1,458

* NALGO = National and local Government Officers Association, NUPE = National Union of Public Employees, and COHSE = Confederation of Health Service Employees

Source: *The Lifestyle Pocketbook* NTC Publications (2001)

Statistics, in 2003 2.8 million children were living in families claiming a key benefit. In the same year, 231,000 children were living in families classed as 'unemployed' (those claiming Jobseeker's Allowance) and 1.57 million children lived in families classed as 'lone parents'.

Furthermore, for many, homelessness is the big issue – this conviction spawned a publication of that name sold largely to fund its vendors. John Bird, its founder says there are 25,000 homeless people under the age of 24 in Britain.

Alongside the growth of poverty have come riots in very poor urban areas such as Toxteth (Liverpool), Moss Side (Manchester), Handsworth (Birmingham) and Brixton (London). Despite the undoubted affluence of some areas of Britain, in 2001 there were riots in deprived areas of Oldham, Bradford and Burnley. Street begging and the 'cardboard cities' of homeless people in London and other major cities are other symptoms of a new harsher climate. Even diseases such as diphtheria and tuberculosis are making a comeback. This 'underclass' is excluded from the 'flash' car, the Vector Bank account, and Gold Blend coffee. Many of the new poor go to 'car-boot sales' where people sell second-hand goods, usually from the back of a very ancient car which really does 'take your breath away'. In many areas

FIGURE 5.1 A law firm seeking business in a run-down area presents the concept of personal freedom as an optional consumer choice

of inner-city Britain, crime has risen to record levels, drug addiction resembles the American inner city and unemployment is over 60 per cent. A recent study showed that one in five households now has no adult in any sort of employment. In 2006 there were 1.7 million unemployed people. The growth of one-parent families in Britain is higher than in any other European country. Contrary to the 1950s image, the working-class woman of the 2000s is often depicted as an unmarried single mother living on a council estate.

Social change

This out-of-work underclass is divided from those in work. If they are on Social Security benefits, they are often in a so-called 'poverty trap' where their benefits are reduced if they work. They are thus cut off from both opportunities to learn skills and interaction with people who might be of some benefit to them. They thus become further isolated in society

Meanwhile, there has been a sharp decline in male manual workers, a group always seen as the core of the traditional working class. In 1951, 70 per cent of the workforce was made up of manual workers. In 2006 they made up only 24 per cent of workers.

The greatest revolution, however, has been in housing choice. In 1950 over 80 per cent of skilled and unskilled manual workers lived in private rented or council-owned properties. In 1988, 72 per cent of skilled and 55 per cent of semi-skilled manual workers owned their own home. A recent opinion survey showed that 90 per cent of manual workers who lived in council property would like to buy their own homes. Since 1981, 33 per cent of all council tenants have bought their council houses.

Today, housing remains a huge problem in Britain. Because of a number of factors, including the government's unwillingness to release more land for development, house prices are sky high. According to the Halifax Building Society, in the last ten years the average house price in Britain has risen from £64,441 to £179,601. This rise of 359 per cent far outstrips the rise in the Retail Price Index of 76 per cent over the same period. House prices are a constant topic of conversation for people who want to buy or move house. It means that young people have great difficulty getting onto the housing ladder even if they are prepared to burden themselves with debt. This generation is thus made more reliant than previous ones on parental financial help (assuming they leave the parental home at all). Those unable to buy are forced to rent, mainly in the private sector, with considerable financial, social and class consequences. The extent of this pattern of buy-to-let housing has not been seen since the 1950s.

Life has changed for ordinary people in other ways too. The modern working-class manual worker spends less time with workmates at the pub (increasingly the preserve of youth) or the football match (increasingly attended by the middle class) and much more time at home. The growth of DIY superstores and encouragement from TV programmes has led to more working-class men spending time making their homes more attractive. Industrial change has radically altered many former working-class communities which depended on heavy industries such as coal mining, shipbuilding, dock work, railways and steel making. New industries have tended to be located long distances from where workers live.

An additional change in the traditional pattern of working-class life has been in the role of women. A majority of working-class women are now going out of the home into either part-time or full-time work. Thus, female members of the working class are actually much less home-centred than ever before. Of course, much of this work is poorly paid and part-time. Nevertheless, more opportunities for women in expanding service sectors such a retailing, banking and insurance exist and over 30 per cent of households now boast a female breadwinner. Hence, working-class women are much less reliant on males. This has resulted in more all-female social activities outside the home. A recent example is the popularity of male groups of strippers, the most famous being the Chippendales, who are viewed by women as sex objects. The idea of a working-class woman accepting a traditional-housewife role is declining. The novelty of the househusband has emerged in the working class. There is also evidence that an unemployed male is increasingly being seen as a poor marriage partner – hence the sharp increase in one-parent families.

Increasingly, the majority of working-class people aspire to higher levels of consumer spending. The power to withdraw one's labour has been eroded – and replaced by the power to buy goods. This has led to a climate in which 'we are what we buy'. Working people have become more money-centred, family-centred and individualistic. House and car ownership in working-class areas has become a symbol of rising status.

However, this cultural revolution has not completely led to the working class no longer feeling working class. When account is taken of what the working class say about class, we find they still differentiate themselves from the middle class. They still consider class to be an important part of British life. They see themselves as part of a particular class and few believe they live in a classless society.

The nature of politics

There are numerous organisations which agitate for political change out-side the formal channels of government power. Some prominent examples include Greenpeace and Friends of the Earth which are concerned with environmental matters, the Campaign For Nuclear Disarmament (CND), which agitates for the adoption by the government of a nuclear-free British defence policy, the National Farmer's Union (NFU), which lobbies government on behalf of the agricultural community, the Confederation of British Industry (CBI), which represents the interests of big business, the Trade Union Congress (TUC), which lobbies on behalf of workers, and Shelter which speaks on behalf of the homeless. British pressure groups are proliferating at a rapid rate and enjoy the support of people whose ordinary lives are nowhere near as radical. Yet these groups are primarily interested in a single issue rather than a broad range of policies. They all seek to influence the government in London.

It is clear that the dominant mechanisms of power still reside with the Parliament at Westminster. Many writers would suggest that the power of central government has never been stronger. Equally, the power of local government and pressure groups has never been weaker. In 1979, when Mrs Thatcher took office, she promised to end the 'enlarged role of the state'. But this bold claim never really came true. In 1979 the state was responsible for 43 per cent of the economy and in 2001 the state was *still* responsible for 43 per cent. Indeed, Britain is the most centralised state among all the major Western industrial democracies.

While claiming to devolve power to the regions, the government has in fact continued to centralise and to take on itself all sorts of tasks theoretically devolved. Power has increasingly been concentrated in the hands of the prime minister and the Cabinet. The power of central government has been extended since 1979. In 1988 British universities came under central research and teaching regulation for the first time. British schools now have a national curriculum. In the 1994 Police Act, the police, previously organised on a local basis were brought under the control of the Home Secretary.

New Labour promised to decentralise education by giving local schools what they called 'earned autonomy'. The outcome of their policies was the opposite: £35 billion of the educational budget was moved from local to central government.

Regional health authorities have been abolished and the National Health Service is now under the control of the Health Secretary. The power of local government has been dramatically weakened from 1979 to the present. Local authorities no longer have the right to build homes. The introduction of rate-capping (limits on the amount of money raised through local taxation) has turned local councils into little more than the agents of central government. Until 1999 London was the only major world capital without an integrated local government agency. (The government then reluctantly granted limited autonomy to a new London administration under the mayor Ken Livingstone.) Other centrally controlled agencies have appeared, including the Child Support Agency, the Student Loans Company, and the National Rivers Authority. Even the National Lottery, though privately managed, is under central government control. It was partly to address the accusation of centralisation that Tony Blair's government pressed ahead with a programme of political devolution. Assemblies were set up in Edinburgh and Cardiff where locally elected representatives could look after the interests of the people. This has been welcomed by members of those assemblies, naturally, but others complain about the costs of another layer of administration, and say that the amount of real power devolved is limited.

In theory, centralisation should enable the government to deal better with national emergencies such as the 2001 foot-and-mouth crisis. In practice, the experience for rural Britain was catastrophic with government seeming more inclined to manage the news rather than handle the disease. Over 3.5 million animals had been slaughtered and burnt by mid-year; meat was being imported from countries which had endemic foot-and-mouth and used vaccination, which the UK government itself refused to do.

Not since the days when the monarchy dominated Parliament has power been so centrally controlled as it is from Westminster today. Yet, since the English Civil War in the seventeenth century, the power of the monarch over Parliament has dwindled. It has always been claimed that the British monarch reigns but does not rule, whereas the American president rules but does not reign. Today, Queen Elizabeth II remains the head of state but is little more than a ceremonial figurehead. She even pays income tax. The actual power of the Queen over Parliament is reflected in the State Opening of Parliament, which takes place each November. At this ceremony, a messenger of the monarch (Black Rod) has the door of the House of Commons slammed in his face, to symbolise Parliament's independence from the monarchy, before MPs decide to listen to the 'Queen's Speech', which outlines the legislative programme of the government for each year and is written by the prime minister.

The whole ceremony may seem to be one of those peculiarly silly British rituals. Yet it emphasises the way power has shifted from the monarch to Parliament which is made up of two Houses. The less important of these is the House of Lords. This is an unelected body based on hereditary and life peers. Until 1911 the House of Lords had a veto over government legislation. These days it acts as a body which gives advice on government legislation. The Labour government has reformed its membership – at the time of writing, hereditary peers are reduced to 92, elected by their fellows, and the remaining 524 life peers are nominated, but see pp. 197–8.

The dominant political forum is the House of Commons. In 2006 this was composed of 632 MPs. Each MP represents a particular part of Britain known as a constituency and is elected at general elections held every four or five years. The growth of the power of the House of Commons has been accompanied by an expansion of the electorate through various parliamentary reform Acts (today everyone over the age of 18 has the right to vote) and the growth of organised political parties with leaders, national organisations and competing policies. After a general election, the party leader who wins a majority of seats in the House of Commons forms a government from members of her or his party. The Prime Minister selects a Cabinet, which is composed of ministers individually and collectively responsible for carrying out the legislative programme of the government. The dominance of the prime minister and the Cabinet over the British system has led to charges that the British political system is an 'elected dictatorship' of the party leader (and the leader's closest associates) and an Opposition leader (and Shadow Cabinet organised on a similar basis).

Party politics

The two main parties in Britain are the Conservative Party and the Labour Party, and they have dominated elections since 1918. From 1950 to 1970, a total of 92 per cent of votes went to the two major parties. Even in 2005 the Conservative and Labour Parties took 73 per cent of the votes cast.

The Conservative Party emerged in the 1830s from the 'Tory' grouping in Parliament. In the later nineteenth century, under the leadership of Disraeli, the party was concerned with defending traditional institutions such as the monarchy, the aristocracy and the empire. Disraeli also popularised the idea of 'One Nation' Conservatism. This suggested the Conservative Party was the only true national party which could rise above class and special-interest groups to represent the people as a whole. After 1918, and the creation of a mass electorate, the party has constantly and successfully adapted its policies to suit prevailing trends in British society. In the 1930s the party started to shed its aristocratic image and was led by businessmen. In the 1950s the party accepted Labour policies such as nationalisation and the welfare state. This led many commentators to speak of Britain from 1951 to 1979 as having a consensus politics in which there was very little difference between the two major parties. Under Mrs Thatcher, the party moved away from 'One Nation' Conservatism towards a set of policies aimed at business, the consumer and the upwardly mobile. Thus, the Conservative Party, once the party of the Establishment and the classic aristocratic, stiff-upper-lipped ruling class became associated with the business and commercial sections of society. However, the legacy of Mrs Thatcher's conviction politics for the long-term electoral appeal of the Conservatives remains uncertain. Since her fall from power in 1990, the party under John Major, William Hague, Ian Duncan Smith and David Cameron has been greatly divided on the way forward. However, it is always dangerous to write off political parties. Labour were in opposition for eighteen years from 1979 to 1997 and after they failed to win the election against John Major in 1992 at a time of Conservative unpopularity, people said they were finished. They returned to power in 1997 with a landslide which led to a mood of national euphoria. People delighted in iconic TV moments of Tory minister Michael Portillo losing his seat and independent MP Martin Bell winning Tatton. The Conservatives went away to lick their wounds having lost safe seats up and down England and every seat in Scotland. Its leaders claimed that the low turnout cost them votes. They said people had abstained from voting because of despair with the political process not because they disliked the Tories. However, a *Today Programme* poll three months after the election found that of 1,000 people who had not voted, 53 per cent said they would have voted Labour and only 19 per cent Tory. So the Tory case was even worse than it seemed. Since 2001 it has routinely been the case that more people vote to throw people out of the *Big Brother* house than do in general elections. Furthermore, membership of all political parties is less than that of the RSPB (a bird charity).

In the 2001 and 2005 general elections Labour's majority was only slightly reduced, and they seem secure in 2007, but presumably at some point in the future, the Conservatives also will return from their wilderness. Over time the Conservative Party has been the most consistently successful British political party and even at a low point in 2001 had more actual party members (318,000) than the party in power, Labour (311,000). Moreover now, for the first time in ten years, 53 per cent of Britons say that looking after one's own interests rather than those of the community will lead to greater well-being for all. This shift to individualism might benefit Conservatives more then Labour.

It may pay off for David Cameron as Tory leader to have established himself as something of a maverick. He has embraced environmentalism, rides a bicycle and promotes social inclusion. This is meant to establish the fact that he is not a toff, siding with the landed interest, a 'hanger and flogger', but a compassionate individual. When he expressed concern for young people and suggested that the hooded tops which they wore were not threatening but a form of camouflage, his stance was ridiculed by Labour as 'hug a hoodie'. However, providing he can bring substance to his policy statements on crime, his forthright, non-traditional approach should stand him in good political stead.

The Labour Party is Britain's second major party. It was formed in 1906 from the Labour Representation Committee (LRC) with the financial backing of the trade unions to represent the interests of the working class. In 1918 the party made a firm commitment to the 'common ownership of the means of production'. The first Labour government came to power in 1924. By 1929 the Labour Party had replaced the Liberals as one of the two major parties. The Labour Party gained a spectacular victory in the 1945 general election. This government introduced several important social reforms, most notably, the National Health Service, the social security system, mass education and the nationalisation of several leading industries. The party won power again under Harold Wilson from 1964 to 1970 and was in office again from 1974 to 1979. However, while the Labour Party has established itself as one of the major parties, until 1997 it had never ruled for longer than five-and-a-half years. Labour had spent the majority of time in opposition. The failure of the Labour Party to dominate politics was attributed to its image as a party of the labouring working class in major industrial cities. The close link with the trade unions also put off many voters. This may explain why the party had difficulty in winning support from non-union members and from those living in affluent middle-class suburbs or rural areas.

However, under Tony Blair, the Labour Party attempted to ditch its old 'cloth-cap' image. The party constitution now gives greater powers to individual members. The former dominance of the trade unions over the party is downplayed. In 1995, the party revised Clause Four of its constitution and thus ended the historic commitment of the party to state ownership. The party is now portrayed as 'New Labour', but it is probably a change in personnel rather than policies which has led to greater electoral success for the party. The 1997 Labour government contained more women (Blair's Babes) and minorities than hitherto, and this has evidently contributed to its effectiveness.

The success of Labour under Tony Blair and Gordon Brown is also attributable to their having controlled the unions and the left wing, and brought about fiscal stability while reducing unemployment. Blair has had a highly successful PR machine, initially under his press secretary Alistair Campbell, which is credited with managing the information flow ('spin') to the government's advantage. This has meant timing the release of bad news to coincide with national distractions (Transport Department spin doctor Jo Moore was forced to resign after sending an email an hour after the New York bombings of 11 September 2001 which read: 'It's now a very good day to get out anything we want to bury'), or repeating news of allocations of money to the National Health Service, etc.

Some commentators fear that Labour have cultivated a presidential style and undemocratically seeks to bypass Parliament. For example, Britain's involvement in the War On Terror in Afghanistan was undertaken without discussion in the House of Commons. When 'President' Blair set about reforming the House of Lords, formerly made up of unelected, hereditary peers, he set up a Royal Commission chaired by Lord Wakeham. This reported in January 2001 and proposed that the new Lords should have about 550 members. Most would be appointed by an independent committee, but a 'significant minority' would be elected from the regions. The Conservatives were suspicious of Labour's plans, because the House of Lords has always been a Tory stronghold. (Even after the first phase of reform, the Conservatives have 223 peers, compared with Labour's 200.) The then Tory leader, William Hague said Labour intended to 'get rid of the hereditary peers, stuff it with a load of people from the Labour Party and then forget about it.'

Labour continued with its plans. In April 2001 the first tranche of 'people's peers' (a term spin-doctored from Downing St.) was appointed. The fifteen people chosen by the House of Lords Appointments Commission all had an Establishment background and included seven knights and three professors. Four of the fifteen were women and four were from ethnic minorities. But nine lived in London or the South East and only one, Victor Adebowale, Chief Executive of the Centrepoint charity, was under 40 years of age.

In November the government produced a White Paper which proposed that only 120 of the 600 members of the new Lords would be elected, well short of the 190 suggested by the Wakeham commission. The proposals included the removal of the remaining 92 hereditary peers. Thus, only a fifth of the new chamber would be elected by the public, another fifth nominated by an appointments commission (set up by the government) and the majority appointed by political parties. Furthermore, the new chamber was expected to be only a 'revising and deliberative body', in which the prime minister reserved to himself the right to put forward a 'limited number of holders of very high office' for life peerages. The struggle continues.

The third largest party is the Liberal Democrats. This was an amalgamation of the old Liberal Party and the Social Democratic Party, the latter being a breakaway group from the Labour Party, formed in 1981 by the 'Gang of Four' (Roy Jenkins, Shirley Williams, Bill Rogers and David Owen). The Liberal Democrats advocate policies based on freedom of the individual and support for the adoption of proportional representation at elections. However, in spite of its desire to 'break the mould of two-party politics' it remains a minority party which draws support from voters dissatisfied with the two major parties. This may explain why its most spectacular victories are in by-elections in single constituencies. Thus, the Liberal Democrats are a party of protest rather than a real alternative for government. The image of the party is moderate and appeals predominantly to middle-class people, often in rural areas. In 2006 they had 62 MPs, including their Scottish leader Menzies Campbell.

The other parties represented in parliament are the Ulster Unionists who largely campaign on the question of Northern Ireland remaining part of the UK, the Scottish Nationalist Party which demands independence for Scotland and Plaid Cymru which makes similar demands for Wales. There are all manner of small fringe parties who have no representation in parliament. The most prominent examples are the Socialist Workers Party (SWP) which advocates a socialist society on the principles of Marx and Trotsky, the Green Party which champions environmental policies and the National Front, which advocates 'Britain for the British'.

Such parties may be insignificant in terms of voting strength, but they can nevertheless influence policy. For example, the 'Monster Raving Looney Party' run by 'Screaming Lord Sutch', which advocated free ice cream, at a by-election in Bootle, Merseyside in 1990 actually gained more votes than the Conservative candidate. This exposed the political process to ridicule. Again in 2006, when the BNP leader Nick Griffin was acquitted of race-hate charges in the High Court, Gordon Brown immediately pledged to bring about a change in the law.

Voting behaviour

The most important part of political activity for the average person is voting at elections. The way people vote has become the subject of enormous discussion. Between 1951 and 1966 over 90 per cent of voters strongly identified with and voted for one of the two major political parties. Table 5.3 gives an indication of the two-party dominance in the House of Commons. The three major parties between them accounted for 90.66 per cent of the votes cast.

The 1992 election was the fourth consecutive victory of the Conservative Party. However, the Liberal Democrats who polled nearly 6 million votes were hampered by the 'first past the post' system. This system gives a seat to the candidate who wins the most votes in each constituency instead of giving a number of seats to each party based on their percentage of all votes, as is the practice in systems with proportional representation. Not surprisingly, the Liberal Democrats favour the adoption of a proportional representation system and the Conservatives are the strongest supporters of the present system.

It has long been claimed that in Britain class is closely related to voting choice at elections. At the 1964 general election, for example, there was a 2:1 chance in favour of a person from a manual working-class background voting Labour and a 4:1 chance in favour of a person from a non-manual middle-class background voting Conservative. The major anomaly for pollsters has been to explain why 33 per cent of the working class do not

TABLE 5.3   General elections

MPs	1992		1997		2001		2005	
	No.	%	No.	%	No.	%	No.	%
Conservative Party	336	42.8	165	31.4	166	31.7	198	32.3
Labour Party	271	35.2	419	44.3	412	40.6	356	35.3
Liberal Democrats	20	18.3	46	17.1	52	18.2	62	22.1
Welsh and Scottish Nationalist Parties	7	2.4	9	1.7	9	2.7	9	2.7
Northern Ireland Parties	17	2.3	18	1.8	18	2.8	17	2.8
Turnout		77.7		71.4		59.4		61.3
Overall majority	21 (Cons)		179 (Lab)		167 (Lab)		158 (Lab)	

Source: *The Times* (June 2005)

FIGURE 5.2   A pensioner expresses his doubts about Tony Blair's credibility

vote Labour. Indeed most Conservative election victories have included at least 30 per cent of votes from the working class. The classic example of the working-class Tory in popular culture used to be the character of Alf Garnett in the popular comedy series *Till Death Us Do Part*. He voted Conservative because he thought they were patriotic and well-born. He wanted to be ruled by what he saw as his betters not his equals. At the 1987 election, Neil Kinnock, the Labour Leader, was castigated by working-class Tory voters in opinion polls for 'not sounding or looking like a prime minister'.

However, many writers have suggested that class voting is in decline. The result is a growing apathy with both major parties, accompanied by an upsurge of support for centre and fringe parties. In the nine General Elections since 1970 the share of the votes of the two major parties has fallen from 92 per cent to 73 per cent. It seems more and more people are willing to vote for the Liberal Democrats, or the Scottish, Welsh and Irish nationalist parties. At by-elections, the share of the vote for numerous fringe candidates has grown enormously. The number of 'floating' voters who switch their votes to different parties at each election has also grown. Nowadays most people are less attached to any political party than ever before. In 1964, 48 per cent of voters said they identified strongly with one party. But in 2005 this figure had fallen to 21 per cent. This growing apathy may also explain why the number of non-voters has increased. This is especially true of the 18–24 age group. In the 1992 General Election less than 40 per cent of such people bothered to vote at all. After a century of around 75 per cent of the total electorate turning out to vote, in 2005 the figure was 61 per cent.

This apathy may also be linked to the fact that the public standing of politicians has never been lower. They have become figures of ridicule. On *Spitting Image*, a comedy show which uses caricatured puppets, leading politicians were portrayed in negative and often ludicrous terms. Indeed many politicians have complained about the images presented of them in the programme. Some of the most memorable images include: Kenneth Baker (Conservative), who was depicted as a slimy, crawling snail; Norman Tebbitt (Conservative) who was portrayed as a leather-clad cockney 'bovver boy'; Roy Hattersley (Labour) as a spluttering fool; David Steel (Liberal Democrat) as a fawning dwarf; Tony Blair (Labour) as an overgrown schoolboy; and Peter Mandelson (Labour) as a slimy half-worm, half-snake. This programme has served to hold up politicians as figures of ridicule rather than admired leaders.

Another reason for the low public standing of politicians has been the reporting of their sexual activities outside Parliament. A long list of political sex scandals has been eagerly discussed in the tabloid press during the early years of the twenty-first century. Indeed coping with a daily diet of new allegations of political sleaze has become a central aspect of British political life. The popular tabloid press has a mighty appetite for such stories. All the participants in such scandals are offered enormous sums of money by newspapers to 'tell all'. For example, when it emerged that the Liberal Democrat leader Paddy Ashdown had once had an affair with his secretary, he was dubbed by the *Sun* newspaper as 'PADDY PANTS-DOWN'. Similarly, the *News of the World* bought the story of an unemployed actress who had had a torrid affair with the Tory Cabinet Minister David Mellor. It was revealed that Mellor had made love to her wearing a Chelsea Football Club shirt. Not surprisingly, he was forced to resign. Norman Lamont, the Tory Chancellor of the Exchequer, created a scandal by renting out his basement flat to a 'bondage-queen'. The reporting of the sad and lonely death of a Tory MP who had asphyxiated while engaging in an obscure sexual activity which involved a plastic bag and an orange seemed to plunge the standing of politicians to an all-time low. New Labour's contributions have been supplied by David Blunkett, John Prescott, Ron Davies and others. This climate of sleaze, heated up by the tabloid press, has no doubt contributed to the growth of political apathy among voters.

It seems that even for those who do vote, single issues are playing a vital part in voting choice. During the 1992 election campaign, voters put the Labour Party well ahead on all the 'caring' issues such as social welfare, the NHS, education and unemployment. Yet the majority did not trust Labour on taxation and keeping inflation down and so voted for the Conservatives again. This suggests the key issue at the election was the 'pound in your pocket', which indicates that the likely victor at future elections will be the party which allows the consumer greater economic stability and more opportunity to consume. In practice, this is likely to mean the party which keeps tax down and inflation low. Thus, the slump in Labour's fortunes from 1979 to 1992 can be put down to offering policies which were unattractive to the consumer's needs. Hence, a user-friendly leader who deals in 'sound bite' politics, in the style of Tony Blair, may prove popular with these volatile single-issue voters who have ceased to be aligned to any party.

Another factor which was noticeable in the four election victories of the Conservatives from 1979 to 1992 was the growth of stark regional differences. At the 1983 general election, for instance, the Labour Party, excluding London, won only three seats south of the Midlands. Most of Labour's seats were won in big inner-city areas with high proportions of working-class people. At the 1992 election, the Conservative Party held less than ten seats in Scotland and Wales put together. In fact, the Labour vote in many of its working-class heartlands has increased from 1979 to 1992. In Wales, 69 per cent of the working class voted Labour. However, Labour has lost the support of the working class in the south of England: only 30 per cent of voters there chose them in 1992. Thus, the Conservative dominance at elections since 1979 has been in the expanding working-class Tory vote in the Midlands and the south of England. This strongly suggests Mrs Thatcher's hardcore support came from areas which were not part of industrial Britain in the first place. The yuppie life style of the 1980s was also largely based in the south of England. Hence, the class composition of the south has produced a situation in which, in three-cornered fights between the Conservatives, Labour and the Liberals, it was the Tories who were able to come out on top in 1979 and 1992. By adopting their commitment to consumerism, Labour's Blair was able to reverse those victories in 1997, 2001 and 2005.

Conclusion

For the reasons already cited in this chapter, pronouncing the death of class in British society does seem premature. The stark regional differences between the affluent south and the more impoverished north suggest that Thatcherism represented a rather narrow class appeal. In fact, Mrs Thatcher never won more than 44 per cent of the vote at any general election, while in 1950 the Labour Party polled 51 per cent. The link between class and politics has not been completely broken. It seems the overwhelming majority of manual workers still vote for the Labour Party. Yet this group, due to the decline of manufacturing industry, has fallen within the workforce. Class position still remains the best way of establishing long-term voting patterns. At the 1987 general election, 48 per cent of working-class voters chose the Labour Party, while only 15 per cent of salaried professionals did so. The self-employed are still the staunchest Conservative Party voters. The Liberal Democrats are most strongly supported by salaried professional and white-collar members of the middle class. What has probably happened is that the size of the classes has changed. This has resulted in the middle class growing in size in certain geographical locations in the Midlands and the south and the size of the working class has fallen due to the decline of heavy manu-facturing industry in the north, Scotland and Wales.

Finally, to trace a couple of intersections between this chapter and Chapters 3 and 6, we may ask the question: in which political party were women and members of ethnic minorities to be given the fairest chance of advancing themselves? One of the complaints made against Mrs Thatcher was that she 'never did anything for women'. This may well be so in terms of legislation, membership of her cabinets and furtherance of the interests of those traditional families where women did not work outside the home. Yet many others have argued that Thatcher certainly offered a powerful role model for women. In August 2004 there were 14 female Conservative MPs (out of 163) as opposed to 94 'Blair's Babes' (out of 407).

The Labour Party tried to increase the number of its prospective parliamentary candidates who were women. However, all-women short lists for seats at Westminster were judged to be illegal in 1995. The proportion of women and ethnic-minority MPs in different political parliamentary parties is extremely low. The earlier attempt to introduce 'black sections' in local constituencies was shelved after heated debate. However, individual MPs, including Diane Abbott, Bernie Grant, Paul Boateng and Keith Vaz have raised the profile of ethnic minorities in Britain. These four were all elected labour MPs in 1987 (the first black representatives in Parliament for sixty years) but it was not until 1992 that a Conservative MP, Nirj Deva, was elected from an ethnic minority.

For the future, perhaps the most significant aspect of contemporary politics is the fact that the next generation, Britain's young people, seem alienated not just from allegiance to individual parties but from the whole democratic process. Hence their cultural identity is formed far more by consumer considerations and single-issue politics than by a belief in the potential for party politics to bring about change for the better.

 ## Exercises

1 Offer a definition of upper, middle and working class.
2 To what extent do British people vote along class lines?
3 What is your understanding of the voting systems: 'first past the post' and 'proportional representation'? Which offers the better model on which to base a system for electing a government?
4 How have British class attitudes and styles changed since the 1950s?
5 Name some British people from a range of occupations. Can you place them in terms of class?

 ## Reading

Hutton, Will. *The State We're In* Jonathan Cape, 1995. Wide-ranging, accessible review of Britain's political economy in relation to its competitors.

Jenkins, Simon. *Thatcher and Sons* Allen Lane, 2006. Argues that Margaret Thatcher's reforms and philosophy still dominate politics.

Marr, Andrew. *Ruling Britannia* Michael Joseph, 1995. Popular account of recent British government.

Radice, Giles (ed.). *What Needs to Change* Harper Collins, 1995. Compendium of views of people in politics, social sciences and the arts, including film-maker David Puttnam and Prime Minister Tony Blair.

 ## Cultural examples

Films

Damage (1992) dir. Louis Malle. Cold film about a British politician's love affair and subsequent family crises (an updated fictional treatment of the theme found in *Scandal*, Michael Caton-Jones's 1989 film based on the early 1960s Profumo Affair).

Betrayal (1983) dir. David Jones. Harold Pinter's love-triangle play about British middle-class manners and infidelities.

The Ploughman's Lunch (1983) dir. Richard Eyre. Concentrates on a cynical reporter to give a critical analysis of British morals during the Falklands War.

Life is Sweet (1991) dir. Mike Leigh. Light, poignant comedy, typical of the director's films, about the British lower middle class and working class.

Books

John Braine, *Room at the Top* (1957). Portrays the social ascent of a young man whose education and marriage enable his upward mobility.

David Caute *Veronica; or, The Two Nations* (1989) Critique of Thatcherism taking its title from a novel by Disraeli.

David Hare, *The Secret Rapture* (1988). Allegorical play about morals, materialism and politics in 1980s Britain. Also made into a film in the early 1990s.

TV programmes

Yes, Minister. Comedy series about the opposition between government and the Civil Service in which an MP, seeking change and votes, and his Private Secretary, seeking continuity and bureaucracy, try to out-manoeuvre one another. Every episode illustrates the political, and supposedly British, art of compromise.

House of Cards. Fictional series about a manipulative Conservative MP seeking power whose skill at political evasion and double-dealing was compelling, and whose typical hypocritical expressions such as 'You might think that, but I couldn't possibly comment' and 'I have no ambitions in that direction' became catchphrases.

The New Statesman. Comedy series about an obnoxious but successful ultra right-wing Tory MP. Revived in 2006 as a play about a New Labour MP.

Have I Got News for You. Topical satire on the week's news with Ian Hislop and Paul Merton.

The Thick of It. Armando Iannucci's influential political satire, featuring thinly disguised Alistair Campbell.

Power of Nightmares. Adam Curtis's documentary series suggesting that politicians strive to be seen as visionaries rather than as managers.

Music

Jamie T. A. Wimbledon toff who brings middle-class pride to music.

The Streets. Birmingham white rapper Mike Skinner, who has been called 'Britain's true poet'.

Pulp *Different Class* (1995). Album of vignettes about class politics, drug culture and British social attitudes.

Blur *The Great Escape* (1995). A series of comments on British life from the opening track on 'Stereotypes', through a song on the 'Country House' to 'Top Man' (a clothes shop).

Billy Bragg *Workers' Playtime* (1988). Named after a post-war radio programme broadcast from a factory canteen, this, like all Bragg's albums, is a collection of love songs and political anthems such as 'Waiting for the Great Leap Forwards', 'Tender Comrade' and 'Rotting on Remand'.

The Clash *The Clash* (1977). Archetypal British punk featuring songs like 'White Riot', 'London's Burning', 'Career Opportunities', 'I'm So Bored with the USA' and 'Police and Thieves'.

 Websites

www.news.bbc.co.uk
    Contains in-depth coverage of contemporary issues with lots of links to background stories.

www.labour.org.uk www.libdems.org.uk
www.conservative-party.org.uk
    Web addresses of the main UK political parties.

www.statistics.gov.uk
    These deal with 13 areas of British life; economics, employment, etc.

www.direct.gov.uk/
    Portal for all government departments and publications.

Chapter 6

Ethnicity and language

Gerry Smyth

Timeline

1066	Norman invasion from northern France
1362	English legally recognised
1603	Death of Elizabeth I
1616	Death of Shakespeare
1707	Union of England and Scotland
1800	Union of Britain and Ireland
1870	Teaching Welsh banned
1947	Gaelic banned on Northern Irish road signs
1955	Churchill argued for slogan: 'Keep British White'
1958	'Race' riots in Notting Hill
1965	Race Relations Act
1968	'Troubles' start in Northern Ireland
1976	Commission for Racial Equality
1977	Advisory Council on Race Relations
1983	Black sections in Labour Party
1991	Census question on ethnicity
2003	Employment Equality (Religion or Belief) Regulations
2005	'Life in the United Kingdom' test introduced
2006	Racial and Religious Hatred Act

Introduction

ON THE ONE HAND, there is a drive, by for example Jean-Paul Nerrière in his 2004 book *Parlez Globish*, for the world to adopt a new language of 'Globish': a 1,500-word vocabulary of simple English, with basic syntax and punctuation, that can be used as a standarised lexicon for everyone, including Anglophones, to use at any international meeting. On the other hand, a survey carried out in a number of London schools as far back as 1980 found that only 15 per cent of pupils spoke what their teachers considered to be standard, or 'correct' English. The rest spoke twenty different varieties of English from the British Isles, forty-two dialects of overseas English, and fifty-eight different world languages. Another survey of the same period found that there were at least twelve languages in Britain that could claim over 100,000 speakers. To some people, such linguistic diversity might seem surprising in the homeland of arguably the world's most successful modern language. These statistics, however, are indicative of the multitude of ways used by the citizens of modern Britain to communicate, and the nation's linguistic diversity has only grown in succeeding decades.

These languages, moreover, are closely linked with the ways in which people perceive themselves and their role in British society. For although the United Kingdom is a state, many people within this state think about themselves, their families and their local communities in quite different ways. One way of describing these individuals and the groups to which they belong is in terms of 'ethnicity'. Ethnicity is a highly complex and contentious concept. For the purposes of this chapter however, it can be defined as the patterns of social behaviour, cultural values, and genealogical affiliations shared by certain individuals who come together to form a group within a larger population.

According to the 2001 census, the 58,789 million people in the UK included 4.6 million (7.9 per cent) from ethnic minorities (having risen from just over 3 million in the 1991 census). In terms of distribution, the largest ethnic-minority populations are found in London (45 per cent of total ethnic minorities) and the West Midlands (13 per cent), followed by the South East (8 per cent), the North West (8 per cent) and Yorkshire and Humber (7 per cent).

Additionally, the United Kingdom comprises four separate indigenous populations, one very large – English (approximately 49 million) – and three small – Scottish (5 million), Welsh (3 million), and Northern Irish (1.5 million). What all this means is that there are a large number of people in the United Kingdom – around 20 per cent (12 million people) of the total population – who do not have a straightforward relationship with the political state in which they live. In recent years, this problematic relationship between the state and its ethnic and regional minorities has become the subject of one of the most important debates in modern British life, and in this chapter I want to examine some of the practices, attitudes and strategies which have emerged around this debate.

Ethnic and regional identity can appear in many forms. Historians, sociologists and anthropologists have discovered, however, that one of the most important ways in which ethnic groups identify themselves is through language. Not only is language the principal conveyor of symbols, ideas and beliefs that are of importance to the ethnic group, very often the language becomes a powerful possession in itself, something to be protected and preserved as the main badge of ethnic identity. Much of the time then, the alternative allegiances which constitute ethnic identity emerge specifically as tensions about language and the social status and cultural possibilities of different accents, dialects and vocabularies.

The recognition of ethnic status has significant legal, educational and social implications. But ethnic status, going back to our definition, also has important sociological and psychological implications for the kind of person the individual understands him/herself to be – that is, for an individual's identity. The point of departure for what follows is that a significant part of our individual identity is constituted through language – the language the world uses to communicate with us, and the language we use to communicate with the world. Putting this all together, then, these issues of ethnicity, identity and language are going to be our main areas of focus in this chapter. Specifically, I want to examine three interrelated issues – the usage and status of:

1   'standard' and 'non-standard' forms of the English language and implications for English and British identity;
2   other indigenous British languages – Welsh, Scots and Gaelic – and the challenge to the domination of English;
3   non-English languages brought to Britain by migrants and other groups, such as Chinese and West Indian.

Varietie

In the nineteenth century, the notion of 'correct', 'good', or 'ı
became something of an obsession for many literary critics, phi
educationalists. The result of this anxiety was the invention of an ideaı ı
of the English language, covering aspects of grammar, vocabulary, pronunciation and so on, but also importantly linked to ways of acting, kinds
of belief and systems of value. Such an ideal was needed to support Britain's
self-image as a great industrial and imperial power, and to measure various
kinds of linguistic deviance. The fact that this ideal or 'standard' English
was an invention did not appear to worry those who used it to condemn
the linguistic 'errors' made by the vast majority of the British population. It
must have seemed strange to a person from Northumberland or Somerset
for example, regions with dialects evolved over 1,000 years and completely
immersed in local history and local geography, to be told that the way they
spoke was wrong – according to the arbitrary rules invented by certain
intellectuals and scholars! In the twenty-first century, it has been commonly
argued that in most social situations an upper-class accent is a disadvantage
and there are actually now speech coaches who will help 'posh' people lose
their accents, whereas thirty years ago, everyone else was trying to acquire
them. This has to be linked to the perception that class is nowadays more
about celebrity than breeding, especially as many of the prestigious events
on the social calendar, and the magazines that cover them, will now be
overrun with the famous as much as the aristocratic, the only connection
between the two groups being that both are comparatively rich. Voiceovers
for television advertisements in many ways provide a good indication of
how accents are perceived: Yorkshire accents (e.g. Sean Bean or Michael
Parkinson) are considered trustworthy; London accents are approachable
and savvy but neither regional or posh (e.g. Michael Caine or Bob Hoskyns),
Scottish accents (e.g. Sean Connery or Ewan MacGregor) are popular with
banks and other financial institutions who want a trustworthy and careful
image; Liverpool Scouse accents (e.g. the Beatles or Heidi in the Sugababes)
convey down-to-earth qualities and the Birmingham 'Brummie' accent is used
for comedic appeal (e.g. comedians Lenny Henry or Jasper Carrot); while
only advertisers aiming at exclusivity or irony use people with RP (received
pronunciation) or 'posh' accents (e.g. Joanna Lumley).

The question of the correct way to speak and to write English continued
to exercise a very great influence in British life throughout the twentieth
century. Many people even today adhere to the model of standard English
(or 'received pronunciation' as it is sometimes referred to) invented in the
nineteenth century, believing it to be the real or true English language, a fixed
linguistic structure against which deviations and mistakes can be measured.
These people remain anxious about what they consider to be falling

standards in spoken and written English, feeling that this is in some way related to Britain's wider economic, cultural and political status. Letters are written to the 'quality' newspapers (such as *The Times*, *Independent*, *Daily Telegraph*, and *Guardian*) and to the British Broadcasting Corporation (BBC), both radio and television, about bad practices in spoken and written English. In the early days of broadcasting, the 'BBC accent' was the hallmark of correct spoken English and newscasters are still seen as 'custodians' of the language. But in recent years this 'BBC accent', like its close relation 'the Queen's English', has in itself become a minority form; one of the few people likely to be heard speaking 'the Queen's English' is the Queen herself, in her Christmas Day speeches to the Commonwealth (and even she has been accused of loosening her speech in recent years). The clipped pronunciation and mannered voice of Prince Charles, as well as his constant use of the impersonal pronoun 'one' – as in 'one feels one's responsibilities' – is also somewhat of a throwback to an earlier stage in Britain's linguistic history. Although versions of the 'BBC accent' still exist – for example, in some sports commentary such as tennis, cricket, equestrian events, or in some arts programmes – it is now more likely to be used for satiric or ironic purposes. To an extent, this debate has been won by the pluralists, and been replaced by a new concern over written English. Here, rules and standards are far more deeply ingrained, but the need to write 'correct English' is coming increasingly under pressure as new technologies such as email and text messaging encourage compressed forms of expression. A growing informality is apparent, fuelled by the diversity of 'Englishes' among different ethnic and regional communities, despite concerns in some quarters that, for example, it is possible for a student to gain a first-class degree without being able to write grammatically correct English to the standards upheld by their parents' generation. The counter argument is that visual culture is succeeding a literary culture and that a 'post-literate' society will be a more rounded one in terms of its creative thinking: less hung up on words, more capable of thinking in terms of ideas and images, as Marshall McLuhan argued back in 1962 in *The Gutenberg Galaxy*.

Adequate command of English still constitutes a major part of modern British education, even for those who do not speak the language regularly at home or outside the classroom. One way in which the fixation with the language manifests itself is in the debates surrounding the educational significance of William Shakespeare. Of course, to anyone familiar with it, Shakespearean English can hardly be thought of as a viable means of communication in the twenty-first century. Nevertheless, Shakespearean language is felt by many to represent the pinnacle of British cultural achievement, and it is widely argued that in his poetry and plays Shakespeare captured the essence of English (though not British) identity. To those taking this line, it therefore appears obvious that young British people, of whatever ethnic

origin, should become familiar with Shakespeare's work so that [...]
appreciate the history, idiomatic language, and society of which they [...]
a part. Drawing on these opinions, a 'Shakespeare industry' has [...]
established, linked in many significant ways with other major ind[...]
such as publishing, leisure, tourism and heritage.

On the other hand, some people claim that Shakespeare's releva[...]
only historical, and that modern education should be dealing more with
students' contemporary values and beliefs, and society's modern cultural
forms. Both in terms of theme and language, it is also argued, Shakespeare
has limited significance for those from different ethnic backgrounds
possessing important cultural and linguistic traditions of their own (it is, for
example, widely questioned whether Shakespeare's works should remain
standard texts in British schools). The same could also be said of certain
sections of the indigenous British population which have traditionally been
excluded from the high cultural institutions where 'Shakespeare' has been
enshrined for so long. A Shakespeare scholar has also commented that
watching soap opera is more enjoyable for him than going to see Shakespeare; and one cultural critic has claimed that a television soap opera such
as *Coronation Street*, set in contemporary Manchester and detailing the
experiences of a community of working-class people was of far greater
interest and significance throughout Britain than anything by or about Shakespeare. This was because the themes, vocabulary and accents of *Coronation
Street* were closer to the language most British people experienced in their
daily lives. This is a contentious argument, as it might be seen to deny people
from working-class or ethnic backgrounds access to a valuable cultural
experience; on the other hand, it might explain why a poll to find 'The
Nation's Favourite Poem' resulted in a win for the almost equally traditional
but populist and accessible 'If' by Rudyard Kipling. The emphasis on regional
accents was underscored by the decision in 2001 of the French Government,
in an agreement with the BBC, to help French schoolchildren improve their
English by broadcasting programmes such as *Open All Hours* (set in the
north), *EastEnders* and *Only Fools and Horses* (both featuring cockney
accents and estuary English), in teacher training colleges and secondary
schools. The launch of the initiative, in a Paris School in September 2001,
was scheduled to coincide with the European Day of Languages.

Regional variations in accent, vocabulary and pronunciation, as
practised by the characters in *EastEnders* or *Coronation Street*, are of great
importance in British life, as well as having an important bearing on the
question of standard English. Some of the more easily distinguishable
accents are those of Cornwall, the West Midlands, Tyneside, Northern
Ireland and Clydeside, although to a sensitive ear, there are dozens of
separate regional accents in Britain, and hundreds of minor linguistic
peculiarities which set one region, one town, even one village, apart from

another. The city of Liverpool, for example, has a very strong and recognisable accent, known as 'Scouse', deriving from a mixture of Lancashire, Irish and Welsh influences, and those speaking with this accent are referred to as 'Scousers'. One version of 'Scouse' was brought to national and world attention by the success of the Beatles in the 1960s. The phrases, slang and inflections which characterised the speech of the Beatles however, were but one version of what is in fact a highly complex set of linguistic practices operating within the city of Liverpool.

One factor influencing all the varieties of English in contemporary Britain is the economic and cultural domination of the United States of America. Especially since the end of the Second World War, the issue of American influence on British life has been hotly debated. Some people fear that sharing a language with the most culturally successful nation on Earth will erode Britain's own linguistic identity and also accounts for Britons' woefully poor grasp of other European languages, while others argue that the global dominance of English ensures Britain's continuing cultural vitality. It does seem that through exposure to popular music, cinema and computer technology, British people are becoming more and more familiar with the various speech patterns of the US, even learning to differentiate between them (for example, Southern drawl, New York nasal, Californian rising intonation). Distinctive American rhythms, intonations and slang are becoming common throughout Britain, not only in pubs and clubs, but to an increasing extent also in more formal contexts such as education and the media. Much British popular music since the 1960s, for example, is heavily influenced by American styles. Against this, part of the attraction of groups such as Stereophonics (Wales), The Proclaimers (Scotland), The Divine Comedy (Northern Ireland) or Arctic Monkeys (Sheffield) is hearing the singers using their local accents. At the same time, it is clear that English, albeit American English, remains the dominant language of diplomacy and of popular culture, and it could be argued that this has given British people cultural and economic opportunities they might otherwise not have had.

All the issues raised in this section have important implications for the question of British identity. The ways in which the English language is used continue to be of great importance, for those who adhere to standard English as well as for those who accept and rejoice in the latest slang words and phrases. The number of official or authoritative bodies who accept that language is a constantly changing and vibrant part of culture is increasing. For example, dictionary compilers are more likely to include recent slang words than they used to be. The *New Compact Penguin English Dictionary* has entries for 'pants' (awful), 'manky' (dirty or rotten) and 'diss' (to show disrespect), but there are new words appearing in playgrounds all the time – such as 'bovvered' (don't care), 'iPad' (one-bed apartment) and 'moobs' (male breasts) in 2006. A 2001 survey of 7- to 14-year-olds listed scores of buzzwords, ranging from the familiar such as 'wicked', 'radical' and 'dingbat', to the less common, such as 'savage' or 'vicious' (for excellent), 'trev' (a designer-clothes wearer), 'minging' (ugly or disgusting) and 'talk to the hand' (because I'm not listening), which became the title of a popular book by Lynne Truss on modern rudeness four years later. Unsurprisingly, television shows provide many new catchphrases, from 'Bo Selecta' to 'Am I boverred?' (a British equivalent to 'Whatever' made nationally famous on *The Catherine Tate Show*). Other words, of course, fade out of fashion: only the over-30s would call anything 'brill', 'ace', 'fab' or 'naff'. Rhyming slang is also increasingly common in young street culture, though its connections with cockney are far off, and the emphasis is on using celebrities' names in a way that makes the commonplaces of everyday teenage life more interesting. Some examples are: 'Britney Spears' for beers, 'Wallace and Gromit' for vomit, and 'Brad Pitt' for shit.

The possibility of a single, ideal English language was always remote, both because of its artificiality and because of the active role played in cultural life by accent and regional variation. But such an ideal is becoming less and less viable, given both the speed with which language circulates in the technological age, and the number of British people for whom the English language is deeply problematical. With regard to this latter group, I now want to discuss those non-English languages which are, nevertheless, indigenous to the British Isles.

Gaelic, Scots, Welsh

Before modern technology made travel and the spread of information so much quicker, it was possible for people from different parts of the British Isles never to hear the English language spoken. From the influx of European invaders and migrants who began to come to the islands around 2,000 years ago, a great number of distinctive local dialects, as well as a smaller number of discrete languages, emerged. But as English evolved into the successful international language it is today, these other, mainly Celtic, languages tended to be marginalised. For many people, this predominance of the English language is a problem in that it deprives individuals and communities of a distinctive local cultural inheritance. Instead, it collapses all history and all possible experience into an homogenous yet spurious Britishness. A character of James Joyce's describes a conversation at his school in Ireland with his teacher, who is an Englishman:

> The language in which we are speaking is his before it is mine. How different are the words *home*, *Christ*, *ale*, *master*, on his lips and on mine! I cannot speak or write these words without

unrest of spirit. His language, so familiar and so foreign, will always be for me an acquired speech. I have not made or accepted its words. My voice holds them at bay. My soul frets in the shadow of his language.

> (James Joyce, *A Portrait of the Artist as a Young Man* [1916], Penguin 1977, p. 172)

For many minority language speakers, Joyce manages to capture in this passage the social and personal frustrations of being caught between a way of speaking which is specifically attuned to local experience and local history and an all too 'familiar', too dominant language such as English, in which they are expected to communicate.

Gaelic is the language of the Gaels, Celtic invaders from Europe who came to the British Isles in the second and third centuries before the beginning of the Christian Era. Gaelic rapidly became the principal language of Ireland, and later it was also widely spoken on the west coast of Scotland where many Irish Gaels emigrated in later years. (The census of 1991 showed that out of a Scottish population of 4.9 million, 1.4 per cent – about 70,000 people – spoke Gaelic in some form.) Gaelic remained the first language of Ireland until the middle of the nineteenth century, when the Great Famine (1845–8) decimated the population. Death, mass emigration and the association of Gaelic with poverty and backwardness combined to marginalise the language, so that by the time the southern part of Ireland gained partial independence from Britain in 1922, Gaelic was only spoken in small pockets (called Gaeltachts) in the north and the west of the island.

This marginalisation did not go unopposed, however. During the 1890s a cultural movement known as the Celtic Revival became very influential throughout the British Isles, and this movement was closely linked with the idea of political independence for Ireland. An important part of its programme was the restoration of Gaelic as the first language of Ireland. This was felt to be necessary because, going back to the introduction to this chapter, language was seen as the crucial element of a distinctive identity, and therefore it was not possible for Irish people to achieve real freedom if they continued to speak English.

In 2004, out of the Irish Republic's more than 4.3 million citizens, approximately 1.6 million people claimed a competence in Irish. North of the border, the city of Belfast has bilingual schools, a Gaelic newspaper (called *Lá* , meaning 'Day', which began publication in 1981), and a (very small) number of Gaelic radio and television programmes broadcast by the BBC and independent stations. While use of the language is now declining in the south, voluntary Irish classes flourish throughout Northern Ireland. All this activity is encouraging for Gaelic supporters, although whether the language can truly escape its sectarian heritage and help resolve the political divide in Northern Ireland remains a hotly debated question. The cause was boosted by The Gaelic Language Act 2005, which recognised Gaelic as an official language in Scotland.

One of the most interesting British languages, precisely because of the debate as to whether it is a distinct language or merely a dialect of English, is Scots. Scots is descended from the Northumbrian dialect of Old English, and, at one time, forms of the language existed in all the non-Gaelic regions of Scotland, including the remote Shetland and Orkney Islands. By the sixteenth century one particular form of Scots supported a highly developed cultural and political tradition entirely separate from England. At that point, however, a number of factors combined to force Scots into decline, the most important of which was the union of the Scottish and the English Crowns in 1603. After the abolition of the Scottish parliament in 1707, Scots, like Irish Gaelic in the nineteenth century, began to be rejected as a sign of cultural backwardness, and the ruling classes attempted to purge their speech of any remnants of the old Scots tongue. Despite interest in what came to be known as 'Lallans' (Scots for 'Lowlands', as opposed to the mostly Gaelic-speaking Highlands) among some poets and novelists of the eighteenth century, the language survived only among the peasantry and, after the industrialisation of Scotland during the nineteenth century, among the urban working class.

Scots was under constant threat throughout the twentieth century because, unlike Scottish Gaelic, most people do not regard it as a separate language but as a deformed version of English, or as an artificial dialect invented by the romantic writers of the eighteenth and nineteenth centuries. Both of these misconceptions add to the stereotypical notion of Scots that tends to be reproduced in the popular imagination as the 'sign' of Scottish-ness – words such as 'wee' (small), 'braw' (fine, good), 'lassie' (girl) and so on, as well as a heavily inflected accent when speaking English. Mr Scott, from the original *Star Trek* series (played by an American actor James Doohan), possesses probably the most famous, and least convincing, Scots accent in popular culture. One of the dominant Scots forces in British culture today is the resurgence of indie bands from 'north of the border': Glaswegian groups such as Belle and Sebastian, Franz Ferdinand, and The Fratellis have brought back the idea of Scottish pop which flourished in the early 1980s, when the Postcard record label launched groups such as Orange Juice and Aztec Camera. Welsh pop groups are also flourishing, from the 'idiosyncratic' Gorky's Zygotic Mynci to the mainstream Stereophonics and Manic Street Preachers, or the slightly less well known Super Furry Animals, who in 2000 released a CD in Welsh, *Mwng*, which quickly became the best-selling Welsh language album ever.

Scots received little institutional support in the 1990s. It was not recognised for census purposes, and given the success of Welsh and Scottish Gaelic in competing for what funds *are* available from central government and the BBC, this situation is unlikely to change in the near future. As with the Gaelic language in the Republic of Ireland, it is only among a relatively small number of historians, critics and writers that Scots is still valued; indeed, this intellectual support confers on Scots a sort of cult status, granting the language a vogue somewhat at odds with its shrinking working-class base. The familiar argument is that despite its impoverished condition, the language articulates a way of life, a way of thinking about the world, a way of being Scottish, that cannot be adequately expressed in English. This argument is rejected by many however, and not only by those 'Unionists' who maintain that Scotland's future depends on remaining an English-speaking region of the United Kingdom. The revival of Scots is also dismissed by many nationalists (seeking separate national sovereign status for Scotland) and devolutionists (seeking an autonomous Scottish parliament while remaining part of the United Kingdom) who feel that, given its history of strong cultural and political independence, Scotland does not need the support of an artificially resurrected language. This latter understanding of the relationship between language and national or ethnic identity is in marked contrast to the feelings underpinning the most successful non-English language of the British isles: Welsh.

Like Scotland, since the nineteenth century Wales has had great difficulty in asserting its cultural independence from England. Before the Education Act of 1870, which prohibited teachers from using Welsh as a medium of education, about nine out of ten people spoke the language. As with all the minority languages mentioned so far, however, Welsh became stigmatised as the language of the poor and the backward, and when the southern part of the country began to industrialise, it was only in rural areas such as the counties of Gwynedd and Dyfed in the north and west that Welsh managed to survive.

Since the 1960s, however, a new attitude towards the language has become evident. The rise of Welsh political nationalism has encouraged a pride in the Welsh language, and in recent years the ability to speak Welsh has become a highly prestigious attribute. This pride has manifested itself in many ways, but the basic impetus is towards the conversion of Wales into a fully bilingual country. The Welsh have in general been more successful than the Scottish in basing a nationality on cultural identity. The translation of the Bible into Welsh in 1588 gave a solid basis for the language, Welsh universities study the language and culture of the country, and official jobs may require applicants to be Welsh speakers.

Many people began in the 1960s by abandoning anglicised names in favour of Welsh ones, while for those who had not yet mastered the language, it was possible to assert a Welsh identity simply by using the heavily inflected Welsh accent. Once over the border, all road signs are now given first in Welsh and then in English; as are most job descriptions and the language has had great success at all levels of education. Welsh programmes represent well over 50 per cent of the country's radio and television output, and the success of the annual Eisteddfod festival adds to the sense of an autonomous nation supporting a distinctive national culture. Although the number of Welsh-speakers as a whole dropped from 19 per cent to 18.7 per cent between 1981 and 1991, the number of speakers aged between 3 and 15 rose from 17.7 per cent to 24.4 per cent, a real rise of 21,000, such that by 2001, 21 per cent of the population said they could speak Welsh. This augurs well for the future of the language, and is in marked contrast to Scottish Gaelic where the highest percentage of speakers are 65 years old and over. However, some Welsh nationalists argue that the success of the language has been achieved at the cost of a coherent political programme, and that central government support for various cultural initiatives does not represent a relinquishing of power, but merely a way of redistributing it.

We should remember that Welsh is reviving, not revived, and in the industrialised south, Swansea, Cardiff, Glamorgan and the Rhondda valley, where over half the population lives, Welsh is still to all intents and purposes a foreign language. Even so, the relative success of the language has been difficult for many English people to cope with. One recurring image is that

FIGURE 6.1 'Britain Visitor Centre' showcases the separate countries of the UK

of the English tourist feeling intimidated and offended by their exclusion from the Welsh conversations of local bilingual communities. Stories such as these reflect more, perhaps, on the insecurity of English people who hold an idea of Britishness specifically invented to incorporate the various identities of the British Isles under one, English-led, banner (controversy has been sparked by Parliament repeatedly appointing non-Welsh speaking Secretaries of State for Wales). For it hardly seems strange that Welsh people should wish to converse in their own language, nor that in the absence of political self-determination this should represent a valuable means of identification for them. In autumn 2001, it was suggested that an unofficial citizenship exam for English people planning to move to Wales would be a test of their ability to pronounce Llanfairpwllgwyngyllgogerychwyrndrobwllllantysiliogogogoch, the longest place name in the world after the Maori names of some towns in New Zealand. The town's county council clerk argued that newcomers needed to mix in with the community more, and that pronouncing the town's name correctly would be a good start, especially for people who had moved from England. Local people in fact, however, refer to the town as Llanfair PG, rather than calling it by its full name, which in English means 'The church of St Mary in the hollow of white hazel near the rapid whirlpool by the church of St Tysilio of the red cave'.

It may be that given time and the global domination of American English noted in the last section, Gaelic, Scots and Welsh will suffer the fate of other non-English languages of the British Isles such as Cornish (from Cornwall) and Manx (from the Isle of Man), ceasing to be living languages, preserved only in the artificial confines of the library and the university. Welsh appears to be in a reasonable state of health, but Gaelic and Scots must give cause for concern to their supporters and speakers. It might be wondered why, having been so neglected for so long, Britain's non-English languages have aroused so much interest in recent years. Certainly there has been concern about the fate of Gaelic, Scots and Welsh since the beginning of the twentieth century, but one could argue that it is only since Britain's non-indigenous ethnic minorities began to work for proper recognition of their distinctive cultural heritages that the islands' Celtic minorities have begun to see their languages in a new perspective. I will now turn to those non-indigenous languages.

New languages, new identities

Since the end of the Second World War (1945), immigration has become an issue of national importance for the economy but also of public and political concern in Britain. Not only that, but the very terms in which the question of immigration is considered are also highly charged. If you reread the previous two sentences, you will see that the words I have used at the beginning of this discussion of immigration and ethnicity are 'issue' 'concern' and 'question'; other terms invariably found when this subject is raised are 'problem', 'solution', 'answer', 'debate', etc. For many people, such language is itself part of the 'problem' in that it only allows immigration and ethnicity to be discussed as anomalies in an otherwise efficient system, anomalies that 'we' – that is, the established indigenous population of Britain – need to resolve. Being constituted a 'problem' or an 'issue' or a 'cause for concern' even before their arrival in the country has serious implications for the way in which ethnic communities perceive their relations with the state and with Britishness generally. More recently, political commentators have observed that, aside from cultural benefits, only by welcoming migrants will European countries be able to increase their long-term rate of growth and also pay for the pensions of those currently in work.

People have been migrating to and from Britain for centuries, and as long as this has been so, native and immigrant have been constantly reviewing their mutual relations. In 1596 the parliament of Queen Elizabeth I issued an edict limiting the number of black people entering England. This may be seen as the first of a large number of measures taken by British governments in an effort to define exactly what kinds of people have had the right to enter Britain and claim citizenship. The years since 1945 have seen numerous *Immigration* and *Citizenship* and *Race Relations Acts*, all in an effort to supply British identity with a legal and constitutional basis. Over this more recent period, two opposing attitudes appear to be at work. If, as some commentators suggest, increased population mobility is becoming a characteristic contemporary experience, then cultural and political systems which used to construe immigration and ethnicity as 'problems' may no longer be applicable. Such systems indeed, it is argued, were never acceptable in the first place. On the other hand, with the break-up of the Soviet Union, the re-unification of East and West Germany, and the growth of Europeanism, the issue of borders, national and ethnic identity has become very important throughout Europe. Britain, as we have already seen, has its own internal borders and identities, a situation that has led to its unique political constitution. The exact nature of Britishness however, has become even more complex in the decades since 1945 with the influx of a new range of ethnic identities, and the subsequent emergence of new ways of being British.

There have been well-established black, Chinese and Indian communities in Britain since the nineteenth century, especially in London and some of the bigger seaports such as Liverpool and Cardiff. The post-war period has seen the arrival of people from many geographical backgrounds – West Africa, the Caribbean, Hong Kong, India, Pakistan and so on, countries and regions known as the 'New Commonwealth' (as opposed to the 'Old Commonwealth' of Canada, Australia and New Zealand). Traditionally, the most positive response in mainstream Britain to immigration from the New Commonwealth has been mild interest in the possibility of viewing exotic cultures at close hand. Asians, for example, have been 'contained' by mainstream British culture in terms of the 'colourful' or 'alternative' practices – food, clothes, music, religion and philosophy – brought from their homelands.

The multitude of identities brought by immigrants from that part of Asia are frequently collapsed into one exotic 'brown' identity which can then be more easily accommodated by modern 'multicultural' Britain. The Indian restaurant and the Pakistani newsagent or corner shop are established parts of British life, and certain other stereotypical traits and practices – Yoga, the Sikh and Muslim turban, the raga (the distinctive pattern of Indian music), arranged marriages, as well as of course the 'strange' way of speaking English – have become representative of what to most people seems a tolerable degree of difference within a larger British identity. It is, however, decreasingly appropriate to speak of a homogenous British Asian experience. For example, those of Indian origin, according to government and independent statistics, are the most likely to vote, have considerable savings or achieve top exam results of all ethnic groups (including white), while Bangladeshis are the least likely.

FIGURE 6.2 People from numerous ethnic origins populate Britain

The identity of Indian and other people in Britain is complicated by a history of colonial relations, and this in its turn is linked with the other major form of response to modern immigration. Since the nineteenth century, certain theories regarding the relations between race, nation and culture have led to the development of ideas which cast immigration and ethnicity in a very negative light. Influenced by these ideas, much of the modern British response to immigration has been characterised by xenophobia and racism. Racism in modern Britain can take two forms. An older, biological racism tends to be linked with violence and aggression, as for example, during the 1960s and 1970s when extreme right-wing elements went on 'Paki-bashing' sprees, and even developed political organisations based on repatriation of immigrants. This form of racism is increasingly rare, although it would be a mistake to underestimate the capacity of certain outmoded 'scientific' discourses of race to feed the cycle of racial hatred inherited from earlier times, and racially motivated crimes are an occasional feature of news stories into the present.

The newer, cultural form of racism is more subtle. It claims that it is unfair to ask people from a particular background to accept the kind of changes in lifestyle necessary for them to become proper British citizens. For example, one former politician caused a controversy in the 1990s with his 'cricket test'; Lord Norman Tebbit argued that if people living permanently in Britain support other nations in sporting or other cultural events, then they have not sufficiently adapted themselves to British life, and cannot therefore legitimately be called British. Tebbit used the example of the way in which many black Britons support the West Indies cricket team, but the point was intended to apply to any instance of cultural 'treason'. Indeed, the issue of sporting affiliation has become even more heated since the publication of an article in a prestigious cricketing journal in 1995 which suggested that it would be a mistake to expect any 'ethnic' sportsperson selected to represent Britain, even if born here, to be as committed as a 'real' (that is, white) Briton. Racism has been on the decrease, however, over the last few decades and though there are sporadic flashpoints, Britain is becoming a more tolerant multicultural society with regard to simple perceptions based on skin colour, and one in which religion, especially the differences between the West and Islam, is affecting public debate more than ethnicity.

However, following high-profile investigations into racially motivated attacks, on Damilola Taylor and Stephen Lawrence for example, race relations in Britain reached what some considered a crisis in 2001, when several northern cities were hit by a spate of 'riots'. In Oldham in May, in Burnley in June, and in Bradford in July, clashes between whites and blacks resulted in considerable damage and national fears about Britain's future as a multi-ethnic community. Reasons for the violent outbursts are open to discussion, but facts suggest some of the inequalities behind them: for example, in Oldham, the infant mortality rate among Muslims was three times higher than that of whites, while life expectancy was lower; adult health was worse and Muslims in the town were three times more likely to be unemployed. Government statistics reported that about 50,000 people in the town experienced some of the worst social conditions in the country, and the cotton mills which brought Pakistanis and Bangladeshis to Oldham in the 1950s to 1970s closed down long ago. In Oldham, a temporary eight-foot-high metal mesh fence was erected in the Hathershaw district, and while the Home Secretary said there would be no official Belfast-style ring-fencing, some white and Asian communities in the town asked for more 'peace barriers'.

Questions of citizenship and acculturation have remained high on the government agenda. As a result of a 2003 review led by Sir Bernard Crick and acted upon by the Home Secretary, a 'Life in the United Kingdom' test was introduced in November 2005 for people seeking indefinite leave to remain in Britain and in April 2007 for those seeking naturalisation as a British citizen and rights of settlement. The computer-based test fulfils requirements for English-language knowledge as well as cultural under-standing through its menu of twenty-four multiple-choice questions based on the book *Life in the United Kingdom: A Journey to Citizenship*. The book was criticised on first release in 2004 for being almost exclusively England-focused and for having several historical inaccuracies (such as leaving out Italy in the list of founding members of the EU). A new corrected edition had to be issued in 2007 – the 300th anniversary of Britain's founding in the Act of Union.

It does seem clear that Britain's ethnic minorities do not have a straightforward relationship with the state. People from the Commonwealth coming to live in Britain have as a rule identified with it as the 'mother country', and most have sought to become good citizens. Yet, the uncertainty of status, the petty forms of racism invariably experienced, as well as the very act of displacement from familiar places and practices, means that individuals may wish to preserve, and indeed emphasise, their ethnic identity. Of course, not all ethnic minorities will understand their relation-ship with the host country and the English language in the same way. Each community brings its own assumptions and aspirations, its own cultural values and beliefs, to the relationship with British identity. When one con-siders that there are many such ethnic communities in Britain, all experienc-ing different levels of assimilation and alienation; and when one further considers that different generations will not engage with the available identities in the same ways, then one may begin to appreciate that the question of what is and is not 'British' has become extremely complex in recent years. It now appears, in fact, that the practices, attitudes, beliefs and values that come together to form any identity are enmeshed in an intricate web of similarities and differences, and this web covers every area of modern British life – religion, politics, work, leisure, culture and education. Nowhere can this complicated situation be seen more clearly than through the subject upon which we have been focusing throughout this chapter – language.

Many British people do not use English as a first language, but speak instead the language of their home country, or of their parents' home country. Chinese people living in Britain, for example, have not traditionally placed a high priority on integration into the host community. In a city such as Liverpool, which has the oldest and one of the largest Chinese populations in the country (11 per cent of Chinese live in the North West region), it is clear that Chinese people make less use of the English language than the city's other ethnic minorities. There are a number of reasons why this might be; the extreme difference between the Chinese and English languages; the hope of many Chinese people eventually to move back to their native country; the wish to preserve a valued cultural heritage; the unwillingness to 'lose face' by speaking English badly. Whatever the reasons, the older Chinese population of Liverpool have maintained a low profile in the social and economic life of the city and as a consequence a high proportion of the community still speak very little English. Chinese children on the other hand, whether immigrants or born in the city, learn to speak the language of their parents (usually Mandarin or Cantonese) at home, but have to learn English for school and for their other interests outside the community. This bilingualism can influence the ways in which the younger Chinese population understand their status in the contemporary life of Liverpool. Familiar both with the traditions of their parents and with the facts of modern British life, the younger people appear to possess greater confidence than their parents and grandparents, and are not afraid of raising the profile of their community. The Chinese New Year has become a major event in the social and cultural life of Liverpool and street names in the area known as 'Chinatown' are given in English and Chinese. At the same time, these young Chinese people have problems that are different from the ones faced by their parents and different again from the ones faced by the city's other ethnic minorities. Bilingualism is just as likely to bring a sense of being marooned between identities as it is confidence. Third-generation Chinese, having different familial, religious and cultural values, will accept (or deny) their British identity differently to third-generation West Indians, or Indians, or Irish people. In fact, generalising about such relatively small populations can be dangerous, emphasising once more the political as well as social complexity of issues of ethnicity and language.

One of the most interesting examples of the complexity of modern British ethnicity is illustrated in the language brought by migrants from the Caribbean. People from the West Indies – mostly Jamaica, but also Trinidad, Guyana, Barbados, the Windward and Leeward Islands – were actively recruited for the British labour market in the years after the war when business was beginning to recover and unemployment was low. When these people came to Britain they brought with them their cultural traditions, the most obvious and important one being their language. But what was this language?

Standard English is the official language of Jamaica and many of the other West Indian islands. But most West Indians speak a version of 'Jamaican Creole', a language developed from the slave culture of the eighteenth and nineteenth centuries. Members of many West African tribes were brought over to the West Indies, and they spoke different languages, so to communicate among themselves they developed a form of language known as 'pidgin'. Pidgin drew on the language of the slave-masters – English – but reworked it using the linguistic forms of the numerous West African languages. And this language is basically the same one that has become known as Jamaican Creole (a 'creole' is a 'pidgin' dialect that has become a standard language for a particular community).

Many people would not consider Jamaican Creole to be a distinct language in itself, but merely an exotic form of standard English. This is certainly true at one level, yet according to linguists and anthropologists, it is possible for West Indian people to derive 90 per cent of their vocabulary from English and still speak a language that is not English. This is because language involves much more than words. Language involves complex physical and mental strategies, verbal styles and techniques, narrative genres and traditions, tones of voice, turn-taking protocols, speech rhythms and a hundred other things, some of them immensely subtle. As a gesture towards this subtlety, consider this short passage from a poem called 'I trod', written by the black British writer Benjamin Zephaniah and published in 1985:

> I trod over de mountain
> I trod over de sea
> one ting I would like to see is
> up pressed people free
> I trod wid I eye peeled . . .
>
> (Benjamin Zephaniah, *The Dread Affair* ,
> Arena 1985, p. 86. Reproduced courtesy of
> The Hutchinson Publishing Group)

This example is interesting in a number of ways. The theme, first of all, is one that is very significant in Caribbean history and one that emerges in much black British culture – the search for freedom. The poet uses the device of a physical journey over the landscape to represent the quest for a means to remove the spiritual and political scars of slavery. This theme is supported by the language of the poem, in which there is an attempt to reproduce the accents and pronunciations of Jamaican Creole – 'the' becomes 'de', 'thing' becomes 'ting', 'with' becomes 'wid'. Instead of being 'oppressed', these people are 'up pressed', a 'neologism' (a new word invented by the writer) that suggests both the pressure coming down on the people from above, and the people's determination to resist that pressure. This reworking of the language is also a way of linking past and present, as the refusal of standard English is part of the process whereby black British people resist their 'enslavement' in contemporary Britain. In danger of becoming part of a permanent black British underclass and thereby repeating the cycle of slavery and mastery, Zephaniah celebrates his West Indian identity by emphasising his distinctive speech patterns and rhythms in the face of Anglo-Saxon cultural domination.

The analysis should not stop here, however. The phrase 'I eye' is not typical of Jamaican Creole (in which it would be 'me eye'), but derives from the discourse of Rastafarianism. This religion, which encompasses both a spiritual and a socio-political outlook and which is associated with certain cultural practices such as reggae music, marijuana and dreadlocks (a hair style), originated in Jamaica and has in recent years become one of the dominant images of West Indian identity. Rastafarians reject words such as 'me', 'my' and 'we' in favour of a single word ('I') which celebrates the unique identity of the individual speaker and his/her unique relationship with Jah (the Rastafarian notion of God). At the same time, Rastafarianism is far from dominant among Britain's West Indian population which, typically of the wider British situation with regard to religion, encompasses a range of Christian, Islamic and atheistic positions. In these few lines, therefore, the poet can be seen as identifying with a very specific group. Analysis of the poem also shows the complex connections between contemporary British society, Caribbean history, and a particular religious system.

Two points should be noted. The first is that even from the fairly sketchy reading provided here, it is possible to appreciate that Zephaniah's position is not *typical* of black Britishness, itself a contentious term, but shows instead the diversity of language and identity available to a British person of West Indian ethnicity. The second point is that Jamaican Creole, if not an *actual* separate language, certainly operates as a separate language for those members of the West Indian community who speak it to signal their lack of identity with dominant British culture. If Jamaican Creole is at one end of the spectrum, and standard English is at the other, then a person born in Britain of West Indian parents has potential access to all the variations and nuances of language in between. How the individual from an ethnic community speaks will depend upon that highly complex cultural web mentioned earlier, incorporating different backgrounds, different generations, different levels of assimilation, different desires.

Like all the other languages and dialects mentioned in this chapter, Jamaican Creole has attracted a number of stereotypical images in modern British culture. The West Indian cricket team (known as 'The Windies') has been a Caribbean cultural image with a high profile in Britain. Their extended superiority over the 'English' team in the twentieth century (which over the years has included 'naturalised' players from all over the Commonwealth, as well as from Scotland and Wales) was, as previously mentioned, a source of pleasure to many black Britons and of much resentment to many 'traditional' Britons. On the other hand, in 1999 the English cricket team gained its first captain born in India, Nasser Hussain, and in 2006 one of the heroes of the English team was Mudhsuden Singh 'Monty' Panesar (born in Luton to Indian Punjabi parents), of whom it was possible to download a mask to wear during the Ashes series in and against Australia. Interestingly, the nickname 'Monty' would be familiar to older Britons as that of Field Marshal Montgomery, the 'desert rat' hero of Britain's fight against Rommel in the Second World War.

Other images and role models have helped to reveal the complexities involved in ethnic identity. The Notting Hill street carnival around Ladbroke Grove in London, which began as a local celebration of West Indian culture, is now the biggest event of its kind in Europe, attracting an average of a million people each year (twice the number of black Caribbeans in Britain in 2001). This cultural festival has in the past seen clashes between black Britons, organised racists and the Metropolitan Police, but more recently it has been peaceful and hugely successful, attracting people from all over the country and indeed the world, with myriad multicoloured floats participating in the procession around the three-mile route coming from as far afield as South Africa and Australia. Likewise, the television programme *Desmonds*, about a barber shop owned by a West Indian family, relied for much of its comic effect on the differences in perception between the older generation, born in the Caribbean and speaking variations of Jamaican Creole, and the children, born in London and speaking English with a typical London accent, who are now targeted by new radio stations such as Choice FM and the BBC's 1Xtra black music channel. Both the street carnival and the programmes such as *Desmonds* (or a film such as *East is East*) confront the confusion which arises from the wide range of identities available; both attempt to offer positive, enabling options rather than insisting on a final decision for or against Britishness.

The same can be said of the popular television series *Goodness Gracious Me* which parodied cultural stereotypes of the British, Indians, and particularly Indians in Britain. The show, a comedy featuring four British

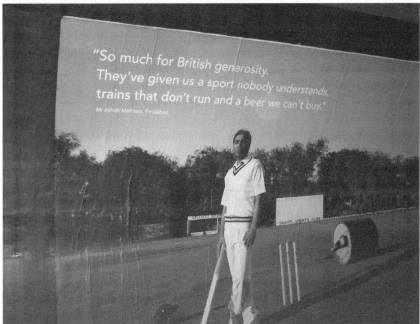

"So much for British generosity.
They've given us a sport nobody understands,
trains that don't run and a beer we can't buy."

Mr Ashish Malhotra, Faridabad

FIGURE 6.3 (a) and (b) Cricket, an archetypically British game, now dominated by Commonwealth teams

FIGURE 6.4   A wedding car (awaiting the newly-weds) outside a Gujarati Hindu temple in Preston

Asian actors, often reversed familiar scenarios: celebrated sketches feature a group of rude and loud Indians going for an 'English', and a party of Indian tourists coming to London for its spiritualism and simple, exotic way of life. Since *Goodness Gracious Me* the BBC have broadcast the Asian radio soap, *Silver Street*, and made the TV drama *Life isn't all Ha Ha Hee Hee*, contributing to the prize of 'Media Organisation of the Year' in the 2005 Race in the Media awards, but it remains true that the Corporation does not have African-Caribbean equivalents to these Asian programmes. Equally important to media representations are steps being made in the professions and in sport, but progress is slow and there are, for example, no British Asian footballers in the Premiership and the Conservative Party has yet to get its first female ethnic-minority MP even though Labour's first, Dianne Abbot, was elected twenty years ago in 1987 (there are, at the time of writing, fifteen ethnic-minority MPs).

Conclusion

What we have seen then, is that regional accents, as well as dialects and languages such as Gaelic, Scots and Welsh, challenge the apparent homogeneity of the English language (and the British identity which it supports) from well-established positions within the state. Further, we have seen that although sharing some of the same concerns and strategies, ethnic groups from Asia, from the Caribbean and from other parts of the world pose a different kind of challenge to British identity. All the issues examined in this chapter have important implications for British identity, and they impact in significant ways throughout the cultural and political life of the country. By way of conclusion, I want to demonstrate this by looking briefly at three areas which are of great importance to British people of whatever background or allegiance – popular music, work and sport. These areas are examined in greater detail in other parts of this book, but here I wish to focus upon them specifically in relation to the issues of ethnicity and language which have been our concern in this chapter.

Music is one of the principal ways in which ethnic identity is manifested. Ireland, for example, has a vibrant folk-music culture, encompassing strong traditional elements as well as an avant-garde interested in experiment and innovation. For Irish people living in Britain, or for British people wishing to identify with what they consider to be an 'Irish' way of life, folk music offers a readily accessible means of ethnic identification. In the absence of a Gaelic language, certain distinctive sounds and rhythms come to be associated with Ireland and Irishness, and these effects are invariably reproduced whenever Irish identity is invoked. This close link between identity and cultural practice is however, always liable to stereotyping, as we have noted with much of the material mentioned so far; the same sounds and rhythms that produce a positive identification for some will suggest a whole range of negative, comic, racist images for others.

Folk music is also very popular and active in Scotland and Wales, where it fulfils slightly different functions while nevertheless continuing to serve as a badge of cultural heritage, such that a National Folk Festival was inaugurated in Scotland in 2002. The English folk scene, on the other hand, although widespread and successful, tends to attract a more specialist audience, and the music does not play the part in national life that it does in the Celtic countries. One possible reason for this is that during the period of the rejuvenation of Celtic folk music – roughly since the 1960s – English folk has had to compete with another kind of music in which England has been consistently successful – rock 'n' roll. This form of popular music developed in the US in the 1950s, and once again, the fact that the vast majority of songs were in the English language meant that young British people had an advantage when it came to producing rock 'n' roll music of their own. There is a widespread belief among both English and non-English speakers in fact, that effective rock 'n' roll, unlike contemporary dance music, can only be produced through the medium of the English/American language. For example, many of the entries for the Eurovision Song Contest – an annual event attracting huge television audiences across Europe but nevertheless evoking much derision and amusement among 'genuine' rock musicians – are now in English, a trend started by the Swedish group Abba in the 1970s. It is certainly true to say that since the 1960s, British rock musicians have been responsible for some of the most interesting and successful innovations in the genre, though the fragmentation of popular music into niche styles and fusions has meant that 'rock' has developed a somewhat antiquated image and older genres have begun to make the charts again, albeit in modern forms: jazz (Jamie Cullum, Amy Winehouse), soul (Joss Stone) and folk (KT Tunstall, who headlined Edinburgh's Hogmanay Celebration in 2006).

Despite legal and voluntary moves towards 'equal opportunities' for all, certain kinds of employment in modern Britain tend to attract certain kinds of people speaking in particular ways. At one level, this is explicable with reference to social class and gender. At another level, however, the way one speaks and the ethnic background with which one identifies have always played a major part in the kinds of work one can expect to find (or not find) in Britain. Certain associations between ethnicity and employment – the Chinese laundry or (food) take-away, the Indian restaurant, the Irish 'navvy' (i.e. building labourer), etc. – have in some cases become so established in popular culture that it can be difficult for individuals from these ethnic communities either to imagine or to be accepted in different employment contexts. Much contemporary popular culture in fact, turns on the comic exploitation, or (more subtly) the dramatic refutation of these stereotypes. The very currency of these images, however, or the desired 'surprise' effect when they are shown to be untrue, points to the fact that most British people still accept them as having some basis in reality, and they apply also to newer migrant populations from the EU, such as the stereotypes of Polish builders and Czech nannies.

A typical example of ethnic employment stereotyping is the association of West Indians with the rail system. Many of the Caribbean people who came to Britain in the 1950s and 1960s were invited specifically to work for British Rail, and this remains an option for second- and third-generation West Indians. At the same time, black Britons are under-represented in almost every other area of employment and especially in the professional sector – medicine, higher education, law, the media and so on. Those who have made the breakthrough into higher paid, more prestigious jobs, tend to be haunted by the ambiguities of 'tokenism' and 'positive discrimination' – that is, the racist accusation that they have been selected especially to give the impression of equality of opportunity rather than on personal merit.

Whereas Welsh, Scottish and Irish accents appear to be acceptable as indicators of certain kinds of 'natural' ethnic qualities, it is very rare to hear a lawyer or a politician or a media broadcaster speaking Jamaican Creole. This is a result, as already indicated, of institutional pressure certainly, but also it seems, of personal choice. Black British professionals tend as a rule to speak a version of standard English, apparently because they (or their parents, if it is the language of the home and family) have decided that this is more suitable to their professional status.

One area in which black Britons have made a major contribution to national life in recent years is sport. Indeed in some sports, such as athletics, boxing and soccer, people of Afro-Caribbean ethnicity far outstrip their level as a percentage of the population. The success of people of West Indian origin in representing Britain in sport has generally not been equalled by other minority ethnic communities – Indian, Chinese, etc. – and the reasons for this are not clear. However, while some regard the success of black athletes as a positive thing – the full identification of people of Afro-Caribbean origin with Britain – others see it as a sign of the lack of opportunity for black Britons in other areas of society, as a way of diverting dangerous social and political tensions into harmless leisure activity and as a way of consolidating racist myths about the physical prowess of black people, as opposed to the supposed mental superiority of Caucasians.

While sport still does much to concentrate national and ethnic identity, the cultural ambiguities upon which ethnicity relies can help to expose the narrowness of traditional sporting affiliation. Again, Ireland is an interesting case in point. The soccer team representing the Republic of Ireland has had great success in recent years. Many of the players representing the country at international level were in fact born in Britain, but claim Irish citizenship through their immigrant parents or grandparents. A high percentage of these sportsmen, in fact, are of mixed-race origin, possessing English, Scottish and Caribbean ties as well as Irish. This phenomenon has extended, in a highly popular and accessible way, the possible range of Irish identity, no longer restricted to the 3.5 million who live in the Republic itself, but incorporating the huge number of people throughout the world – more than 70 million according to some estimates – who identify to some degree with Irishness.

Finishing a chapter on British identity with an example from a non-British country nicely captures the complexity of the issues we have been discussing here. The ethnic, racial and linguistic factors operating in modern British society make for a highly sensitive, highly nuanced set of possibilities, in which identity is under constant pressure, not only from the society in which one lives, but also from the person one believes oneself to be.

Exercises

1 Choose a particular regional accent and try to identify some of the stereotypical characteristics that are associated with it. What are the principal differences between British English and American English – vocabulary, grammar, intonation? List some examples.

2 Why do some British people insist on speaking minor languages and dialects, even when they are bilingual? Try to identify some words or phrases from Scots, Welsh, and Gaelic that have entered into the English language and are used regularly in Britain today.

3 What special 'problems' are faced by minority ethnic communities in Britain? What other factors influence young British people from minority ethnic backgrounds?

4 Try to obtain a current listing of the British Pop Charts. How many of the singers/groups are British? How many are American, or some other nationality? How many are black?

5 Compose a sentence defining exactly what you understand by the phrase 'equal opportunity'.

6 What is cockney rhyming slang and do you know any examples? Can you think of any other similar cases of communities constituted through language, speech or word-play?

7 It was mentioned above that Kipling's 'If' was voted the nation's favourite poem in Britain, following a poll by 'The Bookworm' to celebrate National Poetry Day in 1995. Looking at the language and sentiment of the poem, easily found online, what do you think it says about dominant national characteristics that this verse should be the best loved of all?

 Reading

Buonfino, Alessandra and Geoff Mulgan (eds). *Porcupines in Winter: The Pleasures and Pains of Living Together in Modern Britain* The Young Foundation, 2006. Contemporary portraits of places and people, from Polish migrants to Jamaican transnational families.

Crick, Bernard. *Life in the United Kingdom: A Journey to Citizenship* The Stationery Office, 2004 (revised 2007).

Foster, Roy. *Paddy and Mr Punch: Connections in Irish and English History* Allen Lane, 1993. Series of essays exploring the historical relations between Ireland and England in a scholarly yet readable way.

Gilroy, Paul. *There Ain't No Black in the Union Jack: The Cultural Politics of Race and Nation* Hutchinson, 1987. Influential analysis of race relations in contemporary Britain.

Hughes, Arthur *et al. English Accents and Dialects* Hodder Arnold, 2005. An introduction to social and regional varieties of English in the British Isles.

Phillips, Trevor and Mike Windrush. *The Irresistible Rise of Multi-racial Britain* Harper Collins, 1999. The story of British Caribbean migration.

Sutcliffe, David. *British Black English* Blackwell, 1982. Very accessible account of the varieties of language spoken by Britain's West Indian population. Includes examples and glossaries.

Winder, Robert. *Bloody Foreigners* Abacus, 2005. The long view of migration to Britain.

Cultural examples

Films

Brick Lane (2007) dir. Sarah Gavron. Film version of Monica Ali's novel about a Bangladeshi woman who arrives in London's East End in the 1980s.

Goodbye Charlie Bright (2001) dir. Nick Love. Bittersweet film about five boys growing up on a South London council estate one summer.

Trainspotting (1996) dir. Danny Boyle. Film version of Irvine Welsh's powerful drug-focused and anti-materialist novel of Scottish outsiders.

Twin Town (1996) dir. Kevin Allen. Swansea-set tale of two brothers, starring Rhys Ifans. Sometimes called the Welsh *Trainspotting*.

East is East (1999) dir. Darren O'Donnell. Comedy about cultural differences focused on an Anglo-Asian family, with a white mother, growing up in Lancashire with a stern traditionalist Muslim father.

The Crying Game (1992) dir. Neil Jordan. An exploration of national, political and sexual identity in Ireland and Britain.

Books

Lynne Truss, *Eats, Shoots and Leaves* (2003). Unexpected bestseller on the importance of grammar and punctuation.

Nirpal Singh Dhaliwal's, *Tourism* (2006). London Sikh slacker's life and thoughts in the summer of 2002.

Andrea Levy, *Small Island* (2004). Post-war race relations and themes of empire, migration and prejudice are woven together in a prize-winning story of a white Londoner who takes in black lodgers.

Niall Griffiths, *Sheepshagger* (2001). Acclaimed novel written in rough, native prose of a boy growing up in the Welsh valleys, detailing the highs and lows of contemporary life.

Andrew O'Hagan, *Our Fathers* (1999). Old and new Scotland collide in this novel of social injustice and human spirit.

James Joyce, *A Portrait of the Artist as a Young Man* (1916). Classic exploration of the tensions between family, nation, religion and art.

Hugh MacDiarmid, *A Drunk Man Looks at the Thistle* (1926). A poetic plea for a modern Scots language to support a modern Scottish identity.

TV and radio stations

Zee TV. The first UK television channel specifically for the Asian community. Launched in 1995 with a mix of Bollywood films, game shows, music and drama, it is the most popular channel for UK Asians.

Radio: BBC Asian Network. Can be found at www.bbc.co.uk/asiannetwork/index. shtml?logo.

S4C. Welsh language television station: www.s4c.co.uk/e_index.html.

African Movie Network. African Movie Channel shows movies from 'Nollywood (the hugely popular Nigerian motion picture industry, and the third largest in the world), and other major African film production houses.' www.homechoice. co.uk/tv/african.html.

Music

Apache. Indian singer whose name puns on the native North American tribe of 'Indians'.

Bob Marley. West Indian musician who brought reggae to a worldwide audience, now succeeded by his children Ziggy and Damian.

RunRig. Scottish folk-rock group whose set includes many songs in Gaelic.

Clannad. Irish group crossing folk and popular divide, singing many songs in Gaelic and Breton, the Celtic language of Brittany in northern France.

Roots Manuva. Innovative hip hop expressing the cultural mix of twenty-first century London.

Websites

www.everygeneration.co.uk/
Site aimed at celebrating the black community through history, family genealogy and heritage.

www.100greatblackbritons.com/
Biographies and more of the winners in a poll of Britain's top black figures.

www.askoxford.com
Guide to English usages, grammar and expressions.

http://jewish.co.uk/
Guide to Jewish culture and activities in the UK.

www.angelfire.com/ga/isbglasgow/
Website for the Islamic Society of Britain. Good links page.

www.scit.wlv.ac.uk/~jphb/american.html
Differences between UK and US English.

www.hecall.qub.ac.uk/studying/ukirelan.html
Website devoted to the languages of the UK, including Welsh, Cornish, Manx and Scottish Gaelic and Irish.

Religion and heritage

Edmund Cusick

chapter 7

Timeline

1532	Formation of Church of England
1580	Formation of Congregationalists
1652	Formation of Quakers
1653	Formation of Methodists
1760	Board of Deputies of British Jews
1774	First Unitarian Chapel in London
1833	John Keble: Oxford Movement
1843	The Free Church splits from Church of Scotland
1850s	Broad Church formed
1880s	Christian Socialism
1942	British Council of Churches (all non-Roman Catholic)
1948	World Council of Churches
1972	United Reformed Church (Congregational and Presbyterian)
1978	The London Mosque, Regent's Park
1980	Modern English Church of England Service
1988	Lord Chancellor censured by Free Church for attending Roman Catholic funerals
1994	First Church of England woman priest
1995	Hindu Temple, Neasden Sheffield rave services condemned
2001	Archbishop Carey: 'Tacit atheism prevails'
2006	First black Anglican Archbishop John Sentamu

Introduction

THE TIMELINE OPPOSITE PROVIDES a quick snapshot of key religious movements, milestones and changes in the UK over the last 500 years. Most will be touched upon in this chapter, which will be looking at the importance of public and private religion in the lives of British people and considering the role that notions of 'heritage' have come to play in ideas of national identity in recent years.

A peculiarly British phenomenon is the presence of *established* churches such as the Church of England. These churches have an official constitutional status within the legal and political framework of Britain, and the Christian religion is to some degree woven into every level of British life: government, education, architecture, the arts, broadcasting and many other areas. In Northern Ireland, religion has the extra political significance of marking the line between Catholic and Protestant paramilitary factions. At a personal level, Christianity may have been encountered in the form of prayers or hymns that were taught at school, or personal acquaintance with a local vicar or a chaplain at a hospital. Philip Larkin, in his poem 'Church Going' is not himself a believer, but accepts that there is a role for churches with their 'tense, musty, unignorable silence'. Most British people feel in some way reassured by the background presence of this religion, even if they do not wish to become actively involved with it. Only in 2001 was a voluntary question on religious affiliation included for the first time on the census form. Seventy-two per cent of respondents described themselves as Christians.

Yet, despite the official uniformity provided by an established church, and the shared heritage of, for example, religious music and the Lord's Prayer ('Our father, Which art in Heaven'), the religious experiences available in contemporary Britain form a complex and remarkably varied picture. The fact that Britain is commonly assumed to be a Christian country (and a majority of people feel themselves to be 'Christian' in terms of their general principles) is undermined by a number of factors: the rapidly declining levels of people's involvement with the churches to which they nominally belong; the sharp decline in the value which young people attach to Christianity; the growth of a range of New Age religious practices; and the presence of large

Hindu, Sikh and Muslim communities as a result of post-war immigration. All of these changes result in considerable differences between the religious identity of the segments of society and of different generations.

One way in which this 'ingrained' religious identity of British people is communicated is through the physical landscape. The historical evolution of British religion is visible to any visitor. In the countryside, every village will have one or more churches, and even quite small English towns usually have a range of different churches, representing Protestant and Catholic belief, most of which have been present in Britain for two centuries or more, though in larger towns and cities new churches such as those of the Church of Jesus Christ of Latter Day Saints (the Mormons), Jehovah's Witnesses, or Christian Science and Friends' Meeting Houses (Quakers) may also be seen. The visitor will also notice a large range of church buildings which are no longer in use as places of worship. Some lie derelict, while others have been converted to new uses as apartments, restaurants, warehouses or even nightclubs.

Alongside this decline in Christian practice over the last fifty years, particularly in the big cities, there has been a rise in other faiths (see Table 7.1). In addition, in every town high street, bookshops have extensive sections devoted to mythology, witchcraft, palmistry, spiritualism and related subjects. Off the high street, particularly in seaside, market or university towns, there are small shops selling incense, crystals, relaxing music, jewellery and books on magic and meditation. In gross terms, the people who attend the churches are few, elderly, and overwhelmingly female. The people in the New Age shops are young, enquiring and unbound by any sense of religious duty, motivated rather by their generation's belief in personal freedom. These all indicate Britain's changing religious environment.

Another part of this change, is the way in which religious buildings have become a part of what is called 'British heritage'. One obvious example is the 'marketing' of a number of great cathedrals which are to be found across the UK, though this is particularly noticeable in medieval cities such as Chester, York, Winchester and Durham. These buildings are now both religious centres and centres of tourism. A new meaning to the term 'heritage' has arisen – heritage now reflects the intervention of the tourist industry to recreate images and artifacts from Britain's past. The 'Heritage Industry' has grown rapidly to become one of the fastest developing, and most visible, of Britain's areas of employment and enterprise. It is also one that promotes a particular version of Britain which celebrates continuity, tradition and conservative values.

Partly for this reason, Christianity in Britain is in many ways more of a cultural force than a spiritual one. Table 7.1 indicates that the number of practising Christians is in fact much more in balance with, than exceeding, that of other faiths.

TABLE 7.1 Attendance at religious ceremonies (000s)

	1992	1998	2001
Christian denominations			
Anglicans	1,808	980	800
Roman Catholics	2,049	1,230	900
Presbyterian	1,242	1,010	850
Church of Scotland	700	600	550
Methodists	458	379	350
United reformed church	148	121	115
Baptists	170	277	250
Quakers	18	15	13
Other faiths			
Muslims	1,200	1,000	1,600
Hindus	400	350	559
Sikhs	500	400	336
Jews	410	285	267

Sources: 2001 Census, *Religious Trends*, No. 2 (2000/2001), Christian Research Association, *Whitaker's Almanac*

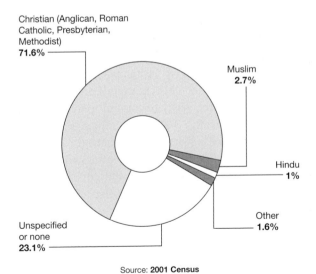

Christian (Anglican, Roman Catholic, Presbyterian, Methodist)
71.6%

Muslim
2.7%

Hindu
1%

Other
1.6%

Unspecified
or none
23.1%

Source: **2001 Census**

FIGURE 7.1 Religion breakdown

Source: 2001 Census

TABLE 7.2 Church members by country (% of adult population)

	1985	1992
England	11.6	10.1
Wales	17.0	15.0
Scotland	32.4	29.4
Northern Ireland	81.6	82.7
Total	15.6	14.4

Source: UK *Christian Handbook* (1994/5) Christian Research Association

In the 1990s there were, nominally, 27 million Anglicans in Britain – that is, almost two-thirds of the adult population claimed to belong to the Church of England. However, at the same time the Anglican church had less than 2 million registered members. Membership signifies active involvement with the church, for example in attending services and offering financial contributions. Between 1960 and 1985 the Church of England's registered membership halved, while the number who think of themselves as belonging to the Church, in comparison, barely changed. This apparent contradiction between those who choose to think of themselves as Anglicans and those who are actively committed to Anglicanism is perhaps the single most important feature of British Christian life, and is discussed in more detail below.

There are 5 million Catholics in Britain. However, on any given Sunday more Catholics than Anglicans will attend a church service – it has been estimated that in Britain 40 per cent of Catholics registered as church members actually attend regularly, as against only 11 per cent of non-Catholics. Nevertheless Catholic church attendance is also in decline. The north-west of England, and the west of Scotland (particularly Liverpool and Glasgow) have had historically, and retain today, a distinctively Roman Catholic heritage. Liverpool is Britain's only Catholic city.

There have, however, been sporadic exceptions to the story of Catholic attrition in Britain. In the political arena, the advent of the Blairs made Catholicism fashionable for a time. (Cherie Blair is a Catholic and their children were sent to the smart Jesuit Catholic school Brompton Oratory.) And again, although the decline in numbers of vocations to the priesthood and the retirement of priests have led to closure or amalgamation of churches, some parishes have been revitalised by young priests coming from India or Africa.

In 2001 pessimistic sound bites on religion were attributed to two senior clergymen, the Anglican Archbishop of Canterbury, Dr George Carey and Cardinal Cormac Murphy-O'Connor, the Catholic Archbishop of Westminster. Dr Carey, addressing a congregation in the Isle of Man, declared Britain to be a country where 'tacit atheism prevails'. He said that British society concentrated only on the 'here and now' with thoughts of eternity rendered 'irrelevant'. Cardinal Murphy-O'Connor, speaking to a gathering of 100 priests in Leeds, said 'Christianity as a background to people's lives and moral decisions and to the Government and to the social life of Britain has almost been vanquished.'

Both statements generated considerable publicity. There were laments about the state of the nation, on the one hand, and complaints about the churches' defeatism on the other. However, both clergymen went on to offer rays of hope. Dr Carey said that despite massive changes, religion had survived and there was growth in churches in Africa, the Far East and 'signs of real life' in Europe. Cardinal Murphy-O'Connor said that clergy should use this difficult period in the Church's history 'to change the culture of Catholicism'. He believed the answer for the Church could lie in new movements, such as Youth 2000 and New Faith, and the building of small Bible-study and prayer groups. He said 'these small communities are the secret for the future of the Church.'

From the 1960s till the present day religious issues in Northern Ireland have been overshadowed by 'the Troubles' – the continuing violence generated by the unresolved political issue of whether Northern Ireland should form part of the UK or of a united Ireland. The religious differences between Protestants and Catholics have thus been exacerbated, as Nationalists want Northern Ireland to be part of a Catholic country (with the South) while Unionists want the province to belong to a Protestant country – that is, the UK. It is often implied by British people that 'the Troubles' are based on religion, but it is probably more accurate to see the conflict as political, or even tribal, at root, a stand-off in which the communities have both looked to their differing Churches for support. At no time has either Church condoned the use of violence in the dispute. And, in fact, meetings between religious leaders, including that between Pope Benedict and the Archbishop of Canterbury, Rowan Williams have helped to reduce religious strife. As Table 7.2 shows, church membership in Northern Ireland, like attendance, far exceeds that in evidence on the mainland of the UK, and this is the case in both Catholic and Protestant communities. This is probably largely for political and cultural reasons, as churchgoing is an important way both of establishing solidarity within a community, and of defining its differences from other communities.

Wales has a separate religious tradition in which Methodism and the Congregational church have traditionally played an important part, both churches laying an emphasis on individual devotion and strict adherence to puritanical rules of abstention from worldly behaviour, such as drinking and

FIGURE 7.2   The Church in Wales offers services in English and Welsh

fornication (sex outside of marriage). 'Chapel' (the word means a small, simple church) has come, in Wales, to represent the ordinary people who embraced non-conformism (a form of Protestantism comparatively extreme in comparison to the Church of England). Welsh chapels are plain, and unadorned, and Welsh non-conformist Christianity has traditionally had no concept of the minister as priest (one with unique spiritual powers and authority to administer sacraments such as the Eucharist, or Holy Communion) but has a strong sense of the prophetic tradition (preachers inspired directly by God). There has been no established church in Wales since 1920 – the Anglican church in Wales is known as 'the Church in Wales'. Nearly all Welsh denominations hold at least some of their services in Welsh, particularly in Welsh-speaking areas. The past devotion of the Welsh (as well as changing population patterns) is evident in the appearance of chapels, many of which are now neglected, in the most remote areas, and the smallest of settlements.

Ironically, as sectarian tensions ease in Northern Ireland, on the British mainland Communities Secretary Ruth Kelly launched a Commission on Integration and Cohesion, saying:

> the fact that Britain is open to people of all faiths and none, has been a huge strength of this country . . . But what we have got to do is recognise that while there have been huge benefits, there are also tensions created. The point of the Commission . . . is to try and examine how those tensions arise and what local communities can do on the ground practically to tackle those and make a difference.

The Commission is aiming to re-establish the sense of community which religion used to supply but now doesn't, but one suspects that, however worthy, initiatives from above cannot make people get on better together.

The established Church

The Church of England occupies both a political role, and a spiritual one. The organisation is referred to as 'the Church of England' when considering its place in the constitution or life of the nation, and as 'the Anglican church' when its spiritual or theological identity is at issue. Because it is the body chosen by, and connected to the British political system of government, the Church of England is the established Church (it differs, however, from the Church of Scotland). It is thus formally tied to both Parliament and to the monarchy.

Partly because of this link, the relation between religious principles and the personal morality of members of the Royal Family is closely observed and, as noted in the introductory chapter, is of continuous interest to the British people and the tabloid press. Though the monarch's religious role no longer includes 'the divine right of kings' (the idea that the monarch's rule is endorsed by God), people still expect the royals to set personal standards in social and religious institutions such as matrimony. Revelations in the mid 1990s about the adulterous liaisons of both Prince Charles and Diana, Princess of Wales, compounded by speculation about possible future marriages, matter to many people because the reigning monarch is still the head of the Church, the institution which above all others is supposed to offer moral guidance to the country. Likewise, prominent politicians in the UK are still expected to endorse religious belief and to attend church occasionally, while the Church is expected not to get involved in party politics.

The fact that the Church of England has also been known as 'The Tory Party at Prayer', has less to do with any identification with the political policies of Conservative governments in the 1980s and the 1990s than with its role as a guardian of the past, and of established views. It is, as British people will say, conservative with a small 'c'. On rare occasions the spiritual and the perceived political function of the Church may come into conflict – the memorial service held after the Falklands war aroused anger from many Conservative politicians because of its emphasis on the Christian values of forgiveness and compassion for all in the war, including the relatives of Argentinean forces killed, an attitude not shared by those who felt that the national church should identify itself only with the victorious British forces. The Church of England is, in fact, also represented within the armed forces – every regiment has its chaplain, and barracks have their own chapels. It is not unusual to see stained glass windows commemorating British Armed forces (through the flags or insignia of local regiments) or of Royal Air Force squadrons within English churches, and particularly in cathedrals.

The presence of the established Church is evident in numerous ways in British life. British coins bear the head of the monarch plus the Latin initials 'F. D.' signifying that the monarch is Defender of the Faith, a title given to Henry VIII by Pope Leo X in 1521. In 1995, Prince Charles caused some controversy among traditionalists by suggesting that at his coronation he would like to be known as Defender of the Faiths (plural) in recognition that Britain was no longer an exclusively Christian country. He again caused controversy in 1996 when he suggested that money from the 'millennium fund' (a fund of money from the National Lottery which is intended to finance projects to enhance Britain's cultural life and National Prestige) should in part be spent on mosques. Despite many moves towards multi-culturalism in Britain, sections of the tabloid press reacted with hostility to this suggestion, seeing mosques as a symbol of a foreign and minority religion despite the fact that British Muslims now outnumber adherents of most British Protestant denominations. Meanwhile, even Government proposals to reform the House of Lords in 2001, rejected the idea of giving a formal place in the Lords for religions outside the Church of England.

Westminster Abbey

Methodists, Presbyterians, Baptists and Quakers share much the same struggle as Anglicans and Roman Catholics to retain the interest of the population at large. The divisions within Christianity which separated the denominations alienated potential members, and, although they have been addressed by the reconciliatory ecumenical movement, none of the churches is really thriving.

At all levels of society, Britain's churches are involved in its cultural life. Church halls are used for whist drives, jumble sales, play groups, badminton, barn dances, sales of jam by the Women's Institute, and an array of other events for charity and local causes which may be entirely secular. Most of the Church's cathedrals hold concerts of classical music, both secular and religious, and may also hold exhibitions of painting. Nearly all British cathedrals have a gift shop, for buying cards, tapes, ornaments and books, and many also have a 'coffee shop' or cafe where visitors are encouraged to come and eat. It is perhaps because of this greater flexibility in their use, as well as because of the aesthetic or historical appeal of beautiful buildings and stained glass, that, while churchgoing is in marked decline, attendance at cathedrals (both by tourists and by worshippers) is on the increase. In 2005, Canterbury Cathedral had 1.05 million visitors – more than London Zoo.

Religious tourism for recreation is also very popular, taking the place that pilgrimage for a spiritual purpose held for previous ages, and converging on the same sites. Holy Island (Lindisfarne), for example, which is situated off the Northumbrian coast near Berwick, and which combines a peaceful atmosphere and dramatic setting with the sites of some of the earliest Christian settlements in Britain, receives more than 300,000 visitors a year, most of them British. Such spiritual tourism is not always welcome, however – such is the demand for property for retreat houses and meditation centres that local people complain of not being able to afford houses on the island, which cost twice as much as they do on the mainland.

Throughout the period between the 1960s and the turn of the new century the Church was in a state of change. Conscious of its rapidly diminishing appeal to the population at large, it attempted to change traditions, in some cases hundreds of years old, in order to be more modern and hence attract more worshippers. The decision in 1992, to admit women as priests and bishops, in particular, proved controversial and divisive, resulting in many priests leaving the faith to take up holy orders in the Roman Catholic church. Those Church of England priests who were most opposed to women priests may feel at home there but, ironically, many Catholics do not welcome what they see as their male chauvinism, and themselves see the advent of Catholic women priests as both desireable and inevitable. Meanwhile the issue of ordination for homosexuals remains extremely divisive.

A further illustration of the shift in the manner of religious expression occurred in 2001 when Tony Blair offered the Americans the redundant Greenwich Dome to cover the site of Ground Zero, the New York site of the Twin Towers destroyed in the 11 September attack. He was perhaps intending to capitalise on the melding of religious belief with heritage, to cement the Anglo-American 'special relationship' and to bolster the flagging tourist industry. His offer was not taken up.

Background religion

The English capacity for compromise can be seen to have emerged in what we could call 'half belief' or 'passive belief'. While membership of all Christian churches in Britain, and churchgoing, are in steep long-term decline, active Christianity in Britain is not, in general, being replaced by atheism, but rather by a less taxing, and harder to define 'passive Christianity' (a vague belief in a God, and a vaguer belief in Christ, but a strong adherence to the idea of being Christian). As suggested earlier, the contradiction at the heart of Christianity in Britain is that while most of the population believe themselves to be in some sense Christian, they have no commitment to, little knowledge of or belief in things that the Church regards as central to Christianity. There is in many quarters of the non-churchgoing population an assumption that being English automatically qualifies one for membership of the Church of England and hence confers the right to be considered a Christian. This position is made easier to hold by the Church of England's status as the established Church. As the Church's rituals of baptism, marriage and funeral have traditionally been extended to anyone who lives within the parish of a particular church, it has been easy to assume that membership of the Church, too, is a right that everyone shares. Thus the English choose the Church of England, but choose to stay away from it – preferring a loose sense of association with it to actually attending its services. Despite this, overall more people still attend church on Sunday than football matches on Saturday. Moreover, events such as the 2001 Twin Towers bombings spark an increase of up to 20 per cent in attendance. Surveys of religious attitudes in Britain regularly reveal a higher percentage of people who claim to be Christian than of people who claim to believe in God, implying a 'cultural Christianity' in which no orthodox spiritual faith in a divine Being is necessary, however strange such a concept may be to a traditional believer.

Most British people, it can be said, live in a state of 'popular religion', which, while loosely based on Christianity, would not be recognised as faith by most priests. In moments of crisis, it is the Christian God in some form to whom they will turn in private prayer. Such religion requires no active participation, but may be satisfied for example by listening to radio or TV broadcasts. A Sunday Service is broadcast nationally every week while morning radio programmes have 'Thought for the Day' or 'Prayer for the Day' slots – uplifting spiritual thoughts offered to the nation. The foremost news

TABLE 7.3 Main ethnic groups in Great Britain, by religion, 2001 (percent)

	White British	White Irish	Mixed	Indian	Pakistani	Bangla-deshi	Black Caribbean	Black African	Chinese
Christian	75.7	85.7	52.3	5.0	1.1	0.5	73.7	68.8	21.1
Buddhist	0.1	0.2	0.7	0.2	—	0.1	0.2	0.1	15.1
Hindu	—	—	0.9	44.8	0.1	0.6	0.3	0.2	0.1
Jewish	0.5	0.2	0.5	0.1	0.1	—	0.1	0.1	0.1
Muslim	0.1	0.1	9.7	12.6	91.9	92.4	0.8	20.0	0.3
Sikh	—	—	0.4	29.2	0.1	—	—	0.1	—
Any other religion	0.2	0.3	0.6	1.7	0.1	—	0.6	0.2	0.5
No religion	15.7	6.2	23.3	1.8	0.6	0.5	11.3	2.4	53.0
Not stated	7.7	7.4	11.6	4.7	6.2	5.8	13.0	8.2	9.8
Total (=100%)									
(000s)	50,366	691	674	1,052	747	283	566	485	243

Sources: Census 2001, Office for National Statistics; Census 2001, General Register Office for Scotland

and current affairs radio programme, 'Today', early morning on Radio 4, has not only daily interviews with prominent politicians but a message from spiritual leaders. Radio 4 also broadcasts 'Something Understood', a Sunday night reflection on spiritual matters. Similarly, *Songs of Praise*, a weekly televised Christian act of worship which focuses on hymn-singing, regularly attracts a greater audience than does *Match of the Day* – the most popular weekly showcase for Britain's national sport, football. The same enjoyment of passive religion is evidenced by the local and national newspapers which carry a weekly column on spiritual decisions written by a pastor. In Scotland, some local papers carry a daily sermon. Across the UK, religious broadcasting, which produces thoughtful programmes of high quality, is surprisingly popular. On an average Sunday in Britain six hours of religious programming will be broadcast by the BBC and independent television companies, and four hours by BBC radio. In general, it is the older generations who watch such programmes. In keeping with British reticence on the subject, religion only occasionally features in television drama. One exception was *Brookside*, a now defunct soap opera set in Liverpool, whose story lines have included a Catholic priest who leaves the church after an affair with one of his parishioners and one which dealt with a cult of extreme evangelical Christians. On BBC television, *The Vicar of Dibley* is a comedy drama series based around the life of a woman priest in the Church of England, and derives much of its humour from the clash of expectations between the traditional role of a clergyman and the new clergywoman.

Other world religions in Britain

Britain has approximately 1,597,000 Muslims, the majority of whom were born in the UK. Others have arrived from the Indian subcontinent or from African countries. The larger Muslim communities are concentrated in the industrial cities of the Midlands, in London, Bradford and Strathclyde, and in the textile towns of Yorkshire and Lancashire where in the 1960s the clothing industry attracted workers from overseas. Additionally, immigrant communities who arrived in Britain from colonies and ex-colonies in Asia, West Africa and the Caribbean in the 1950s and 1960s tended to concentrate in particular areas – notably London, Birmingham, Glasgow and the big industrial towns of northern England, and this has led to large communities of Muslims, Hindus and Sikhs in these areas. Glasgow, Newcastle and Leeds have sizable Muslim populations. Britain's Muslim population is predominantly Sunni, with only around 25,000 Shias. For the first generation of Asian settlers, the practice of Islam and the heritage of Asian culture are inextricably intertwined. For their children, who have grown up in Britain, however, Islam is a cultural and religious force in its own right, so that many young

Britons of Asian origin may think of themselves as British Muslims, rather than as Asians or as black Britons. Whereas in the 1980s only a fifth of the Muslims in Britain claimed to actively practise their religion, in the 1990s that figure rose to half.

For this generation the challenge is to continue to find ways to integrate the religious traditions of Islam into contemporary British life and to create a new British Islamic identity. It is a process which involves some difficulty, exacerbated by the fact that although Britain has laws of blasphemy which could be invoked when Christians were offended by Martin Scorsese's film *The Last Temptation of Christ*, Muslims who objected to Salman Rushdie's *The Satanic Verses* had no legal recourse. The Rushdie Affair, as it came to be known, in many ways started abroad. Objections to Rushdie's blasphemy against the Prophet in his book were first voiced in India, and later in Pakistan and, of course, Iran, from where the Ayatollah Khomeini issued his *fatwa*, which Rushdie heard on Valentine's Day 1989. In Britain, the famous organised book burnings only began the month before. The Affair raised awareness of Islam in Britain and several groups emerged into the public eye. For example, the Bradford Council of Mosques attacked Rushdie, while trying to create a political Muslim collective, and the Women Against Fundamentalism group defended him while trying to dislodge stereotypical views of Muslim women. Meanwhile, British law did not recognise that any blasphemy had occurred.

In 1996, there was a widespread boycott by Muslims of religious education classes in schools (which, by law, may teach about other religions but must be predominantly Christian). Despite there being state-funded schools offering an education which is distinctively Anglican, Catholic or Jewish, no state money had by then been awarded to assist in creating a Muslim school. (This situation was not redressed until the year 2000.) The anomaly arose possibly because Islam was still seen as intolerant, or even as a threat, by many conservative Britons, whose folk-memory of Islam was in terms of the medieval Crusades (a word used with a positive emphasis in Britain generally, but which must have adverse connotations for Muslims). Young British Muslims, however, represent an important strand in British identity, feeling themselves to be in the forefront of the development of Islam in Europe. Positive cultural public images have been supplied by the cricketer Imran Khan and Yusuf Islam, the pop singer formerly known as Cat Stevens.

The bombings on the London Underground in July 2005 ('7/7') prompted some unpleasant anti-Muslim feeling when it was discovered that the perpetrators were from northern England. However, they also concentrated the minds of the majority-peaceful Muslim community to whom this form of extremism is every much as threatening as to the British mainstream population.

The government remains apprehensive about relations between Christian and Muslim groups and continues to seek mediation and compromise. For example, in 2006 it proposed that 25 per cent of places at new faith schools should be made available to children not of the dominant faith. However, it then swiftly backtracked on this proposal in response to a negative reaction, mainly from the Catholic Church.

The history of the presence of other faiths and peoples, and their role in public life in Britain, is not widely known. For example, Asian performers are recorded in London in the seventeenth century, and Indian sailors, called Lascars, were living in London at the end of the eighteenth century. England had several Indian professors in the 1800s and a British India Society was established in 1839 (under the influence of the first widely known Indian nationalist Rajah Rammohun Roy) followed by a London Indian Society in 1872. Already, by the middle of the nineteenth century there were significant Indian communities in London, Southampton and Liverpool, though they were smaller than other black communities in Britain. As an indication of this level of cultural presence, it is worth noting that Queen Victoria – who never visited India – asked a Muslim servant, Abdul Karim, to teach her Hindustani. The founding President of the London Indian Society, Dadabhai Naoroji, also one of the early presidents of the Indian National Congress, was the first Indian elected to the British Parliament, in 1892, when he stood as a Liberal candidate in East Finchley, while another Parsi, Mancherjee Merwanjee Bhownaggree, a merchant from Bombay, was elected Conservative MP for Bethnal Green North-East in 1895.

There is therefore a long cultural heritage of Asian people and faiths in the UK. This was well demonstrated in 1995, by the opening of the largest Hindu temple outside India, in Neasden in London. This event attracted much media interest since it was the only such structure to be built outside India for a thousand years. It used largely volunteer labour and was paid for entirely by donations from the Hindu community. Now, the majority of Hindus live in Greater London although Birmingham, in the Midlands, has also become a centre of the community. Many British Hindu families came from India and Sri Lanka but considerable numbers also arrived from Uganda and Kenya, when they were expelled by the authorities there in the early 1970s. There are now Hindu temples across the UK in major cities and towns. The Sikh community is also well represented in Britain and is concentrated in particular areas – for example, in Southall, and Gravesend in Greater London. Most early post-war migrants, in the 1950s, came from the Jat caste, and were predominantly men. At first they would hold a *diwan* or religious meetings at home, often in all-male households, but soon set up *Gurdwaras* (Sikh Temples) for Sunday services. Their families followed from the Punjab in the 1960s and stronger domestic and religious ties were established.

FIGURE 7.3   Local Lions welcome Indian performers to the Llangollen Eisteddfod

Britain has the second-largest Jewish population in Europe. Most Jews live in London, but there are several hundred Jewish congregations in the UK, many Jewish schools, and synagogues serving both the Orthodox faith and the minority Reform group. Fears have been voiced that nowadays half of Jewish men are marrying non-Jewish women and that this will lead to a decline in faith and religious observance.

Finally, the Rastafarian religion has had a sizable cultural influence in Britain. Rastafarians' philosophy of life was originally based on their adaptation of the Christianity they experienced in the colonial West Indies. They see themselves as Israelites displaced from their homeland, and Babylon is the collective name for all countries of exile outside Africa. Rastafarians have been influential in many cultural ways in Britain. Their 'dreadlocks' hairstyle is shared by some New Age travellers or crusties and they were probably influential in promoting a climate of tolerance towards soft drugs, a major aspect of their religion, in the 1980s. They staked out their territory in urban areas of cities like Liverpool with graffiti such as: 'Toxteth Not Croxteth' meaning that marijuana was welcome in Toxteth, but not the heroin which was available in another district of the city.

Though the religious group is small, millions appreciate the characteristic Rastafarian music, reggae, and particularly that of Bob Marley and the Wailers. Marley's music has been enormously influential, even with many British white punk bands such as The Clash, Stiff Little Fingers and The Ruts, plus more mainstream groups like Culture Club and UB40. Among other black British groups displaying Rasta influence are Aswad, Misty in Roots, and Steel Pulse. Also, the critically acclaimed and widely published Rastafarian poets Benjamin Zephaniah and Levi Tafari have raised the profile of Rastafarianism, promoted the interests of ethnic-minority groups generally and contributed to the transformation of British cultural identities.

Religious festivals

One of the most obvious examples of religion in contemporary British life is in the progression of the year through festivals and significant dates. Oxford University's terms are named Michaelmas (feast of St Michael the archangel), Hilary (St Hilary) and Trinity (a Sunday in June). The Anglican church has traditionally divided the year according to a liturgical calendar – basing the year around a number of key religious feasts and thus creating holidays such as Whitsun, named after the feast of the Pentecost which is celebrated on the seventh Sunday after Easter, when the Holy Spirit appeared to the apostles. British life is punctuated by such national holidays, some of which still have a religious meaning, but many of which are now largely secular festivals. An example of the latter is Mother's Day which is based on Lady's Day (25 March), a celebration of the annunciation to Mary that she was pregnant with Christ, who was to be born nine months later on 25 December. Some public festivals have roots in the pagan religions that held sway in Britain before the arrival of Christianity, lost religions whose customs are being recreated and celebrated by a new generation of 'pagans', who celebrate seasonal events such as the winter and summer solstices (mid-points), by meeting out of doors at ancient sites of worship, most famously at Stonehenge.

The name Easter is derived from the name of the Saxon goddess of spring, Eostre (related to a Mediterranean pagan goddess mentioned in the Bible, Astarte). In some areas, Easter rituals, as well as celebrating the resurrection of Christ, include ceremonies which were once probably part of pagan fertility rites, though now performed in a spirit of secular fun, for example, the rolling of eggs down hills or the eating of pancakes on Shrove Tuesday, at the beginning of Lent, the period of fasting before Easter (observed by few Christians in Britain, in contrast with the month of Ramadan, observed by Muslims). For most non-religious British people Easter is an occasion for the exchange of chocolate, though this chocolate is usually in the shape of an egg or a rabbit (the Easter Bunny), both symbols of fertility. Many British people who never normally go to church will attend a service on Easter morning. The day after Easter Day, Easter Monday, is also a public holiday.

The first of May or May Day is a public holiday introduced by a Labour government. It is a socialist revival of a much more ancient pagan festival of Beltane which is still celebrated by Morris dancers, who dance traditional dances, clad in straw hats and with bells on their ankles, around a Maypole. In places such as Oxford (where there is a tradition of greeting the dawn on May Day morning), Morris dancers are likely to be joined by neo-pagans – young people dressed in the fashions of youth counter culture – ex-army coats, trousers and boots, dreadlocks, strings of coloured beads or leather thongs worn as bracelets or necklaces, and pierced noses and ears. That such people will share the same celebration as well-heeled middle-class students and conservative middle-aged people points to the deeper rhythms of British life which unite people who otherwise feel themselves to be profoundly different, politically and culturally.

Hallowe'en, on 31 October, is a British festival which now shows many traces of American influence. For example children are now beginning to play 'trick or treat'– that is, to call at houses on Hallowe'en dressed in macabre fancy-dress costumes and ask for sweets. This new and growing fashion, pagan in origin, can be contrasted with the Christian tradition of groups of carol singers going from door to door at Christmas, singing in exchange for coins or refreshments. Carol singing is in marked decline. Some people feel uneasy about Hallowe'en. It was originally a pagan festival of remembrance for the end of the old year (according to the pagan calendar) and of communion with the dead (it falls on All Souls' Eve). It is celebrated principally by children, who enjoy the frightening atmosphere created by make-up, masks and costumes on the theme of ghosts, witches, spectres and skeletons. While in the 1960s and 1970s schools would enthusiastically participate in Hallowe'en, from the 1980s onwards many schools, particularly in Scotland, which had a particularly strong Hallowe'en tradition, banned the celebration, because of pressure from Christian parents who believed the festival was connected with black magic and witchcraft, or because it encouraged children to go out unsupervised, at night.

Guy Fawkes Night (the fifth of November) also known as 'Bonfire night' or 'Fireworks night' is another example of how a festival which is now seen as entirely secular can grow from religious origins. While, again, its origins lie in pre-Christian pagan customs (a fire festival to welcome the winter) this custom of gathering to light outdoor bonfires, and, to burn effigies symbolically representing the old year, was adapted by the Christian state in the seventeenth century to commemorate the defeat of a Catholic plot (the gunpowder plot) to blow up the Houses of Parliament. Like Christmas, Bonfire night is remarkable in being one of the few customs which actively unite British people. All across the UK, everyone is acutely aware of, if not participating in, festivities typically consisting of a display of fireworks around a bonfire, on which a human effigy of Guy Fawkes is burned.

The role of the traditional churches as part of the British state is most obvious on Armistice Day (the Sunday nearest to 11 November). This day is also known as 'Poppy Day', as many British people, particularly of the older generations, will wear a red paper poppy to show that they remember those who have died fighting for their country. (In the First World War many British soldiers were killed in battle in the wheat fields of Flanders, which had poppies growing in them.) All over the country, ceremonies which combine military drill and Christian ritual are held to remember the war dead, especially those killed in the 1939–45 war. This is principally a time of mourning and of celebration for the generations who have lived through the Second World War, and those who died. However, even many young people, who feel uncomfortable about the solemnity and emphasis on the past of Poppy Day, also feel that some of their sense of identity as British subjects is defined by this day. Even if the themes of patriotism and military service are not those with which they personally identify, the commemoration ceremonies held in schools, churches and town centres provide an annual reminder of another history of British identity – one which now needs to be negotiated alongside strengthening links with the EU.

For those without significant religious festivals, Christmas (25 December) is without question the single most important event in the British social, religious and cultural calendar (though it should be noted that in Scotland, where it was not until the 1950s that Christmas Day became a public holiday, the alternative celebration of 'Hogmanay' or New Year has historically been of much greater importance and, in the Highlands of Scotland particularly, remains so). Christmas Day is the one time when people feel the need to re-enact the importance of the family and most young people who otherwise live elsewhere will still spend that day with their parents. For most British families the Christmas period is the only time, apart from weddings and funerals, when the 'extended family' – including different generations and the children of different branches of the family, are gathered together. It is the time when, as John Betjeman put it in his poem 'Christmas': 'girls in slacks remember Dad / And oafish louts remember Mum'. For many people, this proves to be something of a strain, as British people are not used to sharing their lives so closely with so many other relatives for several days and this is reflected in statistics for violent domestic crime.

While the Christmas festival, celebrating the birth of Jesus, is of course a religious one, it could be argued that for most British people, any religious meaning is very slight, and the celebration consists chiefly of drinking and eating (especially Christmas dinner of turkey, roast potatoes, Christmas pudding (a very rich fruitcake), mince pies (sweet fruit pies of mixed dried fruit and brandy), the giving of presents, and the watching of special Christmas programmes on television. Passive religion, however, is more popular at Christmas than at any other time, with many people listening to carol services on the radio, such as that broadcast by the BBC from King's College in Cambridge. For many British people, the Christmas story has sentimental appeal, if only because it reminds them of when they first heard it as children, and it is this, rather than religious faith, which makes the church seem more attractive at Christmas. Generally speaking, public performances of the nativity story of Jesus' birth, which is primarily reserved for children's school plays, take a second place to pantomimes and productions of Dickens's *A Christmas Carol* across the country. In 2006 for the first time the Royal Mail's Christmas postage stamps omitted any religious reference.

Some Christmas traditions are of fairly recent manufacture. Prince Albert, Queen Victoria's consort, introduced the Christmas tree to Britain from his native Germany. The red uniform and white beard of 'Father Christmas' or 'Santa Claus' are said to have been inspired by a Coca Cola advertising campaign in only the 1920s. Despite the widespread commercialism however, most British people do derive some religious meaning from Christmas and, for this one time in the year, will participate in Christian ceremony. They will also listen to the monarch's only annual talk to the nation, which has an ostensibly religious purpose. It is broadcast on both radio and television and the queen or king asks for God's blessing on the British people. For most of the nation this is a dated occasion devoid of any religious meaning, and indeed, of any meaning at all. While in the 1970s up to 27 million people, more than half the population, watched this broadcast, in 1994 this number had fallen to around 15 million, and in 2005 to 8 million. One may only speculate on why 8 million British people watched the broadcast, and what they got out of it. For many it is simply 'a tradition' – part of the Christmas ritual.

The New Age

'New Age' is a broad term devised to describe the renewal of interest in a range of approaches to the spiritual dimension which promote individuals' ability to discover and develop their own spirituality. Whereas Christianity is seen by many as emphasising adherence to a strict moral code (for example through the ten commandments, the Bible, confession or sermons) New Age religions concentrate on developing the spiritual awareness which they believe is present in each person. Their practices have a huge variety in their origin – some being revivals of the pagan magical and religious systems that Christianity replaced in Britain, some being extensions of Eastern meditative and religious practices, and some, such as Yoga and T'ai Chi, being concerned with physical exercises.

It may be that the presence of an increasingly diverse multi-ethnic community in Britain has boosted the popularity of some practices. For example, interest has grown in vegetarianism and veganism (large Hindu and other communities have added a considerable market for vegetarian food, which has in turn stimulated British caterers and retailers, and thus aided their popularity) and while twenty years ago vegetarian options on a pub menu were rare, they are now standard. The practice of Chinese medicine, meditation and yoga are also rapidly increasing in Britain.

The belief in reincarnation, which many young people who have been influenced by paganism adhere to, is one which, while alien to older generations brought up under Christianity, is fundamental to Hinduism for example. Similarly, it is not unusual for young British people involved in the New Age to talk about 'karma' (a religious idea of divine cause and effect passed on through different acts and incarnations), they have derived from Hinduism. Other New Age practices have a distinctly European origin, stemming from a revival of interest in Celtic myth and culture, or from new publicity given to old systems of occult knowledge through, for example, the Kabbalah or palmistry. Hundreds of thousands of people are involved directly in activities such as meditation or astrology (the belief system where people's personalities and destinies are determined by the star signs under which they are born). But more significant is the effect of these beliefs on the overall sense of how British people see themselves and their world. A quarter of British people, for example, claimed in a recent survey to regularly read their horoscope as published in a magazine. Many more will read their horoscope as a form of light-hearted entertainment, but will still hope for good news. TV programmes which explore 'inexplicable' phenomena, are also extremely popular. As was Mystic Meg, a TV seer formerly on the BBC's weekly National Lottery show who predicted the type of person destined to win the jackpot each week. Also, business people have adopted many alternative spiritual practices, as a cure for stress and as a source of inspiration or energy. Feng Shui is also used to create a comfortable working environment for offices. Finally, a small but growing number of people among the professional classes are choosing Buddhism.

The term 'New Age' is used to link all of the above activities, and this grouping has some justification, not least because those who have an interest in one of these practices often also have an interest in others. The term itself is derived from astrology, which holds that every 2,000 years the solar system enters a new age. The Piscean age (from the sign of the fish) which started approximately at the birth of Christ was the Christian age (Pisces is seen by astrologers as the sign of self sacrifice and mass movements), while the New astrological era will be that of Aquarius. (Aquarius is the sign of individualism, and hence of any religion which allows individuals freedom.)

Some of the increasingly popular practices which have been placed by the media in the New Age category are distinctively religious. For example Wicca (witchcraft, or worship of British forms of the Mother Goddess, often associated with the practice of magic) and Buddhism are religious preoccupations. Interest in oriental medicine, health food and yoga, however does not require or imply faith. Many facets of the New Age, such as the interest in astrology or in Eastern meditation, are religious in the sense that they involve establishing a link between individuals and a spiritual realm. However, in other ways these activities seem more like hobbies than parts of organised religions because they involve individual study or meditation rather than a formal organisation with its own hierarchy and moral code. New Age groups are thus the antithesis of the highly controlled, brain-washed 'cults' which fascinate newspaper editors in Great Britain (such as followers of the Unification Church, known as 'Moonies').

New Age practices, in the widest sense, are the most important, and most rapidly developing area of religious change across Britain, and must be considered seriously. Aspects of the New Age have permeated very different sections of British society: from business people turning to meditation as a release from the stress of pressurised, urban, executive life, to the Donga tribe – young pagans who have abandoned normal British society and who live, largely, out of doors, and who came to national prominence for their role in actively protesting against the government's appropriation of sites of rare natural value to build new motorways.

In many ways, currents of New Age religion have enabled changes which have occurred in British Life since the 1990s to find a religious expression. The rising tide of concern for the environment, for animal welfare and rights (a subject the British think themselves very concerned with, though they have fewer domestic animals per capita than for example the Dutch), for conservation, and for green or ecological politics, has helped to create a climate in which religions such as paganism, which celebrate the earth and its wildlife, fulfil a need for many people. A powerful element within the identity of young British people is a sense of identification with the countryside, and a resentment of the loss of countryside to modern building, and in particular, of the road-building programme, which successive governments have pursued.

Famously, while statistically very few young people seek active involvement in any of the national political parties, and there is generally much cynicism about politics in British life, concern for the landscape is an area for which there is genuine enthusiasm. Many environmental protesters endure poverty and physical hardship to fight new road building. Such activity earns considerable sympathy from many Britons of all generations. TV coverage of campaigners against the Newbury road bypass and a new runway at Manchester airport turned one young male protester 'Swampy' into a national hero. Far more young people are involved in such 'single issue' protests than in party politics, as referred to elsewhere in this book. Whereas for previous generations the sense of belonging to a nation may have been expressed through such institutions as the Church, the armed forces, or in some cases, a university or a public school, many of the young generation find their ideals, and their sense of belonging in nature and in the land itself.

While Christianity is identified politically with authority, the Establishment and the older generation, many New Age beliefs, and paganism in particular, are identified with the young and the disaffected. The most visible adherents are 'New Age Travellers', who, in the hot summers of the 1980s, fought annual battles against the police to reach Stonehenge, Britain's most important ancient site, because they believed that they had both the right and the duty to celebrate the summer solstice, and, in particular, to name their children there. The latter idea offers an example of how quickly an idea essential to identity – the ritual of naming – can become part of British sub-culture, and how the New Age generates its own 'instant' mythology through which people define themselves.

The British appetite for passive religion, and the commercial forces of tourism show their influence on pagan sites as well as Christian ones. Stonehenge is one of Britain's most popular attractions, receiving 750,000 visitors a year, many of whom are drawn by a vague, but powerful, sense of communion with some other world, or mystic power, which lives on in the imagination of the visitors, if not in the stones themselves. The young New Age pagans who worship at the stones are in a sense a natural extension of British instincts rather than a violation of them, despite their anti-Establishment posture.

Religious differences: age and sex

The decline of Christianity in Britain is not due to individuals' losing their religion, but rather to a process of generational change. A generation which was very religious, at least in terms of church attendance and social attitudes, and which has been the mainstay of church life in England over the last thirty years is literally dying out, and being replaced by a generation which cares far less for church observance, and for Christianity in general. Christianity is associated for young people with the unfashionable and unnecessary code of restrictive, negative morality of the value systems of their parents or grandparents. Many associate a figure such as the Pope with an authoritarian patriarchal Jehovah and tend to see Christianity, and Catholicism in particular, as a series of prohibitions – 'don't take drugs', 'don't have sex', 'don't get drunk' and 'don't swear'. As such it has very little appeal and has also been seen as male-centred, dictating women's lives: under Catholicism, women cannot be priests, or use contraception, or have an abortion. Attempts by some within the church to integrate elements of 1990s youth culture into worship, including some ideas borrowed from New Age spirituality and others from the 'rave' music scene, have caused problems and controversy. They have been backed by many bishops as an attempt to bridge the enormous cultural gap between the Church and young people, yet resisted by many ordinary worshippers who cannot reconcile flashing lights, amplified electronic music and cinema screens as part of recognisable Christian worship. A visitor to a church service in Britain will be struck by the advanced age of the worshippers: many congregations are largely made up of women in their 60s or 70s, or even older. The chief exceptions to this are evangelical congregations, both within the Church of England and outside it in churches such as the House churches, Baptists or Pentecostals, which place a strong emphasis on a dramatically emotional conversion-experience, and conservative moral values and family structures (for example, no sex except in marriage).

One example of the gulf between the Church and society was the Church's hostility towards the National Lottery. The Church was once again seen as basically prohibitive. While some serious commentators on national life agreed with its reservations about the damaging effects particularly on poor people of the compulsion to gamble, and those of extreme wealth on the winners, the week in 1996 when the Church raised its strongest objections was also one in which nine out of ten British people bought a lottery ticket for a £40 million jackpot. The church may still try to exercise its role as moral guardian of the nation, but few people take this seriously enough to be guided by it in their own lives. This is even more the case with the young. For them, Christianity is profoundly unfashionable. It is significant that, almost in imitation of the sub-cultural pagan practice of wearing occult jewellery whose meaning is known only to another 'initiate' of the subculture, Christians have, in Britain, increasingly embraced the symbol of the fish (an ancient secret sign used when Christianity was itself a minor religion, a cult) rather than the cross, as a badge to identify themselves only to other believers.

Church weddings, despite the aesthetic attraction of historic church buildings and music, are in decline. The comment of one future bride, 'We're not religious at all, we don't believe in God but we want to get married in a church' sums up the confused motives behind many such weddings – the fact that the wedding is a Christian ritual, involving religious vows, is somehow invisible to those used to passive religion. The hit film *Four Weddings and a Funeral* offered an illustration of the lack of religious interest in the Church at English and Scottish weddings, which is, paradoxically, matched by the cultural importance to the upper classes of having a church wedding. Christening – the Christian rite of baptism – is now becoming rare.

It should be noted that, while the Church is dominated by men, surveys reveal that in groups of every age women are more likely to acknowledge the importance of religious experience than are men. In both New Age groups and in Christian churches, it is women who predominate. It may be that British women are more open to spiritual practice and belief than men (a survey conducted for Channel 4 found that roughly half of British women believed in astrology, while only a quarter of men shared that belief). It may be that men are simply more reluctant to show religious feeling outwardly. No men's magazines have astrology columns, but almost every woman's magazine has its own named astrologer. Two-thirds of the private clients of leading astrologers are reported to be women.

The heritage industry

A major cultural change in British life from the 1970s through to the present has been that Britons spend more leisure time and money on visiting historical sites and exhibits. It has been argued that the growth in the heritage industry has in some ways filled a gap left in people's lives by the loss of a religious dimension. Reverence for the past could be seen as replacing the religious reverence of previous generations. Britons who, a generation before, might have gone to church, now spend their Sunday visiting a stately home or exhibition of local 'heritage' – a modern pilgrimage. The Jorvik Centre in York (the town's modern name is derived from Jorvik, its Viking name) was the first purpose-built centre for heritage tourism. The life-size plastic Vikings of Jorvik have been followed by other exhibition centres showing everything from Oxford scholars to highland Scottish crofters. Such exhibitions use mannequins dressed up in historic costume, in restored or imitation historic houses, shops, castles or factories. They may even be staffed by actors dressed in historic costume. Paradoxically, the increasing secularisation of British life has led to less leisure time on Sunday for many, as in the 1990s shops began to routinely open on Sundays, giving the traditionally quiet Sabbath day more a feel of 'business as usual'.

The attraction of a 'museum culture' does not just extend to the remote past, but applies even to the twentieth century, and to areas of life that have only recently been part of normal life, rather than historical curiosities. In South Wales (where coal mining was until the 1980s the dominant industry, but has now almost disappeared), for example, it is possible to be guided around a redundant coal mine by men who used to work as miners there, but who are now only dressed as miners to show tourists around. While much of this repackaging, particularly in metropolitan areas, might seem to be arranged or created for foreign tourists, in fact most of the visitors to many such attractions are British, being reintroduced to their own past through the professional presentation of a host of corners of its geography and commerce. As justifications for the former 'Greatness' of Great Britain fall away, it could be said that its people turn to the past to find symbols of their identity, and indeed, their importance. Of these, the stately home is one of the most enduring as well as the most successfully marketed to the public.

In some ways the Church has benefited from this – the great cathedrals which combine Christian heritage and monuments from the past, have never been so popular. In other ways, too, the British could be accused of living in their past. Many films lovingly recreate Edwardian England, particularly those of Merchant Ivory, who have specialised in finely detailed costume dramas and adaptations of literary classics such as *A Room with a View* and *Howards End*. Other films, such as *The Remains of the Day* and Keira Knightley's *Pride and Prejudice* are profitably sold around the world as an image of an ideal Britain, and eagerly consumed by Britons themselves as a kind of national myth. The common elements of the aristocracy, venerable buildings, and English eccentrics occur over and over in such films, offering a picture of a quaint, gentle England.

Fantasies of the Britain of previous generations, particularly of rural Britain, predominate in television drama series such as *Emmerdale* or *The Vicar of Dibley* and in advertising – notably for various brands of bread, biscuits and cakes. Historical settings are also used in some of the numerous 'situation comedies' which British people watch. *'Allo 'Allo* and *Foyle's War* for example, are set during the Second World War, a time which many in the older generations look back to with nostalgia and pride. The celebrations in 1995 to commemorate the fiftieth anniversary of VE (Victory in Europe) day were the occasion of a collective nostalgia for the comradeship and certainties of wartime. It should be stressed, however, that children and young people in general know very little about 'the [1939–45] war' – the defining moment in twentieth-century British history – and the flooding of print and broadcast media with images of the war in the half-centenary year 1995 made very little impression on them. For example, a popular television series, *Goodnight Sweetheart*, with a hero who, by means of time travel, has a double life – one part lived in the wartime 1940s, and one lived in contemporary Britain – appealed only to the old, with their hunger for nostalgia. In 2006 a regular sketch on *The Catherine Tate Show* mocks the cheerful poverty of the 1940s and 1950s and the lack of sophistication of the ordinary people.

Another feature of the British fascination with the past is the recreation of the world – particularly in rural areas far from London – as a series of places defined by some cultural product. Thus one is able to go on an

FIGURE 7.4 Several steam railways have been revived by enthusiasts as tourist attractions

excursion not just to another place, but, at least imaginatively, to another time. For example, the Lake District is advertised as Wordsworth's home, the Yorkshire Moors as 'Bronte Country' and even towns used for very recent productions – parts of Yorkshire for the televisions series *Heartbeat* (now known as 'Heartbeat Country'), or *Harry Potter* films – have become marketed in this way, and there is a steady demand from the public for such attractions.

The Harry Potter film of 2001 and its sequels form an interesting glimpse into the way Britain has come to be imagined, and then marketed. Locations for the film include the remote Scottish Highlands at Glen Nevis, buildings such as Oxford's historic Bodleian Library and Alnwick castle, a preserved steam railway at Goathland, and Gloucester cathedral. All of these sites, illustrating the recent industry that has grown up around British countryside, history and nostalgia for the recent past, are already part of 'heritage' Britain. Not on the heritage trail, but more representative of life for the great majority of UK citizens, is the ordinary house where Harry Potter's story begins, filmed in a suburban cul-de-sac in Bracknell. The contrast between these two Britains is reflected in road signs. Alongside Britain's real geography, through which one is guided by blue motorway signs and green trunk-road signs there is an alternative network of reddish-brown road signs – indicating the presence of 'heritage' Britain. This may be formed of real places – castles, stately homes, preserved factories – or of invented attractions. For example, in North Wales it is possible to journey through the tunnels of an abandoned mine now converted into 'King Arthur's Labyrinth' – a site with no connections to Arthurian legend, but one where an underground heritage display has been erected. There was an equally disjunctive *Dr Who* exhibition at Llangollen. For a country declining economically, there is an added commercial incentive to turn to the past – not just for nostalgia but for a product which, for example, is unavailable in the US yet which is also linked to many of the people, the tourists, from that country.

Conclusion

The question of the role that religion plays in establishing British identity is a complex one, and one that reveals great differences between people of different ages in Britain. For a large number of British people over 50, religion is a quiet and distant but important presence in their lives. It is a touchstone of shared British identity at great national or public occasions and a continuing link with the past and although church attendance is in decline, more people go to church in Britain on Sundays than attend football matches on Saturdays. It is also a source of comfort available at times of private or personal tragedy and celebration, such as weddings and funerals, when religion becomes temporarily of far greater importance for all generations.

In England, even many of those who do not believe in Christianity feel a sense of attachment to the Church of England. While they may never attend church services, they like to know that they are there and would feel robbed if they were taken from them. For a number of people, the Church of England encapsulates in its rituals, liturgies, hymns and music a distinct cultural expression of Englishness. For that minority of the population who adhere actively and strongly to Christianity, this element of religion as expression of national identity is also there but is probably less important. In Wales and Scotland, membership of the respective communions of the Anglican church serves more to divide them off from their fellow Welsh and Scottish people. Religion becomes an expression of difference or trans-nationalism, that is, of possible allegiance to Englishness.

For young British people whose parents were born elsewhere in the world, religion – such as Hinduism or Islam – is one important strand of their identity: a key element in the culture that marks their own contribution to Britishness as distinctive and creates a link with another heritage elsewhere. Their religion can be a source of estrangement from the rest of the British population, when they are faced with a hostile tabloid media which talks only of Muslim or Hindu 'extremism'. However, a large majority of them refuse to be alienated, and have come to see all religions as, in the words of Indajit Singh, editor of *The Sikh Messenger*, 'overlapping circles of belief with much in common'.

For most people under about 30, Christianity is associated with a past to which they feel they have little connection. Some will describe themselves as atheists, and many as agnostics, but for those who are interested in spiritual things, the New Age is more likely to attract them. While not part of a formal or organised system, such practices offer people freedom and individuality plus the possibility of exploring spiritual paths for themselves.

Exercises

1   Do you recognise the following phrases? To hide one's light under a bushel, to go the extra mile, to turn the other cheek. What do they mean? How do you feel Christian ideas might be at odds with peoples' lives in Britain today?

2   Many British commentators try to link a decline in religious practice to a perceived deterioration in morals. Do you think this is a fair connection to make, and what signs or changes in Britain do you think lead people to argue that there has been a worsening of moral standards?

3   What are hot cross buns, Shrove Tuesday pancakes, and Yule logs? When would they be eaten? Remembering that dates such as Valentine's Day (14 February) have a religious background, how would you map out the British calendar in terms of first, Christian festivals, and second, significant dates for all faiths?

4   Where would you locate the following ten World Heritage sites (established by UNESCO) on the map in Chapter 1 (p. 40):
   - the City of Bath
   - Blenheim Palace
   - Canterbury Cathedral
   - Stonehenge
   - Westminster Palace
   - the islands of St Kilda
   - the Giant's Causeway
   - Hadrian's Wall
   - Ironbridge
   - the castles and town walls of Caernarfon, Conwy, Beaumaris, and Harlech.

   Do you know, or can you find out, the natural or cultural significance of each site?

Reading

Davie, Grace. *Europe: The Exceptional Case. Parameters of Faith in the Modern World* Darton Longman Todd, 2002. Argues that secularisation is not inevitable.

Dawkins, Richard. *The God Delusion* Bantam Press, 2006. A polemical treatise against Christianity from an atheistic, Darwinian perspective.

Fowler, Peter. *The Past in Contemporary Society: Then, Now* Routledge, 1992. Examines the extent to which our heritage is still with us in the present.

Parsons, Gerald. *The Growth of Religious Diversity: Britain from 1945* 2 vols Open University; Routledge, 1993. Careful and thorough analysis of Britain and religion since the Second World War.

Visram, Rozina. *Ayahs, Lascars, and Princes: The Story of Indians in Britain, 1700–1947* Pluto, 1986. Reveals the largely unknown heritage and history of Hindus, Muslims, Sikhs, and Parsis from India in the UK.

Cultural examples

Films

My Son the Fanatic (1997) dir. Udayan Prasad. Comic treatment of the efforts of a Pakistani taxi driver to clean up the morals of his northern English town.

Priest (1993) dir. Antonia Bird. A social drama exploring the conflicts between Catholicism and homosexuality in an impoverished Liverpool parish.

No Surrender (1985) dir. Peter Smith. Rival Catholic and Protestant Irish factions collide in a Liverpool club.

Bhaji on the Beach (1993) dir. Gurinder Chadha. A trip to Blackpool for a group of Punjabi women becomes a source of mutual understanding and solidarity.

Leon the Pig Farmer (1992) dirs Vadim Jean and Gary Snydor. Young Jewish Londoner moves to rural Yorkshire.

Excalibur (1981) dir. John Boorman. New Age philosophy and Celtic magic projected onto the myth of Arthur's England.

Truly, Madly, Deeply (1991) dir. Anthony Minghella. One woman's private trauma of grief after bereavement.

The Wicker Man (1973) dir. Robin Hardy. A cult movie with a horrifying ending in which a mainland policeman discovers pagan fertility rituals, including human sacrifice, still dominate the society of a small northern island. Inferior remake: 2006.

The Lord of the Rings (2001) dir. Peter Jackson. J.R.R. Tolkien's fantasy masterpiece portrays the struggle between good and evil in a quest for the one magic ring.

Books

Asian Women Writers' Collective, *Flaming Spirit* (1994) eds Rukshana Ahmad and Rahila Gupta. Religion, identity and nostalgia for home are common themes in this collection of stories from Asian women across Britain.

David Lodge, *How Far Can You Go?* (1980). Analysis of modern Catholic faith and responsibility in Britain.

Jenny Newman, *Going In* (1995). A British account of entering a French convent and the relationships between the religious and secular worlds.

Salman Rushdie, *The Satanic Verses* (1988). The novel whose portrayal of Islam sparked a major controversy over blasphemy and free speech.

Hanif Kureishi, *The Black Album* (1995). Novel of Anglo-Pakistani youth growing up in London against the backdrop of the Rushdie Affair.

David Hare, *Racing Demon* (1990). David Hare's intelligent and questioning play about two Church of England priests engaging in theological debate and sociological comment in contemporary South London.

John Betjeman *The Best of Betjeman* (1978). Poems including nostalgic views of his youth but also 'In Westminster Abbey', a devastating critique of English attitudes.

TV programmes

Restoration. BBC Two programme where viewers voted on which heritage building to restore.

Songs of Praise. Perennial Sunday evening favourite in which a congregation and community are visited by the BBC for a weekly service.

Father Ted. Comedy series about three Irish priests and their sometimes less than spiritual lifestyle.

The Vicar of Dibley. Sitcom about a woman vicar written by the author of *Four Weddings and a Funeral.*

 Websites

www.churchofengland.org
> Church structure. What it means to be Anglican.

www.bbc.co.uk/religion/religions/islam/
> Extensive information about the Islamic faith and culture in the UK.

www.buddhanet.net/
> Simple introduction to Buddhism, beliefs, practices and meditation.

www.mysticplanet.com/8diction.htm
> New Age dictionary of terms from 'acupressure' to 'yoga'.

Conclusion: Britain towards the future

Mike Storry and Peter Childs

IF THERE HAS BEEN ONE dominant but underdiscussed cultural trend in the decade since the first edition of this book it has been the continued shift in Britain from metaphysical and mental to material concerns. Britain's traditional anti-intellectual stance, its cultural and linguistic associations with the US, its particular take on ethical and environmental concerns, and the ever-increasing diversity of people's spiritual beliefs may all be factors in this. While the post-war generations were enjoying consumer booms in the 1950s and 1960s they nevertheless believed in respect for the old, the importance of manners, and of course 'class', and a sharp divide between the private and the public, as well as concepts such as spirit, character, personality and honour. These are words from a vocabulary that is dying out as the benefits of science and consumerism impinge on the preoccupations and aspirations of individuals, and our sense of what is important in identity is less predicated on traditional categories of class, religion, family background and politics. There is no longer much talk of the proletarian revolution, of sisterhood and feminism, or even of cultivating the life of the mind to educate oneself in philosophy, literature and systems of belief.

Self-improvement for most people in Britain today concerns going to the gym, eating less, and exercising more. The life of the mind is not the concern that it once was, as visual replaces literary culture, peace of mind replaces spirituality, material possession replaces spiritual self-possession, and networks replace communities. One of the major elements in this is the decline in religious and moral influences on most people's day-to-day lives, and this of course creates tensions in a multicultural society where, though Christians have been used to the changes in mainstream cultural values, religious groups that are newer to the West are less well understood and themselves less comprehending of the way consumerism is changing Western attitudes towards sex, tolerance and general public behaviour.

Another result of globalisation has been a shift in people's worries and hopes; we live in a climate of fear, from terrorists, identity thieves, or simply strangers. Yet, a climate of fear was perhaps always the case: it is just that the 'enemies' have changed, and instead of them being perceived primarily as 'out there', as was the case with the Cold War, they are now felt to be around every corner and among 'us'. The threats people perceive to their safety, and especially that of their children, have increased exponentially as the dangers directly affecting them have consistently decreased (thanks to better hygiene, medicine and food as well as sixty years of peace) and the benefits of modern socio-political stability have increased, making most people's lives in many ways easier and in others simply more complicated. Which is to say that the more prosperous society becomes, the more unhappy people are about the possibility of threats, accidents and injuries of all kinds. With the expectation of a long and successful life for more people in a mass consumer democracy come the fears of possible threat and failure.

In this last chapter I will consider three key aspects to future British society which inspire fear in some and hope in others: the European context, the continued rise of multiculturalism, and the revolutions in behaviour occasioned by technology.

Europe

European union has developed into one of the most important political issues of the present day. Since the Union's conception, Britain has been somewhat slow and reluctant to participate fully, despite the majority perception that European integration is inevitable. It was not until 1 January 1973, following two years of negotiations, that Britain joined the European Community (EC). The decision, taken by the then-governing Conservative Party, who are now divided by the issue of European membership more than any other topic, was not without controversy. A national referendum was called upon the matter in June 1975, and the British populace endorsed EC membership by a two-to-one majority despite considerable opposition from certain quarters. Perhaps the element of EC membership that has caused most dissension between Britain and the EC is the Common Agricultural Policy (CAP). For years this was the central element of the EC budget, commanding over 60 per cent of expenditure, such that if the CAP was unfair the redistributional effects of the whole EC budget would also be unfair. Britain argued that, because of the CAP, the value of its contributions far outweighed the value of benefits received, and consequently the EC established two British refunds in the 1980s.

The Maastricht Treaty in 1992 changed the European Community to the European Union, but other main elements of the treaty included further arrangements for economic and monetary union, including adoption of a single currency (then called the ecu rather than the euro), provisions for an independent European bank, and the development of a common defence and foreign policy. A continued hostility to European integration on the right of British politics led to the 2001 election being fought by the Conservative Party on the platform slogans of 'Keep the Pound' and 'Save the UK from a Federal European Superstate', and to those on the right, the euro and the Maastricht Treaty have transformed the EU from a union of democratic countries into a supra-national empire where decisions affecting citizens are not open to democratic control. The Conservatives lost the 2001 election and the following one in 2005, suggesting that the majority view in the UK on Europe is closer to scepticism than hostility, underlined by the British reluctance to take full advantage of their voting rights: the European Parliament elections of 1999 (23.3 per cent) and to a lesser extent 2004 (38.9 per cent) had a low turnout of the British electorate, but this may change in 2009 if, as some commentators have speculated, a British general election is held on the same day, 11 June. While Britain sometimes seems hesitant to participate fully in European initiatives, Tony Blair has argued that the greatest missed opportunity for Britain occurred when it failed to join the Common Market in 1957, such that rules and precedents had been established by the time of British involvement in 1973.

FIGURE 8.1   (a) The flag of St George has replaced the Union Jack to signify Englishness

FIGURE 8.1   (b) St George English cross on a crusader – outside a bookshop in Brittany

Some commentators in the media have argued that the level of economic and political integration discussed at present will radically change government and life in Britain. The current process of deregulation which began with the creation of a customs union will have radical consequences for national sovereignty if taken to its conclusion. Subsequent further integration, such as adoption of the euro, will mean the sacrifice of certain national economic tools, including control of the interest rate, and a degree of vulnerability to economic conditions in other countries. Those who take a negative view of European union argue that the Chancellor should be able to control the British economy from Westminster and that legislation which governs the British populace, concerning the maximum length of the working week for example, should only originate from the British Parliament. However, others maintain that an increased degree of economic stability will be beneficial to industry while closer union will benefit British traders who can exploit union markets more efficiently.

As Britain under Gordon Brown moves closer to inclusion within a single currency – at present the opt-out clause means Parliament's approval must be sought before such action can be taken – some areas of opposition to European integration have grown more vociferous. Certain members of the Conservative Party, so-called Eurosceptics, have tried to split their party into two camps over the subject of Europe, while the 2005 national election featured 450 (unsuccessful) candidates from the United Kingdom Independence Party, which seeks Britain's withdrawal from European involvement. Britain's economic success appears to be tied to Europe, yet a reluctance to participate fully is as strong as ever in some quarters. This resistance can be most forceful in England, however, because both Wales and Scotland see the prospect of European federation as a means to gain greater cultural and political autonomy in a union of European States within which they are separate and equal voices rather than adjuncts of England within Britain.

A 2001 report from the European Commission warned that public ignorance in Britain of the euro was such that a credible referendum about it could not be held. Only 20 per cent of people felt they were well informed, while 80 per cent of the thousand questioned confessed to a serious lack of knowledge. Almost two-thirds questioned said they believed giving up the pound would mean an end to national independence while 60 per cent said they thought the EU could not be trusted with British interests. The academic asked to review the figures in Brussels concluded that views about the euro were based upon 'prejudice and the innate conservatism of British public opinion'. Many of Britain's largest high-street chain stores will accept euro notes and coins raising the expectation that the currency will become standard in the country before any referendum is held. The phenomenon this is part of, known to economists as 'Eurocreep', will be of benefit to Europeans shopping in the UK, but it is also expected to change the way the euro is perceived in Britain. Richard Branson's Virgin chain was one of the most enthusiastic supporters of the shift to a dual currency and all its tills have been capable of accepting the euro as well as sterling for many years now. Vending-machine operators were also quick to make the change, which cost them about £100 million, though this is only a fraction of the estimated £36 billion the conversion would cost for the whole economy.

Britain's relationship with (the rest of) Europe can be considered in a number of ways, but in general it might be argued that the British have responded positively when the Europeans from the Continent have come to their shores, such as students on the EU's SOCRATES scheme, but have been hostile to legislation which may appear to be imposed at a distance from Brussels. For many people, the European presence in Britain in recent years has been most visible in the national sport of football, where managers like Mourinho (Portuguese, at Chelsea), Benitez (Spanish, at Liverpool) and Wenger (French, at Arsenal) have accompanied stars such as Ballack

(German, at Chelsea), Solskjaer (Norwegian, at Manchester United), and Emre (Turkish, at Newcastle) in a massive influx of European talent since the mid 1990s. The appointment in 2001 of Sven-Göran Eriksson, a Swede, to the position of England Manager caused a national debate, as it was felt in many quarters that the team had to be led by a countryman, who would understand the local importance of football to the English, and the succeeding manager in 2006 was indeed English, Steve McClaren.

Alternatively, Britain has generally been hostile to the ways in which the nation's diet has come under repeated scrutiny by European bureaucrats as they attempt to regulate and standardise agricultural production and markets across the European Community. Rumours concerning legislation over food and drink coming from Europe have become widespread in contemporary folklore, with stories of decrees from Brussels over the size of apples or the straightness of cucumbers fuelling British anti-European feeling. The image of the food mountain, built to stabilise markets and prices, has itself become a powerful symbolic landscape form for Europe. The huge furore around beef and Bovine Spongiform Encephalopathy (a fatal brain disease believed to be passed from infected cattle to humans), which led to a worldwide ban on British beef in the mid 1990s, also brought out the cultural politics of food production and consumption very starkly – especially so, perhaps, given the association of Britishness with beef (the epitome of this is William Hogarth's eighteenth-century painting 'The Gate of Calais', commonly known as 'O the Roast Beef of Old England', which hangs in the National Gallery). The 'beef crisis' provoked in some Britons the 'patriotic' response of ignoring health warnings and continuing to eat British beef, simultaneously mocking people who were more cautious about their consumption habits.

It is widely understood, however, that food from the Continent has had a large and positive impact on British culture. While specialist ethnic supermarkets offer food ranges that compete with those available in 'home' countries and stock items that would be incomprehensible to many traditional Brits, big chain supermarkets now carry multiple brands of products that would have been hard to find twenty years ago: rocket, wild mushrooms, Parmigiano-Reggiano, crème fraiche, filo pastry, dry-cured bacon, pancetta, a dozen kinds of rice, of pasta and of olive oil. However, of all people in the West, the British still spend the least part of their monthly income on food, though the middle classes eat out more and more, expecting to be served foods from around the world that they would not have heard of ten years earlier: pad thai, pho, pata negra, sushi, bulgogi and boutargue. The revolution in British restaurant food has been attributed to the influence of chefs such as the Roux brothers, who opened their restaurant, Le Gavroche, in the early 1970s, and served carefully chosen and prepared 'authentic' French food, as opposed to the imitation fare previously available in London.

These were followed by chefs such as Raymond Blanc and Anton Mosimann, and then Nico Ladenis and Marco Pierre White. Arguably, it is this influence that has led to the enormous success of cookery programmes and TV chefs in recent years. These are sometimes not professional cooks but those who have simply learnt how to eat well for themselves, such as Nigella Lawson and Sophie Grigson. Many are celebrated because of their personalities rather than their cooking (Ainsley Harriott or Jamie Oliver), while still more are valued simply for educating British people about the basics (Delia Smith). It is cookery books, though, that have changed most, as traditional, 'good English cooking' guides by the likes of Elizabeth David and Jane Grigson were superseded in the 1970s by translations from French originals, and hundreds of recipe books by chefs such as Blanc and Mosimann that were subsequently emulated by homegrown authors and publications such as the ubiquitous *River Café Cook Book*, which itself then gave way to the cult of the River Cottage cookbooks by Hugh Fearnley-Whittingstall as more and more people looked to cook with healthy, organic and homegrown produce. For the busy, there is also the prospect of meal-assembly stores where customers can bulk-prepare meals to take home and freeze.

In an *Observer* poll in 2001, Britons were asked which was their favourite European country. The replies placed Spain (26 per cent) over-whelmingly in front, followed by France (13 per cent), Italy (12 per cent), Ireland (11 per cent) and Portugal (8 per cent). These figures were comple-mented by Britons' choice of foreign holiday destinations, recorded in 1999 as: Spain (27 per cent), France (20 per cent), Eire (6 per cent), Italy (4 per cent) and Portugal (4 per cent). These were the top European destinations except for Greece (6 per cent); of non-European countries, only the USA (7 per cent) ranked in the top ten.

Over the last three decades, British people have become increasingly appreciative of European culture. Among the young, Europe is generally perceived positively and associated with many of the good things in life discussed above, from food to holidays, and the failure of the Conservatives to gain any headway on the Labour Government in the 2001 and 2005 national elections indicates that their promise to keep British sovereignty and the pound is not a main priority on most people's agenda. However, many remain concerned about the level of EU migrancy to Britain, which the government says has placed a strain on schools and public services after the addition of the eight 2004 accession countries. Following an influx of over 600,000 migrant workers from Eastern Europe in 2004–6, amounting to 1 per cent of the UK population, the Home Secretary put a cap of less than 20,000 on the number of low-skilled workers from Bulgaria and Romania who would be allowed to work in Britain when the EU expanded again in 2007. While politicians and economists realise that immigration is the only way for Britain to sustain both its population and its position in the world, members of the public are more sceptical, especially from a cultural perspective. Consequently, at the end of 2006, a YouGov survey found that 'what worries' Britons most on a personal level on a day-to-day basis was the 'level of immigration', followed by 'Anti-social behaviour', 'my financial position' and 'terrorism'.

Multi-ethnic Britain

While it is straightforward to offer figures and percentages of various kinds for the overall UK population, as in previous chapters, such statistics are usually more applicable to some social and ethnic groups than to others, and this can be for economic as well as cultural reasons. So, when discussing language, it is important to realise that although more than half of all 16- to 29-year-old Indians and Pakistanis have English as their main spoken language, this is true of only one-fifth of Bangladeshis in that age bracket. These figures are also contextualised by the fact that half the ethnic-minority population is under 24, compared with one-third of the white population. The youth culture of ethnic groups also varies, such that, for example, young people from ethnic-minority backgrounds are a third less likely to use drugs than whites but it is also true that habits of drug-taking will vary across ethnicities. Similarly, 71 per cent of 16- to 19-year-olds from ethnic-minority groups were in full-time education in 2001, compared with 58 per cent of whites. In terms of gender, women from ethnic minorities hold more educational qualifications than white women, and black African women are twice as likely to be qualified above A-level standard. Again, the proportion of Asian women who have separated or divorced is less than half that recorded among whites, while one in ten white women with children is a single mother, compared with half of Caribbean mothers. Last of these indicators, taken from the *Observer's* 'Britain Uncovered' survey in March 2001, is the fact that three-quarters of Pakistani and Bangladeshi women are in partnerships by the age of 25, 50 per cent more than white women.

As with the changes in food and sport occasioned by British society's greater openness to Europeans, the rise of multi-ethnic Britain has signalled great cultural changes for the entire population. Again, food in Britain has been revolutionised by exposure to cuisine from around the world. Every market town now has at least an Indian restaurant and a Chinese takeaway, and Thai restaurants are becoming nearly as common, shortly followed by Greek, Mexican, Iranian, Turkish, and other eateries. This has not been solely because of migrants coming to Britain but also because travel abroad has given the British population a taste for foods new to the mainstream, ranging from halva to green curry. Celebrity TV chefs, such as Ken Hom (Chinese)

FIGURE 8.2   London's diverse ethnic population (London has the most diverse ethnic population in the world)

and Madhur Jaffrey (Indian), have introduced 'exotic' foods to the domestic diet and it has been said that this is a positive part of the rapid mongrelisation of British culture, such that the Foreign Secretary said in early 2001 that Chicken Tikka Masala is now the national dish. Also, alongside the rise of ethnic restaurants has been the enormous increase in the popularity of gastropubs serving high-quality food, and by 2004 Britons were spending £87.5 billion a year on food and drink in restaurants, pubs and takeaways, double that spent in 1992.

In the arts, 'ethnic' and crossover music particularly has become mainstream in recent years, with artists such as Nitin Sawhney, Dizzee Rascal, Zoe Rahman and Ty nominated for the prestigious Mercury Music prize, and music by black women from Corinne Bailey Rae and Keisha White to Jamelia and Alesha dominating the charts. There are now also the annual MOBO (Music of Black Origin) awards solely for black artists and an equivalent ceremony to celebrate the achievements of British Asians in the arts. Since the 1980s Asian musicians in Britain have been experimenting with rap, dub technology, jungle breakbeats, traditional Indian music and rock. In the mid to late 1990s Anglo-Asian artists with sitars, guitars and decks, such as Cornershop, Asian Dub Foundation, Fun-da-mental and Talvin Singh, broke into the pop charts. Though the bands vary in their political engagement, Asian Dub Foundation, for example, released their single 'Free Satpal Ram' in 1998 as a protest against the imprisonment of a Birmingham Asian who defended himself against racist attacks. Across the board, Afro-Caribbeans have exerted a decisive stylistic influence on British youth and mainstream cultures as evidenced by the dance appropriation of aspects of rudeboy, Rasta, hip hop and sound system culture. Soul II Soul perhaps ideally encapsulated the young, black and British cultural awakening of the mid 1980s with their unique synthesis of a black British attitude, music, fashion and philosophy. Hip-hop culture underlines the creative assemblage that defines Afro-Caribbean youth styles in Britain, whether in music (mixing and sampling), dress (arranging assorted fake and real designer labels) or language.

A festival that epitomises the best multicultural aspects of modern Britain is the Edinburgh Mela. This is Scotland's biggest annual intercultural arts festival and its aim is to celebrate Scotland's mix of influences in music and the arts. The festival's roots are in South Asian cultures, and the Mela was originally created by a group of people from Bangladesh, India and Pakistan, yet the festival intends to reflect the diversity of what it means to be Scottish, while also bringing artists from around the world, from the late Nusrat Fateh Ali Khan to Papa Wemba, Bappi Lahiri and Musical Youth. It has become the most significant multicultural Festival in Scotland, attracting people from all parts of the UK, and it showcases global stars such as the bhangra singer Malkit Singh (whose music features in the film *Bend it Like Beckham*) as well as fresh homegrown fusion music from bands such as Jinx, a ska/punk band from Yorkshire.

A debate that has often focused on issues of ethnicity in the early years of the new century has been asylum seekers. The Labour government came under repeated attacks for its scheme of distributing migrants from the ports where they arrive to cities around the country. Several councils declared that they could take no more refugee families and stopped providing homes for those who arrived, while others accused the Home Office of paying self-interested private landlords to house thousands of asylum-seekers in slums rather than use accommodation provided by the local authorities. More than a hundred incidents were reported in Hull alone in the year following the introduction of refugees to the city in the summer of 2000. Around this time, the United Nations estimated that there are 37 million refugees across the world, only 0.5 per cent of whom are in Britain. In 1998 there were fewer than 4,000 applications for asylum, but this rose to 76,000 in 2000, the highest proportion coming from Iraq (9 per cent), followed by Sri Lanka (8 per cent), the former Yugoslavia and Afghanistan (7 per cent each). Of these, 21,565 were granted refugee status or exceptional leave to remain by the Home Office (though, by international agreement, asylum seekers are not allowed to seek work). In 2006, a highly critical Commons report estimated that there was a backlog of between 155,000 and 283,500 failed asylum seekers, whom it would take up to eighteen years to remove from Britain.

As a contrast to those voices who see the demise of 'Britishness' in future years, there are those that consider culture, and identity itself, as pluralistic and multi-layered, while recognising the pressures that are currently

FIGURE 8.3 Long queues form every day outside the London Passport and Visa Office

questioning the limits of Britain. Perhaps most prominently in these quarters, the 'unsettling' of Britain has been detailed by The Parekh Report on 'The Future of Multi-Ethnic Britain' in 2000. The report commissioned by the Runnymede Trust sees seven reasons why the idea of Britain is at a turning-point: globalisation; the country's decline as a world power; its role in Europe; devolution; the end of empire; the spread of social pluralism; and post-war migration. The Report's conclusion is that Britain ought to be recognised as the 'Community of communities' it has now come to be, and for that matter, always was. Changes in the understanding of British culture and in the transmission of appropriate national stories, signs and symbols, can follow through from this appreciation of present and past pluralism.

It is also clear that some British people consider a multicultural society to be a threat not just to their ideas of national identity but their very well-being. The suicide-plane attacks on New York and Washington on 11 September 2001 brought cries of support and outrage from the British press and politicians, but it was also apparent that for some British people these extreme terrorist actions were hard to dissociate from their perceptions of Muslims in the UK, and the week following the American disaster were marked not just by calls for a greater understanding of religious and cultural differences but also by verbal attacks and acts of violence aimed at Muslim individuals and their families.

The feeling of a split in British society reflecting global tensions was exacerbated on 7 July 2005, which has become known as 7/7. On this Thursday morning, several bombs were exploded in central London on buses and underground trains by a coordinated team of attackers during the busy commuter rush hour. Three went off on trains within a minute of each other shortly before nine, and then a bomb on a bus was set off under an hour later. The four suicide bombers were all killed but so were fifty-two innocent travellers. The reasons for the timing of the bombing on 7 July are open to debate but London had just been awarded the 2012 Olympics and it was also the first day of the G8 summit in Scotland; but the date may itself have been sufficient reason. The shock of the events was compounded when on 21 July 2005, just two weeks later, a further four bombs were due to be exploded in London; but they were poorly constructed and only the detonators went off. All the suspects were later arrested and police tracked down a 'factory' where the bombs had been made in an area of Leeds. The revelation that all the bombers had been British Muslims, living within law-abiding communities, born and bred in the UK, was a devastating blow to British self-perceptions and an unprecedented act of violence by British citizens against their fellow country people. A strain has inevitably been placed on relations between British Muslims and the wider society since the attacks. Interestingly, according to the 'Connecting British Hindus' 2006 report funded by the government, many Hindus living in Britain no longer wish to be known as 'Asian', partly as a result of recent media prominence given to Muslims, and prefer the terms 'British Indian' or 'Desi', a Hindi word meaning 'rooted in one's own country'. Although Hindus represent 1 per cent of the population, a disproportionate amount of public focus is given to British Muslims (about 2.7 per cent), and many feel this situation is perpetuated by the blanket term 'Asian'.

Reflecting the tensions of increased ethnic diversity but also celebrating the richness of the cultural mix, literature has provided a number of prominent contemporary examples of multi-ethnic Britain, from Salman Rushdie's *The Satanic Verses* through the works of Hanif Kureishi, to Andrea Levy's excellent novel *Small Island*. To take one celebrated book, Zadie Smith's debut novel *White Teeth*, presents a series of metaphors for the heterogeneity of modern Britain. Her title of course plays with the idea that everyone is the same under the skin, but the novel charts the variety of molars, canines, incisors, root canals, false teeth, dental work and damage that constitute the history behind different smiles. The commonsensical idea of the uniformity of teeth, which can also be divided into a host of shades from pearly to black, is as much a fiction in the novel as the traditional template of Britishness. The prime examplars of traditional Englishness in *White Teeth* are a family called the Chalfens. The Chalfens are taken to be 'more English then the English' because of their liberal middle-class values, and also their tendency towards empiricism. However, they are in fact third-generation Poles, originally Chalfenovskys: not more English than the English, but as English as anyone else. Smith rings this theme of hybridity and cross-fertilisation through numerous extended metaphors, drawn from horticulture, eugenics and the weather.

The most prominent person in the novel who considers herself to be 'a stranger in a strange land' is Irie Jones, whose mother is 'from Lambeth (via Jamaica)' and whose father is a white war veteran from Brighton. In the novel's metaphor, Irie sees no reflection of herself in the 'mirror of Englishness'. She turns to her grandmother and Jamaica for a sense of her 'roots' but concludes that the idea of belonging is itself a 'lie'. The other central family of the book, the Iqbals, have come to England from Bangladesh. Their second-generation children spend their teenage years apart, the one in London, the other in Chittagong. Each finds his identity is located elsewhere: Millat, living in London, wishes to be an American gangsta-rapper before he becomes in the words of his father a 'fully paid-up green bow-tie wearing fundamentalist terrorist', while Magid, in Bangladesh, becomes 'a pukka Englishman, white suited, silly wig lawyer'. Their mother, Alsana, expresses the overall view of the novel: 'You go back and back and back and it's still easier to find the right Hoover bag than to find one pure person, one pure faith, on the globe. Do you think anybody is English? Really English? It's a fairy-tale.'

White Teeth's view of race-relations, though far from perfect, seems more closely to resemble hopes for Britain's future than observations about its past. The book works politically far more at the level of representation than any kind of confrontation. The novel disseminates a multicultural view of London, where currently over 40 per cent of children are born to at least one black parent. And *White Teeth*, as the novelist Caryl Phillips concluded in his review of the novel, ably dramatises the fact that: 'The "mongrel" nation that is Britain is still struggling to find a way to stare into the mirror and accept the ebb and flow of history that has produced this fortuitously diverse condition.' To choose one example of this, there is the genealogy and history of the current 'English' band The Magic Numbers, who are made up of a boy and a girl from two families, the Stodarts and the Gannons: the Stodarts were born in Trinidad the children of a Venezuelan mother and Scottish father, but were raised in New York and then in the mid 1990s moved to London where they met the Gannons, who are of Irish descent.

According to a London University study called Origins Info, of the 200 ethnic groups in Britain, Asian migrants and their descendants are the most economically and socially successful in 2006, followed by the Japanese, Dutch, and Greek Cypriots. The study revealed that Southall, sometimes called 'little India', in West London has the least 'English' gene pool (less than 18 per cent), and Ripley in Derbyshire has the highest (89 per cent). Tottenham in North London is the most diverse place, with 113 different ethnic groups, ranging from Vietnamese to Bretons. The study also shows where ethnic groups have clustered: Italians in Bedford and Waltham Cross, Hispanics in Eastbourne, Ascot, and Crawley, and the Dutch in Plockton in the Highlands in Scotland and Llanwrtyd Wells in Wales. The study also reveals facts about employment: for example, that there is a disproportionate number of migrants in law, medicine and business: so, of Britain's 2,651 voting-age Armenians, 1,600 run businesses and a high number live in West London, the most expensive property area in the country. It is clear beyond all else that the ethnic-minority population is rising, and in mid 2006 there were 690,000 children from an ethnic-minority background in primary schools in Britain, which amounts to over 20 per cent. Britain's future is multi-ethnic and quite soon there will be entire urban areas where the majority population is non-white (Leicester, Oldham, Bradford) as Britain moves towards the 'plural cities' of the future. However, the government acknowledged that this would not be an easy transition when, on the third attempt, it finally introduced the Racial and Religious Hatred Act in 2006, which creates an offence of inciting hatred against another on the basis of religion, often perceived as the primary element of cultural difference in relation to ethnicity since 2001.

New technology

Finally, nothing seems to look to the future more than technology and nothing seems more dated with a few years hindsight. In the last ten years, a number of machines have materialised in a sizable number in most British homes. These include digital cameras and camcorders, Playstations and Gameboys, which have become firmly established as an aspect of cross-generational culture, home cinema speakers and projectors, hard-disk recorders and DVD players, the personal digital assistant and the ubiquitous and multi-functional mobile phone with its professional equivalent in the BlackBerry, Wi-Fi devices and MP3/4 players, while High Definition means new televisions and media will undoubtedly soon be with us. The trend is away from hard and towards soft media, meaning that CDs and DVDs may soon be a thing of the past and every home will be able to access every song and film ever made, possibly for free if enough advertising accompanies it; and the rise in internet advertising is threatening the viability of the UK's terrestrial channels. However, the greatest cultural change has been happening online, with blogs, blurbs, podcasts, file-sharing and online gambling all in the ascendancy. But, the major phenomenon online has been the rise of interactive social networks such as MySpace and video-sharing networks such as YouTube, which allow everyone to have their fifteen Megs of Fame and may well transform the broadcast, perception and presentation of cultural identity in the future, both professionally and socially. MySpace is also expected to try to rival iTunes in the music download industry, which has taken many twists and turns in its formative years, and already allows users to download some record companies' back catalogues for free. The underlying message of which is that while the dream of the paperless office has become a myth, it is likely that music, video and most of the rest of the entertainment industry will be stored digitally for instant easy access consumption without the need for disks, or probably wires. From a work point of view, new technology means that more people can work from home, and teleworkers – those who work at least one day a week from home – have increased in ten years to 8 per cent of the population from 4 per cent in 1997.

In 2001, 90 per cent of teenagers under the age of 16 had a mobile phone, and by 2006 a mobile phone has become considered socially de rigueur if not absolutely 'essential' for the entire population, whereas in 1988 the figure for ownership stood at 3 per cent. This is creating an age divide as, for example, 70 per cent of wired 16- to 24-year-olds use social networking websites whereas only 40 per cent of all adult users do; and the figures for blogging or contributing to a message board are a third versus 14 per cent. As a consequence teenagers are watching an hour a day less television than their parents, who are themselves the ones who need to worry about passivity in comparison with their children who choose socially active forms of communication, albeit from their bedrooms. Text messaging (35 billion sent in 2005), msn messaging and email have become the most common forms of communication as people value the flexibility of these forms of communication and many increasingly consider telephone conversations unnecessary or inconvenient. Even the Lord's Prayer has now been translated into a text message as part of a scheme to send church services to worshippers on their mobile phones. 'Our Father who art in heaven' has become dad@hvn, and the rest of the Prayer now reads: 'urspshl.we want wot u want&urth2b like hvn.giv us food&4giv r sins lyk we 4giv uvaz.don't test us!bcos we kno ur boss, ur tuf&ur cool 4 eva!ok?' The Muslim community has also already witnessed the benefits of text-messaging believers with their five daily 'calls to prayer'. And this is perhaps fitting because, if anything does, the mobile phone expresses modern identity in a country such as Britain more than anything else. Children create their sense of identity through their conversations with one friend while walking along the street with another, commuters clutch their phones as they travel on the trains and buses like they were St Christopher medals, and the current generation is one that frets about where 'the mobile' is far more than their keys, particularly as breaking into your house is seen primarily as a threat to your possession and sense of safety, but the loss of your mobile threatens your connection to the world and your sense of identity. As well as an age divide, a gender divide is appearing with technology: of adolescents aged between 12 and 15, 87 per cent of girls and 77 per cent of boys own a mobile, 63 per cent of girls and 54 per cent of boys use the internet, but 66 per cent of boys and only 51 per cent of girls play computer games. For the most part, girls use technology to socialise and communicate more than boys, whose inclination is often towards competing with the technology through gameplay, which may include online gaming environments or MMOs (Massive Multiple Online Role-Playing Games). While it remains a concern that the internet is unregulated, unlike TV and radio which are overseen by a body called Ofcom, oversight through surveillance is another troubling technological issue in relation to identity. The British are in fact 'spied upon' more than any other people in the world: in addition to the proliferation of car number plate recognition devices and the government's long-term logs of websites accessed by people in their homes, a typical Briton will be caught on camera 300 times a day by one of the 4.2 million CCTV cameras around (one for every fourteen people).

Overall, the speed of technological change has been embraced by the British, who have nonetheless been resistant to the rise of a surveillance culture (particularly speed cameras) and the threatened introductions of identity cards (scheduled for 2009), but welcomed new developments such as broadband internet access, handheld scanners, GPS (global positioning

FIGURE 8.4 A range of book tie-ins, serials and documentaries on DVD and tape are sold through the BBC shop

satellite) systems, and digital assistants, even though according to surveys most people do not use anything like half the features available to them on their gadgets. The technological revolution has enormously changed people's lives in the home, challenging the idea of the family 'unit' by turning its members into consumers of myriad domestic leisure activities, while post-war migration has greatly altered the ethnic population, and the rise of the

European Union has meant that British people have thought more deeply about their national identities, some wishing to call themselves primarily 'Welsh/Irish/English/Scottish', others 'British', and others 'European', 'Asian', 'African' or any one of a hundred other labels.

Conclusion

The Britain the essays in this book have described is composed of various contrasting elements: homeless teenagers and moneyed gentry; settled suburban commuters and country farmers; women priests and male nurses; nostalgic OAPs and young ravers – each experiencing a different version and expressing a contrasting view of the country when talking about their relation to Britain. Any of these experiences of being British is a product of individual identity and experience, formed by a range of factors such as employment, gender, region, religion and education, and each of these alternative views would supply a picture of Britain which can only take a place in a mosaic of opinions. As much as if not more than ever, in the twenty-first century it is wrong to think that there is a single British character, rather than a plurality of cultural identities.

Exercises

1   What do you think are the arguments for and against multi-ethnic communities?

2   Despite new age legislation in 2006 to prevent discrimination, many people believe that some employers will continue not to give jobs to those over the age of 50 because they think older people are less likely to keep up with technological developments. To what extent do you feel the proliferation of new technologies adds to a generation gap in society? Are the young's attitudes towards the old different from what they were in the past?

3   Supposedly, the five things that Europeans think of when considering the UK are the Beatles, London, the Royal Family, the BBC, and Shakespeare. To what extent are these things 'British', as opposed to English? What five things that are not English would you list as the most famous aspects to Britain?

4   In this Conclusion, some of the influences of Europe on Britain have been mentioned. What would you consider the main British influences on European countries to be?

 Reading

Alibhai-Brown, Yasmin. *Who Do We Think We Are? Imagining the New Britain* Allen Lane, 2000. Collection of essays ranging over immigration policy, race-relations, immigration policy, and the concept of citizenship in relation to national identity.

Bracewell, Michael. *England is Mine* 2nd edn Flamingo, 1998. Looks at English identity through its (not necessarily English) exponents and icons from Wilde to Morrissey.

George, Stephen. *Britain and European Integration Since 1945* Blackwell, 1991. Charts Britain's post war relationship with the Continent and the EU.

Gilroy, Paul. *There Ain't No Black in the Union Jack* Routledge, 1992. Classic sociological analysis of the British relationship to race and ethnicity.

Modood, Tariq. *Multicultural Politics: Racism, Ethnicity and Muslims in Britain* Edinburgh University Press, 2005. Examines the state of Britain, and attitudes towards multi-ethnicity, post September 11 2001.

Nairn, Tom. *After Britain* Granta, 2000. Polemical attack on the idea of Britain.

The Runnymede Trust. *The Future of Multi-ethnic Britain: The Parekh Report* Profile, 2000. Excellent government-commissioned report produced by a think-tank of intellectuals, academics and social commentators.

 Cultural examples

Films

Dirty Pretty Things (2002) dir. Stephen Frears. Revealing and ultimately shocking story of a woman who befriends a Nigerian 'illegal' immigrant in London. The lead role is taken by French film star Audrey Tatou. Now also the name of a well-known British rock band.

Borat: Cultural Learnings of America for Make Benefit Glorious Nation of Kazakhstan (2006) dir. Larry Charles. British Jewish comedian Sacha Baron Cohen spoofs cross-cultural stereotypes and offends liberal values as a naïve and politically incorrect East European.

Bhaji on the Beach (1994) dir. Gurinder Chadha. Film, mixing British realist and Indian musical styles, about a group of British Asian women from Birmingham on a daytrip to Blackpool.

In This World (2002) dir. Michael Winterbottom. Two Afghan refugees try to escape to Great Britain with the help of people smugglers.

Books

Gautam Malkani, *Londonstani* (2006). Highly regarded twist-in-the-tale story of a gang of Hounslow Indians running phone scams and debating the British Desi experience in a mix of slang, text-speak, Panjabi and gangsta rap.

Rageh Omaar, *Only Half of Me: Being a Muslim in Britain* (2006). A collection of the author's partly polemical essays on a major contemporary issue for Britain and for him, a black British Somali muslim.

Zadie Smith, *White Teeth* (2000). Hugely popular and highly intelligent cross-generational comic novel of multi-ethnic life in London.

Victor Headley, *Yardie* (1992). Jamaican gangster pulp fiction set in 1990s Hackney, London. The novel looks at the post-war Afro-Caribbean immigrant experience in conjunction with the transnational drugs economy.

Jeff Noon, *Vurt* (1993). Novel set in a grim, comic Manchester of the future. In a world peopled by vurt, robo and dog beings, gangs escape cops through the use of cyber-technology.

Websites

www.cre.gov.uk/
    Commission for Racial Equality.

www.wired.com/
    News and anlysis of the technologies driving the information age.

www.cybertown.com
    A site on which you can live an online life with virtual cash in Cybertown.

www.ukip.org/
    British UK Independence Party site.

www.speakout.co.uk
    Campaign to demand a referendum on Europe.

www.geocities.com/yes_euro/
    One 17-year-old's view of why Britain should unite further with Europe.

http://bebo.com/
    One of Britain's top social networking sites (4 million of the 21 million members worldwide are British).

www.yougov.com/
    YouGov professional market research agency portal, with access to past survey and poll results and analyses.

Glossary

Instead of a set of exercises and questions to end the book, we have noted down the following outlines of keywords. We would like you to use these as starting points for thinking about each of the terms, but also as comprising an elementary glossary to which you may want, perhaps with the aid of a dictionary and other books, to add your own terms and short definitions.

Accent is the inflection given to, and modulation of, speech. It mainly indicates social class and should be distinguished from both *dialect* which is a combination of accent intonation and local vocabulary and indicates region, and *slang* which is the use of ungrammatical English among people in the same generational/gender groupings.

Acronyms adopted widely in the 1980s to describe new social and cultural phenomena included: YUPPIES, Young Urban Professionals; DINKIE, Dual Income No Kiddies; NIMBY, people who were in favour of (say) gypsy sites but: Not In My Back Yard. Mrs Thatcher was nicknamed TINA: There Is No Alternative. The word WRINKLY, applied to an old person, was not an acronym.

ASBO, Anti-Social Behaviour Order. Introduced in 1998 to control youths who have been terrorising their neighbours predominantly on housing estates. Those being given ASBOs occasionally see them as something to be proud of: badges of honour.

Bling (from hip hop) is a style of flashy, cheap jewellery worn by chavs. It includes gold sovereign rings for men and fake gold trinkets for women.

Chavs (from the Romani word 'chavi' child) are vulgar young women who wear gold jewellery and counterfeit Burberry clothing.

Consumerism is the idea that consumption, not production is the basis of capitalist society. Hence 'market forces' and 'value for money' can be

brought into all aspects of public life. There are three stages of consumerism: goods; services (TV entertainment/pizza delivery); and
experience (aerobics programmes/travel).

Do-gooders is a term of abuse for well-meaning, left-leaning liberals. They
are seen as sincere but dangerous interferers, rather than as problem-
solvers.

Drug culture is an alternative way of life that has produced a range of
terminology for drugs. Heroin is 'smack'; cocaine is 'crack'; marijuana/
cannabis is 'grass', 'hash' [ish], 'shit', 'slate'. Addicts are 'smack-heads',
etc.

Emos are a subset of Goths, but they are much more serious. They wear
their hair across their faces and may practise self-harm as a form of
exhibitionism.

(The) Establishment is a neutral term for the people who are traditionally
believed to run Britain – the landed aristocracy, hereditary peers, long-
established business interests ('The Beerage'). Alan Clark used it to
distinguish those members of the Conservative Party who represent an
old guard, as distinguished from those who currently hold political
power.

Estuary English is a form of speech distinguished from 'received pronunciation' or 'proper English'. For example 'regimental' is pronounced
'regimen'au'. 'It'll' becomes 'i'uw'. Identified in 1984, by David
Rosewarne, estuary English supplies speakers from different social backgrounds with a means of camouflaging their origins, whether cockney
or public school. It is commonly used by, for example, traders in
London's money markets.

Gender is a division into masculine/feminine which is socially constructed –
as opposed to the male/female distinction of sex, which is biologically
determined.

Generation X is from Douglas Coupland's novel *Generation X Tales for an
Accelerated Culture*. It identifies and defines a group of consumers born
from 1964–9. They appear alienated from the values of their affluent
parents (Baby Boomers) by their own uncertain prospects, but the
difference may be to do with style. They are also known as Busters or
Slackers. They welcome the internet, quirky advertising, grunge fashion
and the idea of defining themselves.

Goths are young people of both sexes who dress in long black clothes and
wear white makeup, to differentiate themselves from their peers. They
are quiet and unlikely to be troublesome.

Grunge was a term used by mid 1980s rock journalists to describe a confrontational form of hard-rock music. Despite its overtones of squalor
and dirt it has come to describe a particular fashion look – one which
is deliberately not smart.

Hegemony, from the Greek word for leadership, refers to a cluster of ideas, practices and connections which enables a small group of people to retain dominance. Formulation of the concept is associated with Antonio Gramsci.

Heritage has overtones of 'inheritance' and is about the transmission of traditional values. It is intended to be a dynamic outgrowth of static 'museum' culture and to indicate concern for the physical and historical environment. Since the 1980s Britain has had a Heritage Secretary. Some see it as just another contender in the struggle between ideologically opposed versions to 'officially' fix British cultural identity. It is thus an aspect of theme-park Britain.

Hoodies are teenagers who cover their faces with their hoods. When they were banned from Bluewater shopping centre, Tory leader David Cameron famously said that instead of despising them, people should show them more love. His approach was travestied by a government minister as 'hug a hoodie'.

Hybridity is mixing different styles of fashion, music, or anything else in order to come up with a better synthesis. Within this fusion the originals (with their conflicting messages) can sometimes still be detected. So BBC TV's 1990s Jane Austen series might place a more feminist overlay on the original texts.

Jobsworths are people who, when asked to be flexible, protest, 'it's more than my job's worth' (to deviate in any manner from prescribed rules). They are presumed to be narrowly bureaucratic, unthinking, time-serving employees, who hide within the public service. The use of this disparaging description may indicate that the speaker is part of a new, non-unionised, entrepreneurial Britain.

Laddism is a male culture which may be seen as a reaction to the idea of the caring, sensitive 'new man' produced by the feminist movement. So laddism is characterised by a climate of rough behaviour, excessive drinking ('lager louts') and all-male attendance at soccer matches. Magazines such as *Loaded* and *FHM* cater to it. It is imitated now by women, known as ladettes.

Moral panics are periodic bouts of hysteria, where the media (particularly the tabloid press) whip-up national feeling about issues which have existed all along but have lacked the 'oxygen of publicity'. Examples would be: chaining of pregnant prisoners; teenage use of the drug Ecstasy; 'social-security scrounging'.

Muffin top is the roll of fat which spills over the waistband of hipster jeans.

Neets is a term given by Whitehall to a group of young people (7.7 per cent of their age group) living on social welfare, who are not in education, employment or training.

New Age is a broad term devised to describe the renewal of interest from the mid 1980s onwards in a range of approaches to the spiritual dimension which emphasise the individual's ability to discover and develop their own spirituality. The term comes from astrology: every 2,000 years the solar system enters a new age, the next one being the age of Aquarius (the sign of individualism). Influences are: Yoga and T'ai Chi. It is associated with alternative culture: the occult, Tarot, astrology and hippy lifestyles. Most visible elements are New Age Travellers and the Donga Tribe.

Outing is the practice of publicly declaring someone to be homosexual. It has been used particularly to identify the sexual orientation of e.g. an Anglican bishop who opposes the ordination of homosexual clergy. Its use is controversial within the gay community.

Pagan was originally either a polytheist or someone who doesn't believe in a God at all, but now denotes a New Age movement aiming to recreate links with nature. Its adherents may be interested in: Wicca (see below), the occult, the book of shadows, spells, magic, witchcraft, athames, and myriad rituals. Some pagans believe in the mind-expanding potential of drug use.

Political correctness is a term used to suggest that people are too sensitive about giving offence to oppressed or special-interest groups, which include women, gays and ethnic minorities. Language has been purged of many words: housewife; actress; stewardess; chairman. The word 'partner' has become substituted for husband/wife or (gay/lesbian/ straight) lover.

Protestant work ethic is the idea that people must take responsibility for their own destinies and therefore not rely on others to support them but must work for themselves to 'justify their existence'. Robinson Crusoe exemplifies a robust self-sufficient practitioner.

Rhyming slang, though originally cockney, is now incorporated into the language at large. To have a butcher's (hook) is to take a look. The nursery rhyme 'Pop goes the weasel' refers to pawning a suit (a 'whistle and flute'). Slang is often used to avoid obscenity: according to *Chambers Dictionary* a 'berk' (a common English word for a fool) is 'short for cockney rhyming slang Berkeley Hunt, for cunt', while 'Aris' (used in films such as *Lock, Stock and Two Smoking Barrels*) means 'arse' because it is an abbreviation of 'Aristotle', which rhymes with bottle, and 'bottle and glass' rhymes with 'arse' (see www.peevish.co. uk/slang/links.htm#british).

Sound bites are short expressions used by politicians and media commentators to compress ideas into an easily memorable form. The idea is that in a fast-paced modern work, where people have limited concentration spans, ideas have to be got over to them in succinct shorthand. Critics fear that their use leads to the over-simplification of complex arguments. Examples are rip-off Britain; spin doctors; Eurosceptics; dumbing down; cronyism.

Spin doctors are public relations people who manage the flow of information and news so as to cast their corporate or political employers in the best light. They time the release of bad news to coincide with major distracting events, arrange publicity stunts and feed positive information about their clients to the media.

Stakeholder society is the term used to describe Tony Blair's vision of 'active citizenship' in modern Britain.

Subculture refers to both alternative culture and to individual groups operating separately from mainstream society. Often it refers to rival gangs of e.g. mods and rockers, skinheads and bovver boys or punks, but it also refers to groupings of (mainly young) people with gentler outlooks: new romantics (from Spandau Ballet); Goths (based on Gothic Rock); crusties.

Tabloids are sometimes also known as 'red tops'. They include newspapers such as the *Mirror*, *Daily Star* and *Sun*. The last named, owned by Rupert Murdoch, is known for its daily nude on page three. Though despised by highbrows, their political influence is as great as that of the broadsheets, because of their greater circulation.

Theme park is an American concept, popularised by Disney based on recreations of fantasy worlds. It replaces the previous generation's seaside piers and amusement arcades. Popular British examples are: Alton Towers, Madame Tussaud's and Camelot. The expression 'Theme-Park' Britain has been applied to attempts to package a slick, plastic, idealised and sanitised version of Britain's past. It is to be sold to foreign and domestic tourists and sustains various hegemonic interests. Traditional versions of Britain have been seen as engaged in this process. Castle banquets at Ruthin (Wales) and Bunratty (Ireland) are part of it, as are stately homes, and such industrial-archaeology sites as Styal Woollen Mill or Llechwedd Slate Mines.

The third way is the term used to describe Tony Blair's policies, which purported to carve a political niche between traditional left and right positions. It derives from the theories of the sociologist Anthony Giddens and in particular his book *The Third Way: the Renewal of Social Democracy* (1998).

Upstairs/downstairs represents the idea of Britain as 'two nations': masters and servants. Particularly in Edwardian Britain, servants lived in the basements of houses and owners on the upper floors. This division was reflected in respective power relations. The concept was revived by a popular TV series of that name and was in evidence again in 2002 in a new television serial of Galsworthy's *The Forsyte Saga*. Robert

Altman's movie *Gosford Park* (2002) observes this social split from a new angle, as did Kazuo Ishiguro's novel *The Remains of the Day* (1989).

WAGs are the wives and girlfriends of footballers. They have become notorious for their rowdy behaviour and partying. There is a lot of moral panic about the example they set. They have been invidiously contrasted with the wives of England's 1966 World Cup winners.

Wicca is a revived witchcraft followed by some New Agers. Its practices include: herbalism, divination and psychic healing. Partly because of its worship of a 'Great Goddess' it has attracted many feminists looking for alternatives to Christianity and Judaism. The popular image of Wicca was exploited by the cult film *The Wicker Man* (1973).

Index

eBooks – at www.eBookstore.tandf.co.uk

A library at your fingertips!

eBooks are electronic versions of printed books. You can store them on your PC/laptop or browse them online.

They have advantages for anyone needing rapid access to a wide variety of published, copyright information.

eBooks can help your research by enabling you to bookmark chapters, annotate text and use instant searches to find specific words or phrases. Several eBook files would fit on even a small laptop or PDA.

NEW: Save money by eSubscribing: cheap, online access to any eBook for as long as you need it.

Annual subscription packages

We now offer special low-cost bulk subscriptions to packages of eBooks in certain subject areas. These are available to libraries or to individuals.

For more information please contact
webmaster.ebooks@tandf.co.uk

We're continually developing the eBook concept, so keep up to date by visiting the website.

www.eBookstore.tandf.co.uk